JOURNAL FOR THE STUDY OF THE OLD TESTAMENT
SUPPLEMENT SERIES
353

BTC 1

Editors
David J.A. Clines
Philip R. Davies

Executive Editor
Andrew Mein

Editorial Board
Richard J. Coggins, Alan Cooper, J. Cheryl Exum, John Goldingay,
Robert P. Gordon, Norman K. Gottwald, John Jarick,
Andrew D.H. Mayes, Carol Meyers, Patrick D. Miller

Sheffield Academic Press
A Continuum imprint

Bible Translation on the Threshold of the Twenty-First Century

Authority, Reception, Culture and Religion

edited by

Athalya Brenner & Jan Willem van Henten

Journal for the Study of the Old Testament
Supplement Series 353

BTC 1

Copyright © 2002 Sheffield Academic Press
A Continuum imprint

Published by Sheffield Academic Press Ltd
The Tower Building, 11 York Road, London SE1 7NX
370 Lexington Avenue, New York NY 10017-6550

www.SheffieldAcademicPress.com
www.continuumbooks.com

British Library Cataloguing-in-Publication Data

A catalogue record for this book is available from the British Library

Typeset by Sheffield Academic Press
Printed on acid-free paper in Great Britain by Bookcraft Ltd, Midsomer Norton, Bath

ISBN 0-82646-029-1

CONTENTS

ABBREVIATIONS

AB	Anchor Bible
ACS	African Christian Studies
ASV	American Standard Version
ATJ	*African Theological Journal*
AV	Authorized Version
BHS	*Biblia Hebraica Stuttgartensia*
BibInt	*Biblical Interpretation: A Journal of Contemporary Approaches*
Biblit	Bible and Literature
BibPostCol	Bible and Postcolonialism
BibSem	The Biblical Seminar
BJS	Brown Judaic Studies
BT	*The Bible Translator*
CEV	Contemporary English Version
FCB	Feminist Companion to the Bible
GCT	Gender, Culture, Theory
GNB	Good News Bible
HTR	*Harvard Theological Review*
JAAR	*Journal of the American Academy of Religion*
JANES	Journal of Ancient Near Eastern Studies
JB	*Jerusalem Bible*
JBL	*Journal of Biblical Literature*
JFSR	*Journal of Feminist Studies in Religion*
JNSL	*Journal of Northwest Semitic Languages*
JRT	*Journal of Religious Thought*
JSNT	*Journal for the Study of the New Testament*
JSNTSup	*Journal for the Study of the New Testament*, Supplement Series
JSOT	*Journal for the Study of the Old Testament*
JSOTSup	*Journal for the Study of the Old Testament*, Supplement Series
JTS	*Journal of Theological Studies*
JTSA	*Journal of Theology for South Africa*
KJV	King James Version
Moffatt	Moffatt New Testament Commentary
NAB	*New American Bible*
NASB	*New American Standard Bible*

NEB	*New English Bible*
NGTT	Nederduitse gereformeerde teologiese tydskrif
NIV	New International Version
NJB	New Jerusalem Bible
NJV	New Jerusalem Version
NRSV	New Revised Standard Version
NXB	New Xhosa Bible
OAB	Old Afrikaans Bible
REB	Revised English Bible
RSV	Revised Standard Version
SJOT	*Scandinavian Journal of the Old Testament*
STAR	*Studies in Theology and Religion*
UBS	United Bible Societies
VT	*Vetus Testamentum*

CONTRIBUTORS

Professor Adele Berlin, Jewish Studies and English, University of Maryland, College Park, MD, USA

Professor Athalya Brenner, Art and Culture, University of Amsterdam, Amsterdam, The Netherlands

Dr Simon Crisp, United Bible Societies and University of Birmingham, Birmingham, UK

Professor E. Fox, Clark University, Newton, MA, USA

Professor Judith Frishman, Catholic Theological University ,Utrecht, The Netherlands

Professor Jan Willem van Henten, Art and Culture, University of Amsterdam, Amsterdam, The Netherlands

Ms M.P. Korsak, Sentier op Linkebeek 7, Brussels, Belgium

Dr S. Noorda, President, The University Board, University of Amsterdam, Amsterdam, The Netherlands

Dr Jeremy Punt, Theology University of Fort Hare, Alice, South Africa

Professor L. De Regt, United Bible Societies and Humanities Free University, Amsterdam, The Netherlands

Professor J. Rogerson, University of Sheffield, Sheffield, UK

Professor Lamin Sanneh, Divinity School, Yale University, New Haven, CT, USA

Dr Caroline Vander Stichele, Art and Culture, University of Amsterdam, Amsterdam, The Netherlands

Dr A. Verheij, Art and Culture, University of Amsterdam, Amsterdam, The Netherlands

Professor W.J.C. Weren, Theological Faculty Tilburg, Tilburg, The Netherlands

EDITORS' INTRODUCTION

Athalya Brenner and Jan Willem van Henten

The Why

This volume is firmly anchored in the Dutch scene of Bible study and Bible translation. It contains, at least for the most part, papers read at a workshop/colloquium organized by the Chair of Bible, Faculty of the Humanities, University of Amsterdam, The Netherlands, in cooperation with ASCA (The Amsterdam School for Cultural Analysis). The title of that workshop/colloquium was *Bible Translations on the Threshold of the 21st Century: Issues of Translation Authority in Religious Beliefs and Cultural Reception*, and it was held in Amsterdam on 29–30 May 2000. This event followed two other workshops/colloquia held in Amsterdam in 1997 and 1998, on *Recycling Biblical Figures* and on biblical *Families* respectively.[1] Our aim, at these workshops, was to refresh approaches to certain topics or to problematize them anew, in response to what we see as changing times and nomadic shifts in interpretive paradigms. We tried to stimulate this refreshing process through an interdisciplinary approach and the engagement of pluriformity for and of scholars coming from various Christian, Jewish and secular contexts.

In that spirit, the subject of the Bible translations was chosen for the 2000 workshop/colloquium because of the local discussion over the new translation of the Bible into Dutch. This translation-in-process[2] has had enormous publicity in the Netherlands and even caused a public uproar. The translation, ostensibly interdenominational and ecumenical, as well as directed at non-confessional (secular?) audiences, became hotly debated. It

1. A. Brenner and J.W. van Henten (eds.), *Recycling Biblical Figures* (STAR, 1; Leiden: DEO Publishing, 1999); J.W. van Henten and A. Brenner (eds.), *Families and Family Relations as Represented in Early Judaisms and Early Christianities: Texts and Fictions* (STAR, 2; Leiden: DEO Publishing, 2000).

2. See the website of the NBG (the Dutch Society for Bible Translation), esp. http://www.bijbelgenootschap.nl/nbv/achtergrond/ and further.

is in danger—at least in the view of several interested sections of the public—of failing to modernize sufficiently, at least in some aspects, thus undermining its own *raison d'être*. On the other hand, other interested parties have argued vehemently that the translation should stick to renderings of biblical vocabulary that have become classics, like Ecclesiastes' 'vanities of vanities' (Dutch: *ijdelheid der ijdelheden*). A case was put forward by some members of the translation committee for rejecting the time-honoured 'translation' of God's name—the Hebrew *Tetragrammaton* Yhwh, usually pronounced *'adonay* by Jewish readers, following the vowel signs in the Hebrew biblical text—from the traditional Dutch (*de*) *Heer*(-*e*) ('[The] Lord') into something more fitting for a (post)modern target audience. Objections to the traditional appellation were voiced especially by feminists, on the grounds that the appellation (*de*) *Heer(-e)* represented and recreated older non-inclusive gender notions as well as hierarchy parameters for God—parameters that should be revised, in the light of changing winds in theology, philosophy, history and culture in the last decades.

The public uproar—including press and other media discussions, signed petitions and bitter altercations between proponents of change and upholders of tradition—ended, quite recently, in the not-unforeseen victory of traditionalists. The *Tetragrammaton* is rendered by *HEER* ('LORD', in small caps) in the new Dutch translation. Consequently, female members of the translation committee resigned and stopped their participation in the ongoing project.[3] While the decision was taken months after the workshop had been planned and had come to pass—at the time we could only guess at the outcome—public debate here convinced us that contemporary Bible translations continue to be of fascination to an audience wider and more varied than religious officials, Bible scholars, historians of religion, translators and other interested professionals.[4] This debate was a forceful reminder that Bible translations—like other major cultural objects—are commodities,

<hr>

3.   See the *Appendix* to this Introduction for a translated paraphrase of the press releases, following the official decision to maintain the rendering *HEER*.

4.   Amsterdam University Press, in conjunction with the university library of the University of Amsterdam, has started an online digital Bible project, pairing off a commentary to the new translation together with relevant visual artwork from the European art tradition. This project, still at its infancy and awaiting the proper financial support that it deserves, was enthusiastically embarked on by library personnel. This is another indication—if one is still necessary—of the fascination that Bible projects still hold for an interested, 'secular' public.

consumer goods that, as such, are subject to change and change producing at the same time. In light of this public debate and the ensuing realization, we decided to organize a small forum to look at some directions, orientations and practices of Bible translation for the present and future—proceeding from the Dutch context but beyond it, into the Bible translation scene as it unfolds now and for the immediate future.

The Participants

The contributors of the main papers in this volume and in the original conference fall into three main categories: creators and practitioners of the art, that is, Bible translators; people who are involved in the production and dissemination of Bible translations (under the auspices of Bible societies, for instance); and professional consumers, that is Bible scholars, who function—among other things—as critics of translations. The demarcation lines between categories are not stable, of course: the translators are certainly scholars in their own right as well as consumers of others' translations; producers and disseminators are usually heavily involved in the translation process and may determine the direction a translation will take, as well as its eventual influence and ultimate fate; Bible scholars are critics and consumers, but tend to create their own *ad hoc* translations as the need arises. These papers relate to the state-of-the-art in the Netherlands as well as abroad (the US, Belgium, South Africa, England, Israel), and the contributors are local people as well as visitors. The respondents to the main papers belong primarily to the second and third categories of producers/disseminators and scholars/critics, and are mostly local people.

Several of the contributors and respondents are Jewish, others are Christians of several denominations or—in spite of or together with their original subscription to a religious community—secular in their approach. Unfortunately, we have no contributions from outside the Judeo-Christian productions/receptions of Bible translation. Several experts on translation theory participated in the discussions, and one of them (L. de Regt) contributed to the volume with a Response. In this way, we hoped, a balance between potential perspectives, a cursory overview of the complexities involved from the angle of various community memberships, as well as the common denominators across such memberships, could be touched upon.

The What and the How

It follows, then, that 'The Bible'—for this volume—means the Hebrew Bible/Old Testament and the New Testament as texts belonging to contemporary culture.

There's no discussion here of ancient translations *per se*, unless such discussion is helpful for reviewing the contemporary scene and for contemplating future developments. To be seen in a proper perspective, though, translation practices in 'pre-modernity' and 'modernity' are referred to. Thus, temporally, this book's scope is rather limited. On the other hand, spatially it covers quite a range. It proceeds from the new Dutch translation-in-the-making (Noorda) to a general discussion of translation practices, especially in the Dutch and English scenes (Rogerson), to recent translations produced in the US and in Belgium and England (Fox, Korsak, Carroll), to the processes and problematics involved in translations for former European Eastern Bloc countries (Crisp) and 'Third World' Africa (Sanneh, Punt), to the mutual dependency of translation and commentary even in Israel, where usage of the Hebrew text for Hebrew Bible/Old Testament study is the norm (Berlin). The target languages referred to are mostly English, Dutch, East European and African languages, with some references to German.

The first (by Noorda) and last (by Berlin) essays in this collection function as an introduction and conclusion, respectively. As such, we felt, no formal responses to them were appropriate. Other essays are followed by individual Responses that, in most cases, are recognizable as printed versions of oral responses. The respondents, as well as the editors, thought that in this way the original dialogic, conversational feel of the verbal exchanges during the workshop/colloquium will be conveyed to the reader, at least in part.

The problems discussed in the individual essays and in the responses to them are varied and different. They range from theoretical consideration to translation practice, from linguistic considerations to theological ones, from the scholarly to the social, from the general to the particular, from the conservative to the innovative. No attempt has been made to be comprehensive, not even about one facet of our supercharged subject. On the contrary: an attempt has been made to supply an overview of problems and possible remedies, or—more modestly still—of reassessments in service of the future.

As stated by Dr Noorda in his essay, Bible translations cannot exist or become influential without being accepted by readers. This is the ultimate test for any translation, and this test is public rather than restricted—as this volume is—to communities of experts. We end as we began, by referring once again to the new Dutch translation, expressing curiosity as to its eventual reception by its target readerly community.

A Personal Note

This volume is the first in a new series, 'The Bible in the 21st Century', published by Sheffield Academic Press. Hopefully, the new series will explore features and issues that are oriented to contemporary culture and the Bible's place within it, issues that are gaining ground but—perhaps— still get less attention than they deserve. Our thanks to Sheffield Academic Press for facilitating this series.

'The Bible in the 21st Century' is the title of our joint research project in the department of Art and Culture at the University of Amsterdam, with the support of NOSTER (The Netherlands School for Advanced Studies in Theology and Religion) and ASCA (Amsterdam School of Cultural Analysis). We started the project together with the department of Theology at the University of Glasgow in 2000; the Translations workshop/colloquium was the second activity (after an Amsterdam/ Glasgow research meeting in Glasgow, April 2000) within this framework. One of the senior members of the Glasgow department, an esteemed friend and colleague, was Professor Robert Peter Carroll.

As stated in a note to Carroll's essay, his contribution to the present volume was the very last paper he wrote. He died in his sleep several weeks before the workshop/colloquium and his paper was read posthumously. We mourn the unexpected demise of a radiant personality, a unique scholar and critic, a compassionate and wise man. Robert has written important studies about Bible translation problems; this was one of his special interests. Therefore we consider it appropriate to dedicate this book, with admiration, as a tribute to his memory.

ת . נ . צ . ב . ה.

Appendix

Statement to the Press: The decision about the rendering of the name of God in the Nieuwe Bijbelvertaling *(New Bible Translation), March 15, 2001.*[5]

The decision about the rendering of the name of God in the project of the *Nieuwe Bijbelvertaling* (New Bible Translation) has been made. It will be HEER ('LORD'). The boards of the *Nederlands Bijbelgenootschap* (NBG, Dutch Bible Society) in Haarlem and the *Katholieke Bijbelstichting* (KBS, Catholic Bible Foundation) in Den Bosch have announced this during a press conference in Amsterdam on March 15. This decision goes together with the commission, by the NBG and KBS boards, of their directors to investigate the possibility of publishing a popular study Bible version of the *Nieuwe Bijbelvertaling,* in which the name of God will be rendered by the actual *Tetragrammaton* (YHWH).

A meeting of both boards has, in fact, opted for the rendering HEER on February 16, after long and careful considerations and consultations. The boards finally acknowledged that the rendering by HEER, in small capitals, goes together best with the points of departure and aims: that is, to offer a translation that is accessible and acceptable for a large audience. The boards have taken several decisions that are related to this choice. The translation's typography will make clear that this rendering of the name is not a personal name but a substitute. Besides, all editions of the new translation will point out to the reader why this rendering has been chosen. Such editions will also be provided with reading aids, such as alternative renderings of the Hebrew name of God for reading the translation aloud.

The rendering of God's name appeared to be one of the most problematic decisions during the entire translation process of the *Nieuwe Bijbelvertaling.* For this reason it was decided already in an early stage that the boards of *both* Societies (NBG and KBS) would make the decision about the rendering of the name. The advisory committee opted already in 1994 for the rendering by HEER, since there were no better alternatives. In 2000 it arrived again at the same conclusion, not without having evaluated this decision extensively. The boards have weighed this conclusion in their own considerations. The decision about the rendering of God's name is, in

---

5.   This text is a paraphrase, rather than an exact translation, of the actual press release.

fact, the only decision made by the boards in connection to the new translation. In all other translation matters decisions were delegated to the project advisory committee and the translators' team of the *Nieuwe Bijbelvertaling*.

The boards are aware of the fact that the decision will invoke positive as well as negative responses. They will explain the process that led to the decision in the NBV information brochure no. 13, which is available from March 15 onwards.[6]

Press Statement by the resigning members of the Translation's Committee, March 15, 2001.
The boards of the *Nederlands Bijbelgenootschap* (NBG, Dutch Bible Society) and the *Katholieke Bijbelstichting* (KBS, Catholic Bible Foundation) have definitively decided to translate the name of God in the *Nieuwe Bijbelvertaling* (New Bible Translation) with 'HEER' ('LORD'). Three supervisors, Dr Anneke de Vries, Dr Caroline Vander Stichele and Dr. Manuela Kalsky, as well as Prof. Judith Frishman, member of the advisory board, have decided to end their contribution to the *Nieuwe Bijbelvertaling* in response to this decision. It is their opinion that the translation of God's name with 'HEER' does not correspond to the project's translation rules. These rules stipulate that the translation will be faithful to the source in the target text, and that exclusive language has to be avoided. The four persons named above regret that, despite numerous protests and good alternatives suggested, it is the most traditional decision possible that was made in this matter.

A. de Vries, C. Vander Stichele, M. Kalsky, J. Frishman

---

6.   See for this brochure (in Dutch) www.bijbelgenootschap.nl.

NEW AND FAMILIAR: THE DYNAMICS OF BIBLE TRANSLATION

Sijbolt Noorda

Introduction

A dual warning to begin with. In the first place I wish to clarify and define the domain you are about to enter: the theme of this paper is not translation, but rather reflection on the context of translation; not Bible translation, but rather reflection on the context in which Bible translation is and has been undertaken, and the way in which the phenomenon usually is being studied.

My own position should be clear from the onset as well. Once, long ago, I was involved myself in the real thing, the actual practice of Bible translation: as a matter of fact, collecting material on specific translation problems was my very first task as junior assistant at the university; later, in the early 1980s, I was invited to be one of the translators preparing a new edition of the Gospels and Acts in the Dutch and Flemish Catholic Bible Foundations' translation. Now I am rather a bystander, an observer. I am involved in a concrete Bible translation project, yet at considerable distance from the actual workplace. My present role is chairing the supervisory board of a joint Dutch-Flemish project producing a new translation of the Bible in Dutch. The project began in 1994 and we hope to finish it by 2004.

Right from the start I wondered why there should and how there could be a new translation. Bible translation is special in the sense that it is somehow a never-ending story. The book is as a matter of fact constantly retranslated, in very many ways and for a variety of purposes. It is one thing to take this for granted, to describe this state of affairs, but something else to reflect on it, to inquire why and how this is the way it is. And this is exactly what I would like to try to do in this paper. Although my thinking on this topic has not come to a firm conclusion yet—it still is work in progress—I would like to present some observations that seem to hold water. At least they are recurring topics in my thinking so far.

Meanwhile I do not want to create the impression that all of this is original. The subject under review has been around for a while. In a way everything that can be said about it has been said already. Or, to put it differently: my present reflections are themselves translations of older versions of the same theme.

My presentation is structured in three parts: first, installing some general background (Bible translation as a socio-cultural phenomenon); then, focusing on a particular theme (the role of the new and the familiar in translation production and in the process of reception); finally, concluding by making some observations on the way we usually approach Bible translation in academic research, and making some suggestions as to how I think we should redirect Bible translation research or at least add a new approach to the existing modes of research. If you like images, you could imagine being seated in a theatre. First, the set is being built up on the stage; then, a particular scene is being played; and, finally, we sit down to talk about it, comment on and evaluate what we have done and seen.

The Socio-Cultural Context of Bible Translation

Remember Jerome's new Latin translation of the Bible?[1] In his day the Greek version of the Hebrew Bible was very much the basis of authoritative Christian theological thinking, not the Hebrew original itself. As a matter of fact, in a letter to Jerome, Augustine expressed his fear that 'many problems would arise if your [that is, Jerome's] translation [from the original Hebrew] began to be read regularly in many churches, because the Latin churches would be out of step with the Greek ones'. He relates an incident, demonstrating how this new translation on the basis of the original Hebrew source text would endanger church identity:

> When one of our fellow bishops had introduced your translation in his church, the congregation came across a word in your version of the prophet Jonah which you had rendered very differently from the translation with which they were familiar and which, having been read by so many generations, was ingrained in their memories. A great uproar ensued in the congregation, especially among the Greeks who criticized the text and passionately denounced it as wrong, and this bishop was compelled to ask local Jews to give evidence. Whether out of ignorance or out of malice, they replied that this word did occur in the Hebrew manuscripts in exactly the same form as in the Greek and Latin versions. And then what? The man was forced to

1. On Jerome's translation see also Rogerson, 'Can a Translation of the Bible be Authoritative?' in this volume, pp. xx.

correct the passage in your version as if he had made a mistake since he did
not want this crisis to leave him without a congregation.[2]

In other words, Jerome's new translation caused great concern in a congregation that founded their beliefs on the basis of an old-time institution
that was 'familiar' and 'ingrained in their memories'. Prevailing tradition
constitutes authority and fosters identity. And tradition must be upheld by
an algorithm proving the old-time version to be a correct rendering of the
'original' Greek, that is, the Septuagint. Interesting, isn't it? Yet not interesting enough. The more important question remains, why did Jerome
break away from this established cultural institution, and how did his
innovation manage to gain ground to the point that, in the end, it in fact
did replace the traditional institution?

Here some intriguing observations can be made. For one, Jerome was
clearly 'part of a culture in which sensitivity to a foreign language was an
integral element'. He could appreciate the merits of works in a language
not his own.[3] And when he actually studied the Hebrew original, he discovered numerous flaws in the traditional Latin translation—expansions,
mistakes, secondary information, omissions. These should be repaired.

But how does one correct inspired Scripture, debug what is considered to
be perfect? Precisely by following a traditional line of thinking that had
been playing a crucial role in the formation of the Christian Church (early
apostolic witness guarantees authenticity, the more original has best claims
to truth), he came to the conclusion that the Hebrew should be the basis of a
new Latin translation. The more original and authentic the better. So, if you
come up with *first* firsthand witnesses, your claims to a new truth may
prevail.

Yet, at the same time, he didn't overstate his case. His 'strategy',
whether deliberate or not, was much smarter. He presented his translation
as an important addition to existing Latin versions, not as a replacement.
And by so doing he reduced the innovative character of his translation, and
thus managed to make his undertaking less threatening to conservative
minds. At the same time he reasoned that his 'Hebrew' translation could
be of enormous value for Christians in their continuing debate with the
synagogue, by removing stumbling blocks and by offering new material

---

2. C. White, *The Correspondence between Jerome and Augustine of Hippo*
(Lewiston, NY: Edwin Mellen Press, 1990), pp. 92-93; translation slightly changed by
the present author.

3. A. Kamesar, *Jerome, Greek Scholarship, and the Hebrew Bible: A Study of the
Quaestiones Hebraicae in Genesim* (Oxford: Clarendon Press, 1993), pp. 43, 48-49.

for attacking Jewish beliefs. By so doing he even corroborated the dogmatic position of Christian traditionalists, rather than disturbing them.[4]

This story shows some key elements of the dynamics of Bible translation. And if one reads the whole history book of Bible translation, similar elements, stories with similar plots appear to be all over the place.

Remember the story of Erasmus trying to do to the Christian Testament what Jerome did to the Hebrew Bible? How he was in his turn correcting Jerome's Vulgate on the basis of more ancient Greek manuscripts and new insights into the Hebrew lexicon, relying on testimonies of minority streams in the Christian past—and, at the same time, advocating new ideals of *latinitas* (the Bible should be more Ciceronian, less vulgar), and forcefully arguing against churchly interests defended by French university professors (who were reading their sacred Latin Bible not only as if Latin could claim to be God's own language, but also as if Jerome's rendering contained all there was to know in theology).[5]

Remember the many stories about new translations into vernacular languages, not sacred, maybe even unholy vessels deemed by many to be unfit for divine revelation. Horrible events of book burning and even the burning of translators and printers, arranged by authorities pretending to save the innocent and uninformed from wicked new interpretations of the traditional faith, thereby in fact trying to save their own necks. And such things didn't only happen in Europe, in the days of Tyndale and Luther.

I won't go into these histories, however. I just wanted to evoke some general images of Bible translating as a societal, institutional phenomenon. I think we need this socio-cultural background to more clearly see Bible translation in its context and in its formative and re-formative role in the establishment, defense and/or innovation of cultural identities.

The New and the Familiar in Translation Production and Reception

I now turn to my central theme, the *New and the Familiar, the Dynamics of Bible Translation*.

Generally speaking, successfully changing traditional states of affairs

---

4. I owe the example of Jerome's translation and its significance for studying the role of cultural identities, explaining the mechanics of translation reception, to Lawrence Venuti, *The Scandals of Translation: Towards an Ethics of Difference* (London: Routledge, 1998), pp. 78-81.

5. H.J. de Jonge, '*Novum Testamentum a nobis versum*: The Essence of Erasmus' Edition of the New Testament', *JTS* NS 35 (1984), pp. 394-413.

requires a mixture of old and new, enough of the old to guarantee continuation, enough of the new to enable change. The reason for this is, simply,
that socio-cultural change cannot happen without acceptance. In the end
the pragmatics of Bible translation decide whether a particular new translation will be effective, accepted, received by the community of readers.
To clarify what is at stake here, I refer to a simple model by which one can
explain what happens in communication, what happens in the process
of producing and reading texts. I mean the traditional sender–message–
receiver model. When applied to the process of understanding texts, the
terms of the model usually are author–text–reader.

This model is of course a simplified representation of what is going on,
because it doesn't account for the special and intricate relationship between
author and text (just remember that in the course of time authors disappear
into their texts; and that even authors who are alive cannot escape reduction:
their texts live on, they cannot change them and—what is even more important—they cannot influence the way readers read their texts). So, in principle, authorship and authorial power are limited. And the same—*mutatis
mutandis*—is true for translations. Here some sort of double authorship constitutes the first term of the model.

Another complication the communication model doesn't account for has
to do with the special relationship between texts and readers: texts do exist
in a formal way without readers, yet they do not really exist when there are
no readers; and when they are being read, it is the readers who decide how
they read, like musicians playing from a score. And again, also in this
respect, translation makes things even more complicated: in a way it dou-
bles the text phenomenon, not exactly duplicating the original but adding
additional information, with the possibility of interference between original text and translated text.

The simple communication model of author–text–reader is usually
enriched and made into a semiotic model: texts are then syntactic arrange-
ments of signs (the syntactic dimension of texts); producing an extra-
textual, non-linguistic reference (the semantic dimension of texts); all in all
exercising effect upon readers, conventionally called its pragmatic dimension. As such, this model is not a static set of equal relationships. With each
instance of meaning, the model is being activated by readers. Readers
structure texts, attribute meaning to textual signs and evoke pragmatic
effect. They don't do this in total freedom of course, but within limits,
limits that are set by the dynamics of convention and innovation in text and
with readers. In this process of creating meaning, readers have the lead.

Readers' attitudes decide meaning. Their interaction with a given text, be it an original or a translation, produces meaning. Attempts to reduce interpretive variation by definition (as by those who think meaning is established once and for all by conventional semantics) are doomed to fail. Interaction leaves no room for monopolies on either side.

Readers decide about meaning. Yet readers do not exist in a vacuum. The actual checks and balances governing the process of interaction between text and reader are a matter of cultural convention. In a cultural setting where consistency and verifiability are accepted as important criteria for valid interpretation, all the signals of a text are to be heeded: one must read it in its proper context, both in terms of language and of history, and one must take its pragmatic intentions seriously.

The effect of all this defining and modeling is—in my opinion—important for our reflections on Bible translation. If readers decide upon meaning, while acting within or outside certain cultural conventions about valid interpretation, it becomes all-important to turn to the socio-cultural setting, the codes, the rules so to speak that govern the process of reader response, of reception by individual readers or by groups of readers.

Let us now leave theory and modeling aside and look at what setting, which codes and cultural rules are at play in the actual context of the project of a new Dutch translation of the Bible.

A first and simple observation: this is a project that could not have been undertaken with any chance of success in the Dutch and Flemish contexts, say, 20 years ago. Bible translation projects of this sort are institutional enterprises. They require institutional decision making, not only because of the enormous investments in time and money involved, but also because of specific group interests. Bible translation societies, just like any publishing company, analyze and decide whether there is a market for a new translation, whether there will be room for innovation.

In our case we expected that there would be a fair opportunity for a new translation across the borders of specific groups that formerly had had their own version. Those groups were Protestant churches of different kinds, a variety of Dutch and Flemish Roman Catholics, diverse synagogues, and last but not least an enormously expanding general readership not any longer associated with churches and synagogues. While, until fairly recently, Bible translation was a topic for theologians and church people, each favoring their own homegrown versions and conventions, it now appears to have become a topic of much more general interest.

Now for a second observation. This expansion of potential readership enabled a choice of translation strategy much more in line with generally accepted translation practice and theory than would have been possible before. Whereas, for instance, traditional Protestant Bible translation had been largely governed by the ideal of a literal rendering of Hebrew and Greek syntax and idiom, it now proved feasible to clearly differentiate between characteristics of source *language* and characteristics of biblical *texts*, and to produce a translation reproducing source language phenomena only insofar they served textual functions. In the case of Jerome's new Latin translation the cultural setting of his day—with its interest in other languages and cultures—played an important role as did his re-rooting of traditional concepts of authenticity. Similarly, in our actual situation, the present broad cultural interest in fresh translations of classics from Greek and Roman antiquity, of Oriental type and from European medieval sources, no doubt contributes to an overall sympathy for a fresh translation of the Bible along generally accepted lines of translation practice.

Yet, it is not only the new that counts. At the start of the translation project, in 1994, I ventured to characterize the new translation as a 'classic' translation of the Bible. I realized that this was a rather presumptuous statement to make. Classics are not made. Classics are results of a future reception process, a reputation to be acquired. Yet, I believe that the actual translation strategy, the actual aims of a translation process to an important degree limit or heighten the chance of a translation becoming a classic. For a new translation to become a classic, a generally accepted version instead of remaining a minority version, its strategy should be aiming at a high-quality text in terms of language and style and a transparent process of making and reviewing, yet at the same time avoiding modernisms and too much clarity.

This may seem strange. Yet we all know that nothing ages faster than modern usage ('those who are married to the present will very soon be widowed'). And outdated versions, with out-of-fashion language, won't live to become classics. And speaking about clarity, recent Bible translation practice has been governed to quite an extent by missionary purposes, helping readers in every possible way to make sense of even the most obscure and inaccessible passages of the Bible. However, ancient texts, and especially ancient religious texts, are not conspicuous by their clarity. We'd better be prepared in their case for some opacity, some obscurity. Of course this is not to say that translation should aim at being difficult and opaque: whenever possible, we shouldn't make the Bible a book of riddles. What I mean is that we should practice restraint, avoiding excessive explanation and explicitation. Books like the Bible live on because they are fascinating to readers, because they are open to imaginative reading. As I said before, at the end of the day readers decide about the quality of a translation. Yet specific translation strategies can help or hinder successful reception.

This brings me to one final observation in this context. Translators are fond of being original. We hate to plagiarize our predecessors, to repeat existing versions. By giving in to this inclination, however, we not only run the risk of producing sub-optimal translations. (Why avoid perfectly adequate prevailing renderings?) In so doing we may also be disturbing a particular quality of books like the Bible: they are texts that some people read again and again, they contain numerous passages that are familiar to many, they belong to extensive intertextual networks, not only in religious language, but in literature and general usage as well. A new translation is a new text, yes, but it is a new version of a familiar text, and what is more important, a rival translation to existing translations and traditional wordings. While there are many good reasons for innovations, there are also many good reasons for restraint and for staying with the familiar. And, as always in the art of translating, what counts is keeping one's balance.

More Empirical Reception Studies Wanted

I have reached the final part of my presentation, with a few practical suggestions for future work.

Translation is essential to human communication as soon as we leave our own family, village or valley. Without translators this world would not hold together, not in spatial terms, and not in temporal terms. This very broad cultural function of translation, explains its insecure position in academia. The phenomenon is simply everywhere and can be studied from about any angle in the humanities and in social studies. It is always at the same time a very specific subject (e.g. requiring highly specialized knowledge of the languages involved) and a very general one (linked to all aspects of human interaction).

In university translation studies there is usually a lot of theory. In actual translation projects there is of course a lot of practical work to be done, with little time for reflection. And when we do find time for it, it is usually the kind of ad hoc reflection we need to solve our problems. This is not only true in general, but as far as I can see—I hope I am wrong in this— also true for Bible translation study: it is either theory and ad hoc reflection on the work of translators, or very practical support for translators.

I would very much like this arrangement to be changed somewhat. When a new Bible translation was being prepared in Sweden in the 1980s (in a special Swedish way, financed in its entirety by the Swedish government), it was decided that royalties from sales would be put to good use. And, among others, university research was to benefit from this. University research groups were asked to engage in empirical research, to study reader response and to check on the effect of translation strategies, both in terms of general analysis and in terms of actual readings.

This is something I would welcome on a much larger scale. If anything, the field of religious attitudes and practice is a field mainly studied by theorists. There seems to be, generally speaking, little interest in empirical research. One rather believes than knows for certain. The same thing is true—and, once again, I am speaking generally—of the reception of translations. If am correct in thinking that in designing translations and translation strategies much depends on reader response, both the future response translators aim at and the actual response to the final product, it would be of enormous value to know much more than we actually do. For now, much as in the field of textual interpretation, most studies of translation are devoted to theory and sometimes to historic reception, whereas it would be quite worthwhile to engage in empirical study in order to test theories and hypotheses. Translation research would benefit enormously from empirical research: we would be able to see for ourselves whether our theories and hypotheses, including our reader-directed strategies, make sense.

The historical dynamics of Bible translation, including the role of the new and the familiar, promise that this kind of research will not be a routine and unexciting thing to do. Bible study often focuses on the supply side only. I would welcome this to be corrected by much more empirical research into actual reader response, instead of testing hypotheses among translators and other experts only. If I am not mistaken, this would lead to an interesting addition to existing Bible translation research, providing socio-cultural material by which one will be able to judge which translation strategies have which effects, which ones are successful and which ones are not, and why this is the case. On the basis of such material not only the success of individual Bible translation projects can be measured, but also Bible translation theory and practice in general may profit. Translation doesn't take place *in vacuo*, but in a specific cultural environment. This is precisely why translation must be done again and again. Wouldn't it therefore be appropriate and promising to study these ever-shifting conditions more closely?

CAN A TRANSLATION OF THE BIBLE BE AUTHORITATIVE?

John Rogerson

The quick answer to this question must be 'yes', if only because within Judaism and Christianity there have been, and still are, translations that are regarded as authoritative. This paper will briefly review them and the reasons for their acceptance as authoritative, in the hope that, in the process, some of the issues and implications of the title will be unravelled.

Anyone who consults rabbinic commentaries such as *Miqra'ot Gedolot* or Rashi's commentary on the Pentateuch will be aware that a Targum such as Onkelos on the Pentateuch or Jonathan on the Prophets is printed alongside the Hebrew text.[1] This indicates the importance of the Targumim as authoritative versions of the Bible, upon which Jewish interpreters and commentators drew in the Middle Ages and earlier. In *San.* 94b Rav Yosef, who flourished in Babylon around 310 CE, interpreted Isa. 8.6 on the basis of the Targum, prefacing his words with the formula:

אלמלא תרגומא דהאי קרא לא הוה ידענא מאי קאמר

> If it were not for the Targum of this verse we would not know what it means.

Rashi, commenting on Exod. 5.23 (Moses' speech to God, 'Since I came to Pharaoh to speak in your name, he has done evil to this people') took הרע as a Hiphil on the basis of the Targum:

לשון הפעיל הוא. הרבה רעה עליהם ותרגומו אבאיש[2].

Frank Talmage, describing David Kimhi's use of the Targumim notes that:

> He cites them copiously, comments upon them and discusses textual variants in them as if they were the biblical text itself; explains their

---

1. See *Miqra'ot Gedolot* (3 vols; Jerusalem: Schocken Publishing House, 1959); M. Rosenbaum and A.M. Silberman (trans. and eds.), *Pentateuch with Rashi's Commentary* (2 vols.; London: Shapiro, Vallentine & Co., 1946).

2. Rashi in Exodus; see Rosenbaum and Silbermann (eds.), *Pentateuch*, p. 24.

> language and methodology; paraphrases them in Hebrew; and expresses
> great astonishment when the Targumim come up with something he cannot
> agree with.[3]

Talmage's last words, as quoted, indicate what can be called a critical and qualified view of a translation as authoritative. The Targumim clearly contained interpretation and philological and grammatical information that was very highly regarded and accepted as authoritative; but they were not infallible, because they had to be read alongside the Hebrew text, to which they had to conform if it was clear that they erred. This type of qualified authority has to be distinguished from an authoritative translation that is *not* read against the original, and which therefore can gain an infallible status.

A good example of an infallibly authoritative translation is the Septuagint, as viewed by the Fathers of the early church. Whatever may have been the reasons behind the composition of the so-called *Letter of Aristeas*, most probably by an Alexandrian Jew,[4] the legend that it contained was extremely convenient for a Christian church in dispute with Jews over the presence or absence of explicit references to Christ in the Hebrew Bible, and which had adopted the Septuagint in preference to the Hebrew Bible. The position is well stated in Augustine's *City of God*. Referring to the 72 translators he wrote:

> Although each of them sat in a separate place when engaged on the task…
> they did not differ from one another in a single word, not even by a synonym
> conveying the same meaning; they did not even vary in the order of words.
> There was such a unity in their translations that it was as if there had been
> one translator; for in truth there was the One Spirit at work in them all.[5]

Augustine held that the translators were so guided by the Spirit of God that if they had omitted anything from the Hebrew or had added anything to it this was in accordance with what the Spirit of God had decided to say.[6]

What is interesting about the authoritative position assumed by the Septuagint in the early, and later, Greek Orthodox Church is that it did not owe

---

3. F.E. Talmage, *David Kimhi: The Man and the Commentaries* (Cambridge, MA: Harvard University Press, 1975), p. 62.

4. For a summary of the various views about the purpose of the *Letter*, see N. Meisner, 'Aristeasbrief', in *Jüdische Schriften aus hellenistisch-römischer Zeit* (Gütersloh: Gerd Mohn, 1973), II, pp. 38-43.

5. Augustine, *City of God* (trans. H. Betterson; Harmondsworth: Penguin Books, 1972), Book 18, ch. 42, p. 820.

6. *City of God*, book 18, ch. 43, p. 822.

this position to the initiative or intervention of an authoritative institution that could control the availability of translations. Of course, the endorsement of the Septuagint by influential Christian leaders and apologists from Justin Martyr to Augustine was not without effect. However, their endorsement was not the cause of the Septuagint's authority, but the recognition of an inherent authority resulting, paradoxically, from the work of Jewish and not Christian translators.

A different process can be discerned in the rise of the Vulgate as an authoritative translation.[7] Jerome was commissioned by Pope Damasus in 382 possibly to undertake a revision of the whole Latin Bible, certainly to undertake a revision of the four Gospels.[8] In fact, Jerome produced a translation of the whole Bible, and in translating the Old Testament from the Hebrew and not the Septuagint, he demonstrated his dissatisfaction with what his contemporary, Augustine, regarded as an inspired translation. With the authority of the Pope behind the new version of the Gospels, Jerome's work might have been expected to be universally accepted; but this was not so. Jerome was attacked. 'How had [he] dared to make alterations in the Gospels against ancient authority and against the opinion of the whole world?'[9] Some of Jerome's other translations fared little better; and there is the well-known story of the riot that broke out in Tripoli when Jerome's translation of Jonah was read publicly, with its substitution of *hedera* ('ivy') for the familiar *cucurbita* ('gourd') at Jonah 4.6.[10]

In fact, Jerome's translation was generally adopted only in Italy; and it underwent many revisions before reaching the point at which it was declared to be an authoritative version of Scripture by the Roman Catholic Church.[11] The main reasons for it being declared authoritative by the Council of Trent in 1546 were, first, to affirm the canonicity of books rejected by Protestants as 'apocryphal'; and second, in the light of Protestant claims that only Greek and Hebrew originals of the Bible were inspired, to assert

7.   See also Noorda's 'New and Familiar', in this volume, pp. 8-16.

8.   H.F.D. Sparks, 'Jerome as Biblical Scholar', in P.R. Ackroyd and C.F. Evans (eds.), *The Cambridge History of the Bible*. I. *From the Beginnings to Jerome* (Cambridge: Cambridge University Press, 1970), p. 513.

9.   E.F. Sutcliffe, 'Jerome', in G.W.H. Lampe (ed.), *The Cambridge History of the Bible*. II. *The West from the Fathers to the Reformation* (Cambridge: Cambridge University Press, 1969), p. 85.

10.   G. Bonner, 'Augustine as Biblical Scholar', in Lampe (ed.), *The Cambridge History*. II, p. 546.

11.   See R. Loewe, 'The Medieval History of the Latin Vulgate', in Lampe (ed.), *The Cambridge History*, II, pp. 102-54.

that the Vulgate was free from dogmatic error and that it should therefore be used in theology and preaching.[12]

The advent of printing in the fifteenth century radically affected the matter of authoritative translations, because printers could be controlled by ecclesiastical and state authorities; and 'authorized' could mean, in practice, authorized or permitted by those in authority. Yet there were notable exceptions to this development. When Martin Luther began to translate the New Testament in December 1521, he had been in hiding from his enemies and masquerading as Junker Georg at Wartburg near Eisenach. When his so-called September Testament went on sale in late 1522 under the simple title 'Das Newe Testament Deutzsch, Vuittemberg', in spite of a printing ban by Herzog Georg of Sachsen and the high price of a half guilder per copy, it sold out so quickly that a second edition was produced in December, and printers in Augsburg, Basel and Leipzig cashed in on the demand.[13] By 1534, however, Luther's reformation had gained the protection of Friedrich, Herzog of Sachsen, to the point at which Luther's Bible was issued with his ruler's privilege, dated 6 August 1534. This specified the names of the authorized printers, and forbade editions printed in other places to be sold publicly in Friedrich's dominion.[14] William Tyndale was able to overcome determined efforts on the part of the authorities to prevent his translation from being distributed, though not without the cost of his own life. However, Tyndale's success made it clear to the authorities in England that if they wished to control the production and distribution of translations of the Bible this would have to be done through properly authorized Bibles.

The first authorized Bibles to be produced in English were those of Thomas Matthew (a pseudonym) and the second edition of Miles Coverdale's Bible, both of which appeared in 1537 and bearing the words 'set forth with the kings most gracyous lycence',[15] the king being Henry VIII. Ironically, these Bibles incorporated much of the surviving work of Tyndale, who had been betrayed and then executed in 1536. April 1539 saw the publication of Cranmer's Bible, or the Great Bible, which was in effect a revision of Matthew's Bible by Coverdale, the production of which was designed to enable the decree of September 1538 to be enforced, that a

---

12. G.P. Fogarty, *American Catholic Biblical Scholarship A History from the Early Republic to Vatican*, II (San Francisco: Harper & Row, 1989), p. 4.

13. H. Volz (ed.), *D. Martin Luther: Die gantze heilige Schrifft* (Munich: Deutscher Taschenbuch Verlag, 1974), III, pp. 51*-61*.

14. The decree is printed in Volz (ed.), *Heilige Schrifft*, I, pp. 4-5.

15. F.F. Bruce, *The English Bible* (London: Methuen, 1961), pp. 64-65.

copy of the Bible in English should be set up in every parish church in England. The authoritative nature of this Bible was indicated by the iconography of its title page. In the centre was the title 'The Byble in Englyshe': above the title sat the English monarch enthroned, and simultaneously handing copies of the Bible to the chief representatives of spiritual and secular power in the land: Archbishop Cranmer and Thomas Cromwell. These in turn were distributing the Bible to the clergy and to the laity, all of whom were uttering their gratitude with the words 'vivat rex'. As Diarmaid MacCulloch has put it:

> In the Great Bible the message was one of unity: two estates, clerical and lay, harmoniously and gratefully receiving the word of God from the hands of a benevolent monarch, and drawing from it his preferred message of discipline and obedience.[16]

Yet what we might call 'authorization from above' was not the only principle that emerged from the production of translations into the vernacular languages of Europe. In fact, 'authorization from above' was an attempt to control the inherent attraction of the versions put out by such as Luther and Tyndale; and that attraction lay in the way in which their translations expressed the theology of the Reformation. The principle was being born—a principle to which I shall return—of the authority of a translation residing in its conformity to particular theological opinions.

This can be seen particularly in the Geneva Bible, which was produced in 1560 by English exiles from the reign of the Catholic Queen Mary. The Geneva Bible has often been discredited as Calvinist or Puritan, and it is best known as the 'Breeches Bible'—a foolish nickname which, intentionally or otherwise, has enabled its importance to be diminished. (It owes this name to its rendering of Gen. 3.7, according to which Adam and Eve sewed fig leaves together and made themselves 'breeches', a word denoting in English a pair of trousers that comes down as far as the knees.) In fact, the Geneva Bible contained many features that need to be taken into account when considering the question 'can a translation of the Bible be authoritative?' These included division of the text into verses, cross-references, concordances, maps, pictures and explanatory notes. It used Roman and not Gothic type, was imaginatively designed, and was also, apparently, the first Bible in English to be produced in an edition that could fit into someone's

---

16. D. MacCulloch, *Thomas Cranmer: A Life* (New Haven: Yale University Press, 1996), p. 238.

pocket. In 1593 it became the first Bible to be printed in Scotland.[17] Such was its popularity that it remained in use for a hundred years before being suppressed, after the restoration of the monarchy in Britain in 1660.

One of the reasons for the production of the Authorized or King James Version of 1611 was because of the dislike of the Geneva Bible by James I (James VI of Scotland), with its uses of 'congregation' for 'church' and 'presbyter' for 'bishop'. At the Hampton Court conference in 1603, soon after James's accession to the English throne, James said:

> I profess I could never yet see a Bible well translated in English; but I think that of all, that of Geneva is the worst. I wish some special pain were taken for a uniform translation, which should be done by the best learned in both Universities [James chose to ignore that Scotland had *five* universities at this point]; then received by the Bishops; presented to the Privy Council; lastly, ratified by Royal authority, to be read in the whole Church, and no other.[18]

In these remarks, James laid down what came to be regarded as some of the necessary conditions for the production of an authoritative translation of the Bible in English: that it should be undertaken by learned scholars from the universities, and that it should be reviewed and approved by the churches, in the form of bishops and their equivalent.

In spite of the combined authority of the king, the learned men of the two universities, and the bishops, the 1611 Authorized Version was unable to oust the Geneva Bible. It was only after the restoration of the monarchy in 1660 and the passing of the Act of Uniformity in 1662 (an Act that allowed public worship to be conducted only according to the Book of Common Prayer) that the Authorized Version came into its own. It was used for the Epistles and Gospels that were printed in the Book of Common Prayer and was given a boost by being referred to in the preface of the Prayer Book as 'the last Translation', which was to be read and used 'for a more perfect rendering of such portions of Holy Scripture, as are inserted with the liturgy'.

Before I turn to other issues, I want to mention the fate of two other attempts to produce 'authorized' translations of the Bible into English, namely, the Revised Version of 1884 and the New English Bible of 1970. The proposal to produce a revision of the Authorized Version came from the Convocation (i.e. the bishops and other clergy) of the Province of

---

17. Bruce, *English Bible*, p. 91.

18. Adam Clarke, *The Holy Bible, with a Commentary and Critical Notes*, I (London: Ward, Lock & Co., 1825), p. xviii.

Canterbury in 1870, and among its resolutions were:

> That it is desirable that Convocation should nominate a body of its own members to undertake the work of revision, who shall be at liberty to invite the co-operation of any eminent for scholarship, to whatever nation or religious body they may belong.[19]

The revision was thus seen as something initiated and controlled by the Church of England; and although liberty was given to involve non-Anglicans and non-English/British scholars (an American Committee was also set up that would produce the American Standard Version), it was certainly not envisaged that any non-Christian would be involved in the work.

The Committee appointed to revise the New Testament began its work in the Jerusalem Chamber of Westminster Abbey on 22 June 1870, the venue underlining the ecclesiastical and Anglican nature of the project. Not all of the translators were Anglicans (or English), however, and this fact immediately caused trouble.

The broad-minded Dean of Westminster, A.P. Stanley, thought that it would be fitting for the translators to begin their work with a service of Holy Communion. This was duly held in the Chapel of Henry VII in Westminster Abbey on 22 June, and among those attending and receiving Holy Communion were several Scottish Presbyterians, English non-conformists and one non-subscribing Unitarian, that is, a Unitarian who accepted the divinity of Jesus as described in the New Testament, but who refused to subscribe to the Nicene Creed.[20] Reaction to this ecumenical service was hostile in some quarters of the Church of England, and one newspaper went as far as to declare that: 'There can be no possible defence for such an act of desecration as the administration of the Holy Communion to Presbyterians, Baptists, and Unitarians.'[21] Among the many resolutions and memorials that were subsequently issued in the wake of this Communion service was one passed by the bishops of the Convocation of Canterbury in February 1871:

> That it is the judgement of this House that no person who denies the Godhead of our Lord Jesus Christ ought to be invited to join either Company to which is committed the revision of the Authorized Version of Holy Scripture, and that any such person now on either Company should cease to act therewith.[22]

19. Revisers' Preface to the New Testament.
20. R.T. Davidson, *Life of Archibald Campbell Tait, Archbishop of Canterbury* (London: Macmillan, 1891), II, p. 63.
21. Davidson, *Life of Tait*, II, p. 65.
22. Davidson, *Life of Tait*, II, p. 73.

This resolution expressed what, to my mind, is the dubious principle in the production of an authorized translation even for ecclesiastical purposes, namely, a test of religious orthodoxy as a necessary qualification for a person to be a translator. The bishops' resolution put forward this principle rather crudely; but it has arguably been applied implicitly to church-sponsored translations until quite recent times, as though the orthodoxy of translators would somehow guarantee the authoritative nature of the translation.

The New English Bible originated from a motion submitted in 1946 to the General Assembly of the Church of Scotland, which quickly led to the establishment of a Joint Committee that represented all the major churches in Britain. Although 'denominational considerations played no part in the appointment of panels',[23] the leading role of the Church of England was indicated by the fact the Chairmen of the project were successively the Anglican bishops of Truro and Winchester, and the Archbishop of York, while the Joint Committee with overall responsibility for the project met in the Jerusalem Chamber of Westminster Abbey. While the Old Testament was being translated I happened to be studying Semitic languages under G.R. Driver, who was the dominating figure on the Old Testament panel, and who not only made frequent allusions to this work but sometimes showed me drafts of the translation for my comments. He was often contemptuous of what he called 'the theologians' on the panel and of what appeared to him to be their unwillingness to accept his brilliant but eccentric suggestions, which were based upon his unrivalled but often undisciplined knowledge of comparative Semitic philology. A sad outcome for the Old Testament part of the New English Bible—which, incidentally, was continually referred to as the New English Targum by our Dutch colleagues at a joint British–Dutch congress in 1973—was that it needed such extensive revision that this remedial work was put in hand only four years after the publication of the New English Bible. The result was the Revised English Bible of 1989, one of the purposes of which, as its director Professor W.D. McHardy told me, was to remove the 'Driverisms' from the NEB Old Testament.

In their different ways, the Revised Version and the New English Bible were failures as translations, in spite of being sponsored and produced by the churches in Britain for use in church. The Revised Version failed because of its decision to use only one English word to render any one

---

23. Preface to the NEB.

Hebrew word (e.g. זרע is always rendered as 'seed') regardless of context; and because churchgoers were shocked by the loss of familiar passages and phrases as the New Testament translators adopted a text of the Greek Testament that sought to get closer to what the New Testament writers had written, and departed from the so-called 'received text'. The New English Bible Old Testament failed because the dominant figure of G.R. Driver swayed the panel to accept theories about comparative Semitic philology that subsequent research called into question. What the failure of these translations shows is that ecclesiastical sponsorship and execution do not guarantee authoritativeness, and that such projects can be affected by the prevailing state of scholarship or the dominance of particular scholars. These officially sponsored projects raise the question of the value of translations undertaken by representative committees. After all, Luther and Tyndale, while not working alone, were not sponsored by or subject to representative committees, and yet their work became the basis of German and English translations that influenced readers of the Bible for several centuries.

Yet before we conclude that the work of individual scholars is preferable to that of committees, it is necessary to consider a translation that has aroused a good deal of hostile reaction, especially in the Netherlands, namely, the Good News Bible. What was unique about this translation was that it was based upon a careful study of translation theory, was backed by the power and influence of American Bible Society, and that it gained or achieved such a measure of authority that its English form became the basis for translations of the Bible into other vernaculars. Whatever one thinks of the Good News Bible, no one who is interested in Bible translation can afford to ignore the books of its originator and driving force, Eugene A. Nida. His *Toward a Science of Translating* (1964) and his jointly authored books *The Theory and Practice of Translation* (1969 with Charles Taber) and *From One Language to Another: Functional Equivalence in Bible Translating* (1986 with Jan de Waard) are based upon both extensive field work and research in theoretical linguistics, and have had a large impact on translation theory.[24] Nida's approach, based upon Chomsky's transformational grammar, seeks to provide dynamic equivalence translations, that is, translations that will produce the same effect upon readers/hearers in a target language that the original text produced in the source language. To

24. See the relevant essays in S.E. Porter and R.S. Hess (eds.), *Translating the Bible: Problems and Prospects* (JSNTSup, 173; Sheffield: Sheffield Academic Press, 1999).

this end, certain principles have to be implemented: the sense of a passage takes priority over its form; the structures and culture of the target language take priority over those of the source language; direct speech is preferred to reported speech. The example with which Nida has worked for many years is Mark 1.4, which reads in the RSV:

> John the baptizer appeared in the wilderness, preaching a baptism of repentance for the forgiveness of sins.

This is a formal equivalence translation which reproduces in English the linguistic features of the Greek original in phrases such as 'baptism of repentance' and 'forgiveness of sins'. In order to produce something that gives priority to the target language, Nida first identifies five kernel statements: (1) John preached (something), (2) John baptizes people, (3) the people repent, (4) God forgives something, (5) the people sin. In the Good News Bible these kernels are then re-structured in English to produce:

> So John appeared in the desert, baptizing and preaching. 'Turn away from your sins and be baptized,' he told the people, 'and God will forgive your sins.'

That this is much more accessible, especially to non-theologians, cannot be denied, and it is also the case that Nida and his associates have done far more research on the languages *into* which they are translating than is true for other modern translations.

I could, at this point, voice severe personal reservations about the concept of 'dynamic equivalence translation', but instead I shall draw attention to the implications of a research project that I supervised in Sheffield. It was undertaken as a PhD by an Australian who had studied linguistics, and who had worked for many years in Indonesia. He had discovered, to his alarm, that 'Good News'-type translations of the Bible into languages in use in Indonesia such as Javanese were reproducing the English Good News Bible in those languages instead of following the declared principle of the priority of the target language.[25] The undoubted success of the GNB-type translations, and above all their sponsorship by various Bible Societies, has shone the spotlight upon a new factor in the matter of the authoritativeness of translation, that of commercial power. Because Bible Societies subsidize the production and sale of Bibles that

---

25. A.J. Nichols, 'Bible Translation: A Critical Analysis of E.A.Nida's Theory of Dynamic Equivalence and its Impact on Recent Bible Translations' (PhD dissertation, University of Sheffield, 1997).

are made available in 'poor' areas of the world, they can establish a monopoly and provide the only version of the Bible that many readers will ever see or hear. This process did not begin with the GNB, and has always been an implication of the work of the Bible Societies since the early nineteenth century: but the GNB project has given the matter a powerful new form. Whereas in the past many Bible Society translators laboured *in situ* with so-called native informants to produce translations, the GNB project, supported by the series of Translators' Handbooks published in The Netherlands for the United Bible Societies, is evidence of something managed centrally and backed by powerful financial resources.

The whole matter is a difficult one. Nida has shown that translation is a professional and academic matter, and that translation requires more than merely an excellent knowledge of two or more languages. Again, the Translators' Handbooks contain a great deal of expertise in biblical studies and translation theory; and yet doubts remain about the theological and theoretical aspects of the project. It is probably here, in Amsterdam, that doubts about the GNB project have been raised more sharply than anywhere else.

In 1984 the Nederlands Bijbelgenootschap (NBG, Dutch Bible Society) published the *Groot nieuws Bijbel, vertaling in omgangsstaal* (Good News Bible: Translation into Colloquial Language). The following year, several essays in vol. VI of the *Amsterdamse cahiers voor exegese en Bijbelse theologie* were devoted to criticizing *the Groot nieuws Bijbel* from various angles. The sharpest, and most interesting, criticisms were voiced by Frans Breukelman[26] and were based upon the principles laid down by the Synod of Dordrecht of 1618–19, which had resulted in the *Statenvertaling* of 1637, and which stated,

> Dat sy altijts bij den oorspronckelijken text sorgfuldelijc blyven ende de manieren van spreken der oorspronckelijcke talen, so vele de duydelijcheid ende eygenschap der Nederlandsche spraken can toelaten, behouden.[27]

This was taken to mean that the form of the original language was to be reproduced as closely as the target language would allow, the theological implication being that this form had been the means by which the inspired

---

26. F.H. Breukelman and B.P.M. Hemelsoet, 'Van "Nieuwe Vertaling" naar "Groot Nieuws". Over het grondbeginsel van bijbelvertalen', *Amsterdamse cahiers voor exegese en Bijbelse theologie* 6 (1985), pp. 9-22.

27. 'It [i.e. the *Staten-Vertaling*] should carefully match the original text and keep to the manner of speaking of the original languages, [but] as much as to allow the lucidity and character of the Dutch language' (Breukelman and Hemelsoet, 'Van "Nieuwe Vertaling"', p. 12).

message had been communicated. This was further declared to be the authentic tradition of Reformed biblical translation as opposed to the Lutheran tradition, which was accused of slovenliness (*slordigheid*) and of the anthropologizing of theology. The Reformed translators of the *Staten-vertaling* are praised for their honouring of God and his sovereignty and for their consequent devotion to the Word. Clearly, a view of Bible translation that attaches primary importance to reproducing as far as possible the *form* of the original text in the target language could not be further removed from, or at greater odds with, the whole philosophy of the Good News Bible.

But this position has an interesting outcome, which is that Breukelman had a high regard for the Martin Buber and Franz Rosenzweig German translation that first appeared in 1925–29. The aim of these translators was precisely to reproduce the form of the Hebrew in German, and Breukelman wrote of their work:

> dat wij in de Staten-Vertaling met een zeventiende eeuwse nederlandse Buber-Rosenzweig te maken hebben en in de *Verdeutschung der Schrift* van Buber-Rosenzweig met een perfecte moderne duitse Staten-Vertaling.[28]

Incidentally, a project had begun in 1974, sponsored by the Nederlands Bijbelgenotschap and the Katholieke Bijbelstichting, to produce a Buber–Rosenzweig-type version in Dutch, the first publication being *Ruth—een vertaling om voor te lezen*. What is interesting about Breukelman's admiration for the Buber–Rosenzweig translation is that we have a Reformed Dutch theologian praising the work of two Jewish translators. We are a long way from the 1871 resolution of the Anglican bishops that wanted to exclude from the Revised Version panels anyone who denied the divinity of Jesus!

A translation of the *form* of the Bible in Hebrew is possible because, curiously, the Masoretic text of the Hebrew Bible has become the basis of all modern translations, in spite of the possibility of preparing and using a critical eclectic text, as has been done with the New Testament. But how does one apply the principle of reproducing the *form* of the New Testament text when what is available is a reconstructed scholarly edition of the text, authorized by the Bible Societies, but a text that was never used in any Greek-speaking church? One solution is to regard the so-called 'textus

28. '…that we, in the *Staten-Vertaling*, have to reckon with a seventeenth-century Dutch Buber-Rosenzweig [translation], and in the Buber-Rosenzweig [we have to reckon] with a perfectly modern German *Staten-Vertaling*.'

receptus' as the authoritative text of the Greek New Testament, and this is certainly behind attempts to produce such versions as the New King James Bible.

This problem is touched upon in an article by Craig Allert, 'Is a Translation Inspired? The Problems of Verbal Inspiration for Translation and a Proposed Solution'.[29] The main concern of the article is with the question of how it is possible to believe in the verbal inspiration of the Bible when the verbally inspired autographs written by the biblical writers no longer exist, and have to be reconstructed by textual criticism. The answer given by Allert is that the notion of inspiration should be redefined to mean a quality in texts that is recognized by a community of faith:

> Inspiration cannot...be defined as being located in the individual 'author', the text, or the 'author' and the text. Inspiration is not seen as something that is inherent in a writing or a writer. It is best seen as applied to an orthodox writing by the community of faith.[30]

This definition of 'inspiration' enables Allert to propose that all translations are inspired if they are recognised to be so by a community of faith.

I shall leave it to others to decide whether or not this is a viable definition of 'inspiration'. However, as a description of how translations of the Bible have come to be regarded as authoritative, and how they could still come to have this status, Allert's view has much to commend it. If a community of faith or similar institution declares a translation to be authoritative, this will have an impact upon users. Two Catholic Bibles that I have to hand, the New Jerusalem Bible and the edition of the Good News Bible with the deutero-canonical books, both carry a *nihil obstat* and *imprimatur*; and I would be surprised if any Catholic congregation in Britain used a translation of the Bible that did not carry this official authorization. On the Protestant side, the same process of authoritative commendation can work through sponsorship and distribution by Bible Societies, or by declarations such as that by the translators of the New International Version that they 'were united in their commitment to the authority and infallibility of the Bible as God's word in written form'. However, as this paper has shown, even the most authoritative 'top down' commendation of a translation by a community of faith can founder if the translation does not strike the right

---

29. In Porter and Hess, *Translating the Bible*, pp. 85-113.
30. Allert, 'Is a Translation Inspired?', p. 111.

chords with those users who are fortunate enough to be able to choose between versions. Those who are not able to choose will be at the mercy, so to speak, of whatever theology or translation principle has driven the one version that they have; a fact that should provide food for thought.

Why a Translation of the Bible Can't Be Authoritative: A Response to John Rogerson

Judith Frishman

Arnold Eisen opens his recent book, *Taking Hold of Torah: Jewish Commitment and Community in America*, with a description of the present-day Jew's relationship with tradition—He writes that for Jews in particular,

> the process of self-commitment has of late become immensely more compli-
> cated than ever before. We must decide matters which in earlier generations
> would have been decided for us, including the matter of whether to *read* the
> story that begins at the Beginning, let alone to step into it. Most Jews in
> America now come to the Torah from afar. They were not raised on the story
> of Abraham leaving his homeland and the house of his father for a land that
> God would show him. In many cases American Jews must literally leave
> their own parents' homes in order to encounter Abraham for the first time
> and must certainly depart their parents' culture—that of secular America—in
> order to 'cross the river' into observance of the covenant that he first
> entered...
>   One exaggerates only slightly, in saying that Judaism in contemporary
> America is a commitment under siege. It is surrounded on all sides by alter-
> natives which at best leave the Torah one of many books on the shelf to be
> taken down at moments of interest or fancy, and at worst reduce the Torah to
> an ethnoreligious myth of greater or lesser appeal depending on the page. It
> is great literature, to be sure, but who could seriously entertain the thought of
> having his or her life altered by a book, however masterful, much less by a
> story? Let Abraham leave the highest civilization of his day for God knows
> what. Most American Jews will understandably stick with what they've got,
> stay where they are, rest content with the culture that is content to have these
> stories somewhere on the margins of what matters to it.[1]

The complexity of the Jewish relationship to Torah is tied to several challenges confronting Jewish identity summarized by Eisen in terms of

---

1. A.M. Eisen, *Taking Hold of Torah: Jewish Commitment and Community in America* (Bloomington: Indiana University Press, 1997), pp. 3-4.

community, tradition and self.[2] The first challenge is the loss of integral community in which individuals are bound to each other by virtue of the fact that all are bound to the same sacred text. Commitment is no longer self-evident but becomes a matter of choice. The second challenge is the relativizing and marginalizing of this—and any—tradition over the past 200 years due to the triumph of scientific-historical consciousness. This meant that 'appeals to Torah no longer settled any argument, for God had not written the text, and Moses probably had not either'.[3] The third challenge is the emergence of a new sort of 'rational' self, with little patience or apparent need for the truths that Jewish tradition—Torah in the wider sense—had heretofore provided. Now if, as a result of the Enlightenment, acculturation and secularization, the very place occupied by Torah, that is the authority attributed to it, has been radically altered, then the answer to the question, 'Can a translation of the Bible be authoritative?', must be 'No', at least not for the majority of those of Jewish and Christian descent today. Nor is it surprising that ecclesiastical sponsorship and execution do not guarantee the degree of authority attributed to a translation. Not because such translation projects are affected by the prevailing state of scholarship or the dominance of particular scholars or are of lesser value when undertaken by representative committees, but because ecclesiastical sponsorship and approval themselves are of so little meaning for so many today.

Why then are new translation projects being undertaken, by whom and for whom? Bible Societies may still be counted upon to sponsor new translations. Decrease in missionary activity—at least activity with the Bible in one's hand as opposed to socio-economic aid—seems to have led to increased activity on the Western home front. The New Bible Translation (NBV)—a joint project of the Dutch Bible Society (NBG, *Nederlands Bijbelgenootschap*) and the Catholic Bible Foundation (KBS, *Katholieke Bijbelstichting*)—was initiated at a time when the new (Dutch) Willibrord translation was on its way to being completed and the *Groot Nieuws Bijbel* was being revised. One may wonder whether the stream of productions really fills a public need, keeping abreast of the video-clip-like quality of everyday life, or rather serves to justify and perpetuate the existence of the Bible Societies themselves. But a Society cannot survive if its products are not purchased and thus where 'top down commendation' fails, sophisticated public relations officers are hired to stimulate public interest and arouse curiosity.

2. Eisen, *Torah*, pp. 4-15.
3. Eisen, *Torah*, pp. 9-10.

The public in mind is not limited to the Bible Society's natural audience: that waning number of supporters and friends (of the Society) for whom the Society's commendations suffice. Rather a much broader public is intended, for example those who have left the church but regard the Bible as part and parcel of the foundation of European 'Judeo-Christian' culture, or as a source of spiritual inspiration to be consulted alongside the works of Buddhist and Hindu sages. The involvement of well-known writers and literary critics in present-day projects such as that of the Netherlands is meant to assure the literary quality—a praiseworthy endeavor, once more aimed at attracting readers from outside the circle of believers or the affiliated.

Previews or pre-publications provoke reactions and even heated debate which are no longer confined to ecclesiastical circles but played out on the pages of national newspapers. An imprimatur may in the end be irrelevant to the success of a translation. The status of bestseller may instead serve as a measure of the inspiration recognized by an increasingly non-traditional and individualized community of faith in any biblical translation. Thus despite doubts and criticism concerning the *Groot Nieuws Bijbel*, this translation has proven extremely popular in educational and cathechetical settings. It would seem to me that the 'authoritative' status of the translation has thereby been confirmed, despite the fact that most intellectuals wouldn't deign to cite that version. The *Groot Nieuws Bijbel* may in fact for many be the translation that most closely approximates Augustine's notion of the *sermo humilis*, and the personal relationship to Scriptures which it entailed.[4]

I would like to end my response by reacting to Professor Rogerson's closing words in his contribution:

> Those who are not able to choose [i.e. between versions] will be at the mercy, so to speak, of whatever theology or translation principle has driven the one version that they have; a fact which should provide food for thought.[5]

In the Jewish past the Targumim did enjoy a certain status, but that status was attributed to them by those who were still bound to each other by virtue of their being bound to the same sacred Hebrew text. As Steven Fraade describes it:

4.   G. Stroumsa, 'The Christian Hermeneutical Revolution and Its Double Helix', in L.V. Rutgers *et al.* (eds.), *The Use of Sacred Books in the Ancient World* (Contributions to Biblical Exegesis and Theology, 22; Leuven: Peeters, 1998), pp. 9-28 (24).

5.   J. Rogerson, 'Can a Translation of the Bible be Authoritative?', pp. 17-30 in this volume.

> To employ a musical metaphor, the performance of Targum may be said to
> have been neither that of a soloist nor that of an equal partner in a duet, but
> that of an accompanist to the principal performance of the scriptural
> recital... Just as the musical accompanist enunciates and thereby enhances
> the performance of the soloist through the subtleties of his or her
> interpretations, so, too, Targum in relation to Scripture. But in both cases,
> the accompanist must share the stage unobtrusively, that is, without draw-
> ing attention away from the principal performer. It is for both of these
> reasons that the accompanist performs on a different instrument than that of
> the performer. Thus the voices Torah and Targum, of Hebrew and Aramaic,
> worked well in the performative ritual and scriptural enunciation and eluci-
> dation, even while the two remained visibly and aurally distinct from one
> another in quality and status.[6]

But, what to do in a time when the accompanist's voice has been raised
above that of the principal performer, when in fact the principal performer's voice has nearly been silenced?

Already in the eighteenth century Moses Mendelssohn undertook the
project—nearly on his own—of producing a new Targum, a Targum
whose aim it was to educate Jews in two languages at once: *hoch Deutsch*
and Hebrew. Mendelssohn thereby hoped to bridge a gap between the
fading integral community of the past, and the society of European culture
at large which had just begun to open its doors to the Jews. His project—
the authority of which was contested despite Mendelssohn's claim to be in
line with tradition when employing the name Targum—could not salvage
what had once been. As Eisen writes:

> Tradition, when it is distinguished from mere nostalgia, provokes anxiety
> about the sort of authority which brooks no disobedience or creativity. And
> the vision of a substantively Jewish self seems to fly in the face of auton-
> omy: to a modern self perhaps the most precious gift of all.[7]

Those who are not able to choose between versions of biblical translation
may be at the mercy of whatever theology has driven the version they
might happen to have. But those who are not able to choose are also often
those who refuse to distinguish tradition from mere nostalgia and—consequently—reject any new translation, denying it a priori any authority or

---

6.   S.D. Fraade, 'Rabbinic Views on the Practice of Targum, and Multilingualism in
the Jewish Galilee of the Third–Sixth Centuries', in L. Levine (ed.), *The Galilee in Late
Antiquity* (New York: The Jewish Theological Seminary of America, 1992), pp. 253-86
(283).

7.   Eisen, *Torah*, p. 14.

inspiration. Perhaps they are not so much at the mercy of an arbitrary translation principle but, rather, the translations themselves are at their mercy.

In conclusion, in a post-Enlightenment world, no translation will ever occupy as important and universal a place as that which the Targum in Jewish life or the Septuagint in Christian life had occupied.

ICON OF THE INEFFABLE?
AN ORTHODOX VIEW OF LANGUAGE AND ITS
IMPLICATIONS FOR BIBLE TRANSLATION

Simon Crisp

Much in the 'classical' theory of dynamic or functional equivalence in Bible translation, as expounded from the late 1950s onwards by Eugene Nida and his successors, seems at the dawn of a new century to be the child of its time and place. At the symposium on Bible translation held at the Roehampton Institute in London in 1995, for example, some presenters gave the central idea of functional equivalence—the attempt to reproduce for the reader of a translation the impact of the original text on its first readers—a fairly rough ride. For Brook Pearson this kind of 'remainderless translation' reflects a kind of:

> Romantic hermeneutics, where the interpreter needs to get into the head, as it were, of the original author, *recreating* the document in the process of interpretation. This approach to hermeneutics is, first, outmoded, and secondly, demonstrably impossible.[1]

And as John Rogerson pointed out at the same meeting—quoting remarks made already 20 years earlier—there is actually no way, 'short of a time machine', of recovering this information about the original impact of the text. 'Was there only *one* such impact?', he asks.[2]

There is of course a danger of caricature in such brief characterizations of a theory elaborated in detail over many years and applied (to a greater or lesser extent) in a large number of actual Bible translation projects—

---

1. Brook W.R. Pearson, 'Remainderless Translations? Implications of the Tradition Concerning the Translation of the LXX for Modern Translational Theory', in S.E. Porter and R.S. Hess (eds.), *Translating the Bible: Problems and Prospects* (JSNTSup, 173; Sheffield: Sheffield Academic Press, 1999), pp. 63-84 (84).

2. J.W. Rogerson, 'The Old Testament Translator's Translation—A Personal Reflection', in Porter and Hess (eds.), *Translating the Bible*, pp. 116-24 (118).

and indeed, both the authors just referred to are careful to stress their positive evaluation of many aspects of Nida's approach. We should also remember that Nida himself was far from being sanguine about the extent to which the ideal of reproducing the original impact of the text is achievable in practice—witness his remarks on this subject both in the now classic *Theory and Practice of Translation*,[3] and also in his extensive—but less frequently quoted—other writings.[4] The accusation remains nevertheless that dynamic or functional equivalence (the two terms are treated here as identical in meaning, following de Waard and Nida, *From One Language to Another*[5]) implies a rather high degree of optimism about the process of translation, and about the possibility of establishing the original meaning and impact of the text.

From this point of view modern English translations of the Bible, for example, have been severely treated by some literary critics. Stephen Prickett's quarrel with modern Bible translations (and with the Good News Bible and the Bible Societies in particular), for example, may be summed up by his dismissal of the aim of the GNB translators to 'use language that is natural, clear, simple and unambiguous…when the Bible is *not about* things that are natural, clear, simple and unambiguous'.[6] He illustrates his contention with the story of Elijah on Mount Horeb, and particularly the nature of the 'still small voice' experienced by the prophet, bringing out the rich ambiguity between natural and supernatural nuances in explaining what may

3. Eugene A. Nida and Charles R. Taber, *The Theory and Practice of Translation* (Help for Translators, 8; Leiden: E.J. Brill, 1969), p. 24.

4. A sample spanning a long career may include the recognition that the specific nature of each individual's command of language 'does not make communication impossible, but it removes the possibility of absolute equivalence and opens the way for different renderings of the same message' ('Principles of Translation as Exemplified by Bible Translating' [*BT* 10/4 (October 1959), pp 148-64 (151)]; the claim that 'descriptive linguistics operates on the assumption that there are no absolute synonyms' (*Exploring Semantic Structures* [Munich: Wilhelm Fink Verlag, 1975], pp. 140-41); and, in the end, the fact that 'one of the distinctive features of all religious language is its nebulous semantics, because people attempt to talk about infinite, absolute truths by means of finite, culture-dependent words' ('The Sociolinguistics of Translating Canonical Religious Texts', in *Traduction, Terminologie, Rédaction: Etudes sur le texte et ses transformations* 7/1 [1994], pp. 191-217 [201]).

5. Jan de Waard and Eugene Nida, *From One Language to Another: Functional Equivalence in Bible Translating* (Nashville: Thomas Nelson, 1986), p. vii.

6. Stephen Prickett, *Words and The Word: Language, Poetics and Biblical Interpretation* (Cambridge: Cambridge University Press, 1986), p. 10.

actually have happened.[7] For Prickett all explanatory translations, in attempting to make something more understandable out of what is essentially an experience without precedent and defying explanation, represent the imposition of ideology on the text, and in the final analysis render that text less rather than more transparent in that they close off interpretative possibilities. A reading of Prickett raises the question of whether the conflict of approaches is irreconcilable—is it simply the case that academic literary critics are lined up on one side and missionary Bible translators on the other, with no possibility of finding common ground?

The theory of dynamic equivalence in Bible translation, just like any other theoretical approach, did not arise in a vacuum, and it may be useful to review some of the presuppositions on which it is based. From one point of view Nida's application of the methods and insights of modern linguistics to the translation process was quite revolutionary for its time: the model of analysis–transfer–restructuring represented a radical step forward from the methods of formal correspondence that had largely (though not exclusively)[8] held sway in Bible translation up to that point. From a vantage point more than 30 years on, however, such optimism about the potential of what is in effect an early form of transformational-generative grammar may seem a trifle naive: today both linguistics and translation theory have moved far beyond the simple distinction between surface structure and deep structure of language.[9] Extensive work on metaphor, to take one clear and specific case, has demonstrated a much more complex and nuanced set of relations between form and content in language,[10] and developments in discourse analysis have revolutionized our understanding

7.   See also Everett Fox's article, 'The Translation of Elijah', and A.J.C. Verheij's response, in this volume, pp. 156-69.

8.   Some examples of the earlier application of functional equivalence may be found in Roland H. Worth, *Bible Translations: A History Through Source Documents* (Jefferson, NC and London: McFarland, 1992); see also Klaus Haacker, 'Dynamische Äquivalenz in Geschichte und Gegenwart', in Carsten Peter Thiede (ed.), *Bibelübersetzung zwischen Inkulturation und Manipulation* (Paderborn: Deutsches Institut für Bildung und Wissen, 1993), pp. 19-32.

9.   The matter is not really helped by the distinction made in Nida and Taber, *Theory and Practice*, p. 39 n. 9, between deep structure and kernel sentences, since this still begs the question about the psychological reality of the latter.

10.   The literature on metaphor is of course huge. Key applications to biblical and religious language include Janet Martin Soskice, *Metaphor and Religious Language* (Oxford: Oxford University Press, 1985), and Peter W. Macky, *The Centrality of Metaphors to Biblical Thought* (Lewiston, NY: Edwin Mellen Press, 1990).

of the sophisticated structure of texts and their constituent units at all levels.[11] These insights are gradually being incorporated into translation theory in general, and Bible translation in particular.

More productive in the context of the concerns of this paper, however, is consideration of the relationship between Bible translation and interpretation of the biblical text. Here perhaps the most fundamental feature of the context in which the dynamic equivalence approach arose is the laudable desire to make the meaning of Scripture as clear as possible to the reader. Translation, and especially meaning-based translation, presupposes access to the (preferably single) meaning of the text, and is therefore dependent in turn on the methods and presuppositions of the historical-critical paradigm with its roots in European Enlightenment values and the rediscovery of classical learning on the one hand, and the rise of Protestantism with its emphasis on the autonomy of the text of Scripture on the other. Both dynamic equivalence in Bible translation and the historical-critical approach in biblical studies, then, share a certain optimism about the possibility of discovering and expressing in propositional terms the original meaning of the biblical text. As modernity gives way to postmodernity in Western culture, this confidence begins to look a little misplaced—perhaps (in Lyotard's terms) it is another 'metanarrative' towards which a degree of 'incredulity' might now be considered to be in order.

A theory of Bible translation thus entails certain presuppositions about exegesis of the biblical text—in the case of dynamic equivalence the historical-critical method as developed in European biblical scholarship since the time of the Reformation. This method of exegesis in its turn presupposes a certain hermeneutic, which might be expressed in the following terms.[12] Biblical criticism as currently practised derives directly from the Reformation view that Scripture is the only or pre-eminent authority in the church. If this is so then Scripture (in the absence of tradition or a church hierarchy to control interpretation) has to be self-interpreting, and biblical criticism is needed as an 'objective' means of determining which interpretations are valid. This hermeneutic of the perspicuity of Scripture, a 'direct reading of a plain text', can itself be linked with a number of assumptions[13]

---

11. See most recently Stanley E. Porter and Jeffrey T. Reed (eds.), *Discourse Analysis and the New Testament: Approaches and Results* (JSNTSup, 170; Sheffield: Sheffield Academic Press, 1999).

12. This presentation owes much to Mary Sanford, 'An Orthodox View of Biblical Criticism', *Sourozh* 26 (1986), p. 25-32 (26).

13. Interestingly enough, the cultural pervasiveness of these presuppositions about

about the nature of language, which may be presented here for convenience in a rather schematic form.[14]

1. All language (if it is not nonsense) must conform to a normative set of rules governing its use.
2. The fundamental building blocks of language are therefore logical propositions having a single meaning.
3. Since these propositions are ruled by a normative use of language, there are general rules for interpretation which apply to all texts.
4. There is thus unquestionable access to the intended meaning of the author, which is identical with the single meaning of the logical propositions.

So far, then, the aspects of the broader context for Bible translation which we have been considering may be expressed in the form of a simple diagram:

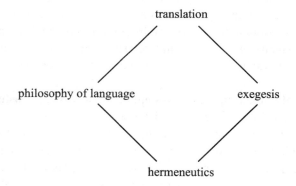

This diagram may be read in two directions. In the case of dynamic equivalence the theory of translation is based on the historical-critical exegetical paradigm, which in turn is based on a hermeneutic of the plain

language goes some way towards explaining why the hermeneutical approach summarized above is common to both conservative and liberal practitioners of historical-critical exegesis. For the former as for the latter a single 'plain meaning' may be derived from the text and expressed in propositional terms: the further use or application of this plain meaning is conditioned by a different set of philosophical assumptions, for instance, about the inherent credibility of the biblical message.

14. Once again following Mary Sanford, this time in her 1984 PhD thesis, 'How Do You Read?": Theology and Hermeneutics in the Interpretation of New Testament Parables' (Canterbury: University of Kent), pp. 68-69.

meaning of the text, and this in its turn relies on a philosophy of language as primarily composed of logical propositions. If we take as our starting point a different philosophy of language and read the diagram in the opposite direction, however, a different picture emerges. If the relationship between language and reality is understood by analogy with an icon, for example, this leads to a hermeneutic of mystery and polyvalency, a hermeneutic which lays more stress on the autonomous life of the text than on authorial intent (and thus finds certain resonances with contemporary exegetical approaches like reader-response criticism and community driven exegesis), and this raises the question of what theory of translation might now be considered appropriate. We shall come back to these questions at the end of this paper—but first it may be useful to return to our starting point.

The dissatisfaction with the dynamic equivalence approach to Bible translation which was noted at the beginning of this paper may be traced back through fragmentation of the exegetical paradigm on which this approach is based, further to the hermeneutical basis underlying this paradigm, and ultimately to the understanding of the nature of language from which this hermeneutic derives. The practical implications for Bible translation, however, are far from straightforward: in reality the primary consequence of dissatisfaction with dynamic equivalence has been a smaller or greater step backwards in the direction of more formal correspondence or more literal renderings (the prime example is perhaps the German *Gute Nachricht Bibel* in comparison with its predecessor *Die Gute Nachricht*). More creative developments may be expected from the interaction between Bible translators and those at the sharp end of general translation studies,[15] but it may also be of interest in this context to ask what other traditions, and other views of language and Scripture, have to offer to the theory of Bible translation. In the remainder of this paper I shall attempt to explore the contribution that the Eastern Orthodox tradition, with its specific understanding of the role of mystery on the one hand and the limitations of human language on the other, might make to this process.

At the level of exegetical techniques, the main distinguishing feature of

---

15. I have in mind particularly the work of Hatim and Mason on the exigencies of translating sacred text: see Basil Hatim and Ian Mason, *The Translator as Communicator* (London: Routledge, 1997), especially ch. 7, 'Form and Function in the Translation of Sacred and Sensitive Text'. Also relevant is the section on 'Sacred Texts' in Karl Simms (ed.), *Translating Sensitive Texts: Linguistic Aspects* (Amsterdam: Rodopi, 1997), pp. 187-243.

Orthodox biblical scholarship is probably its faithfulness to patristic tradition. If for scholars from other backgrounds the interpretations of the Fathers are at best a matter of historical curiosity, the sense of the continuity of tradition in Orthodoxy means that patristic exegesis cannot be considered simply a pre-modern approach belonging to a different (and superseded) world: instead, it is a living tradition with which subsequent interpreters stand in a relationship of direct continuity. Patristic exegesis, in other words, represents an overtly community driven exegesis rather than a search for 'objectivity'; in the context of the claims made in the preceding part of this paper, however, we might be justified in asking whether this approach is in fact any less culture bound than the historical-critical paradigm.[16]

At the level of hermeneutics, the isolation of the Orthodox world from the processes of Reformation and Enlightenment taking place in Western Europe means that the biblical text has maintained its primary role in an ecclesial and liturgical context (e.g. the veneration of the Gospel Book during the liturgy itself at the time of the Little Entrance) rather than being treated in the same way as other ancient texts whose meaning needs to be recovered and reinterpreted using tools developed for the study of texts in general. In Orthodox understanding the text of Scripture functions in a way more analogous to an icon, namely as a window onto another world, rather than as a source of propositionally expressed information.

The analogy of the icon, however, is perhaps most powerful when applied to understanding the nature of language in general, and sacred language in particular. (Given the primary function of the Bible in the Orthodox liturgy, the issue of sacred language assumes particular prominence.) Orthodox tradition views language as an intrinsically inadequate tool for comprehending the holy, and therefore as performing verbally a symbolic role analogous to that enacted visually by icons. Just as the icon makes no claim to be a photographic—or even essentially pictorial—depiction of the scene or event it represents, but rather a window onto the timeless reality to which it testifies and a mysterious means of mediating that reality to the worshipper, so the language of Scripture cannot be a series of logical propositions with a single intended meaning; instead, 'it is intentionally polyvalent, having several intended meanings, because what is being communicated is generally too

---

16. Analogies with other traditions of exegesis, for instance that of the rabbis, might also be worth exploring. A good starting point is Raphael Lowe's article on 'Jewish Exegesis', in R.J. Coggins and J.L. Houlden (eds.), *A Dictionary of Biblical Interpretation* (London: SCM Press, 1990), pp. 346-54.

complex to be communicated in clear and simple statements. It is not that kind of language'.[17]

A full study of patristic material on the nature of (sacred) language remains to be done (although several suggestive steps in this direction have been taken by Ioannis Panagopoulos[18]). Building on classical Greek philosophy of language (Plato, Aristotle and the Stoics), the Fathers debated the relationship between the word (*fone, onoma*) and the essence or reality (*ousia*) to which it refers. In the writings of St Basil the Great the distinction is drawn in a categorical way that has come to be known as apophatic (as Panagopoulos puts it, 'die Ousia kann, als absolute Realität, nicht begriffen werden. Sie wird nur beschrieben und geschaut'),[19] and has been highly influential in Orthodox theology and spirituality. Furthermore, the influence of apophaticism or the *via negativa* has extended beyond its traditional formulations[20] to poststructuralism[21] and postmodernity. Witness, for example, the dazzling demonstration by Gorazd Kocijančič of the links between postmodernity's 'incredulity towards metanarratives' and apophaticism as a means of protecting the mystery of God:

> It was always obvious to the Eastern Fathers that the biblical verbalisation of the Verbum is not an adequate expression, but a gracious adjustment, God's descent (syngkatabasis) towards people, into the world of human thoughts and words... God reveals himself within human words and at the same time remains hidden in His Otherness.[22]

The implications of this understanding of language for Bible translation are quite considerable. Since the way in which language relates to the realities described in the Bible is seen as a complex and mysterious

---

17. Sanford, 'An Orthodox View of Biblical Criticism', p. 31.

18. Johannes Panagopoulos, 'Sache und Energie: Zur theologischen Grundlegung der biblischen Hermeneutik bei den griechischen Kirchenvätern', in Hermann Lichtenberger (ed.), *Geschichte—Tradition—Reflexion: Festschrift für Martin Hengel zum 70. Geburtstag.* III: *Frühes Christentum* (Tübingen: Mohr Siebeck, 1996), pp. 567-84.

19. Panagopoulos, 'Sache und Energie', p. 572. 'As absolute reality the essence itself cannot be comprehended. It can only be described and demonstrated.'

20. See Dan R. Stivers, *The Philosophy of Religious Language* (Oxford: Basil Blackwell, 1996), pp. 16-20.

21. Stivers, *Philosophy of Religious Language*, pp. 189-92.

22. Gorazd Kocijančič, 'He Who Is and Being: On the Postmodern Relevance of Eastern Christian Apophaticism', in Robert F. Taft (ed.), *The Christian East: Its Institutions and Thought* (Orientalia Christiana Analecta, 251; Pontifico Istituto Orientale: Rome, 1996), pp. 631-49 (638).

process, an Orthodox approach would tend to maintain in some way the status of the text as a window onto another world by preserving a sense of the distance between the (modern) reader and the (ancient) text, and by marking in some way the inherent strangeness or otherness of that text.

One might justifiably argue, however, that this is rather a lame conclusion: if all translations have to be situated somewhere on a scale between exact formal correspondence and free paraphrase, it may appear that an Orthodox approach simply lines up with literary critics like Stephen Prickett and demands a return to more formal, literal translation. There seems to be no intrinsic reason, though, why this marking of distance between the reader and the text should have to be done in opposition to a commitment to make the translation understandable to the reader, by a return to literal renderings or artificially archaic language—more careful attention to the stylistic possibilities of the receptor language could achieve the same result in a more effective way, by giving more attention to conveying to the reader of the translation something of the multidimensionality of the source text. And it is precisely here that the Orthodox tradition may have a contribution to make: not by replacing functional equivalence with a wholly different approach, but by balancing the kind of concerns expressed by literary critics with a pastoral concern for the accessibility of the text. It is no part of the aim of this paper to suggest a wholesale abandonment of the heritage of Nida—but rather to offer the analogy of the icon, with its special combination of conventionality, accessibility and mystery, as one strand in the discussion of where the theory and practice of Bible translation need to move at the start of a new millennium.

Appendix: 'Literary Translations' in English

The purpose of this short appendix is to give some substance to the more abstract presentation of this paper by looking at a sample passage in four English translations with pretensions to literary status. These are the translation of E.V. Rieu (*Four Gospels*, 1952), the New English Bible (1970), the Jerusalem Bible (1966), and the translation of Richmond Lattimore (*Four Gospels*, 1982; *New Testament*, 1996).[23] The text of the Magnificat

---

23. The Authorized or King James Version is not included in this selection because the question of its gradual metamorphosis over the course of time, from being jeered at for its poor English to its apotheosis as the (supposed) sublime example of literary style—so ably documented in David Norton, *A History of the English Bible as Literature* (Cambridge: Cambridge University Press, 2000)—is of a quite different nature.

(Lk. 1.46-55) is reproduced here in parallel columns, with the Greek given as a point of reference. The choice of text, of course, is a deliberate one: a piece of Greek writing in uncharacteristically (for the New Testament) high literary style, and with numerous echoes of the Hebrew Bible—most notably, perhaps, the Song of Hannah in 1 Sam. 2.1-10. The selection of translations also deserves some comment: less in the case of the New English Bible and the Jerusalem Bible—which both include in their respective Prefaces explicit statements of their literary aims (see below for details)—than in that of the two individual efforts by distinguished classicists.

Rieu was for many years the chief editor of the Penguin Classics series ('a library of translations of the world's greatest literature'), and a formidable scholar in his own right. In the "Introduction" to his translation of the Gospels he argued succinctly for the literary merit of these texts: 'The Four Gospels are spiritually supreme largely *because* they are great literature.' Lattimore too is a well-known classicist and translator, with a string of published translations of Greek classics to his name. He pursued a somewhat different aim, which he expressed in the 'Preface' to his New Testament as 'the belief that fidelity to the original word order and syntax may yield an English prose that to some extent reflects the style of the original'. These statements reflect two very different perceptions of the nature of literary translation, and as we shall see they lead to startlingly different results.

Evaluation of the literary merits of these short texts is of course a highly subjective matter, and the observations that follow represent a personal view that will correspond to varying degrees with the perceptions of other readers. Despite the limitations of space and subjectivity, however, it is hoped that examination of a piece of real text will add a sharper focus to the more general issues addressed in the paper itself.

The New English Bible (NEB), whose Preface refers to the appointment of a 'panel of trusted literary advisers, to whom all the work of the translating panels was to be submitted for scrutiny', appears in its rendering of the Magnificat to be more florid than elegant. The opening—'Tell out, my soul, the greatness of the Lord'—is more than an echo of Anglican hymnody (and was wisely amended in the Revised English Bible to, 'My soul tells out the greatness of the Lord'). 'Rejoice, rejoice' has become something of an unfortunate cliché since its use in a speech by Margaret Thatcher (though the NEB translators can hardly be held responsible for this!). 'So tenderly has he looked…humble as she is' suggests a Dickensian picture of obsequious hand-wringing rather than the required image of divine care. The postposition of 'the Lord, the Mighty One' is more awkward than poetic. The rhythm of 'the deeds his own right arm has done' is that of school-children's doggerel. And 'he has ranged himself at the side of Israel' is not at all natural in English, let alone good style (the REB, 'he has come to the help of Israel', is a much preferable rendering of ἀντελάβετο ᾿Ισραήλ).

The Jerusalem Bible (JB), together with its successor the New Jerusalem Bible (NJB), in which as the General Editor's Foreword assures us, 'care has been taken to reproduce the dignity of the originals by a certain meas-ured phrasing and avoidance of the colloquial', does considerably better at rendering the Magnificat in English. It is the only one of the four versions presented here, for instance, to retain the Greek word order in 'holy is his name', which does give the text a certain resonance. 'Exults', 'exalted' and 'mindful' hit just about the right note of fairly high literary style, while yet remaining within the passive lexicon of most English speakers. And 'pulled down princes from their thrones' is a nice alliteration. On the debit side, it must be said that the awkward parenthesis, '–according to the promise made to our ancestors–', is anything but elegant; and the elision of 'he has' in 'the rich sent empty away' does not really come off. In gen-eral, however, we may say that JB represents a fairly successful attempt to combine literary merit with intelligibility, as was suggested in the con-clusion to this paper.

Lattimore's translation illustrates a radically different approach, based as it is on the explicit presupposition that a literal translation will be of inherent literary merit by reproducing the qualities of the original at this level. Hence in his rendering of the Magnificat we meet such curiosities as 'cast down his eyes to the low estate', a purely etymological translation of ἐπέβλεψεν ('casting down one's eyes' means something completely dif-ferent for a speaker of English); 'after now all the generations', where the use of the definite article begs the question 'all *which* generations?'; 'he has taken power into his arm', which suggests (if anything) the possible use of an intravenous drip; and the frankly incomprehensible 'through the memory of mercy' which turns a fairly straightforward Greek construction into an English one of such obscurity as almost to defy interpretation. This version, it seems to me, can be considered good literary style only if the main criterion for such a judgment is opacity.

And so to Rieu, which in my opinion gives—out of the four versions considered here—the most successful literary rendering of the Magnificat. One might well query the parsing of τῷ ᾿Αβραὰμ καὶ τῷ σπέρματι αὐτοῦ as an instrumental subject of μνησθῆναι,[24] but it does give a very elegant construction with which to bring the passage to a conclusion, and 'embraced' for ἀντελάβετο only adds to the vividness of the picture. The addition of the verb 'stretches' smooths out the Greek verbless construction εἰς γενεὰς καὶ γενεὰς (compare Lattimore '*is* for generations and generations', and especially JB '*reaches* from age to age'). 'Wrought a victory' is almost a dead metaphor, but still hits the right stylistic note. 'The conceit of their hearts' is sufficiently original to strike the reader with its freshness. 'Dragged dynasts from their thrones' is an effective alliteration, and higher style than JB 'pulled down princes'. On the negative side, perhaps more could have been done with ἰδοὺ γάρ than the rather lame 'and' (JB 'yes' is a lot more vivid here); and the 'rich *man*' who is to be sent empty away sounds unnecessarily restrictive to a modern, gender-sensitive ear (though it may be necessary here for rhythmic reasons?). In sum, however, this constitutes a rather successful attempt to convey the meaning of the Greek text at a high level of literary English: it is a pity that Rieu's translation as a whole is not better known.[25]

Four short extracts can of course hardly provide a basis for any wide-ranging conclusions—Douglas Hofstadter, by contrast, solicited 88 'wildly diverse renditions' of Marot's short poem *A une Damoyselle malade* for his astonishing discussion of literary translation.[26] But even this brief appendix may show that the hope expressed at the end of this paper, that Bible translations could be at the same time accessible and multidimensional, is not incapable of realization.

24. Marshall's commentary, for example, does not include this possibility among his three listed interpretations of the construction (I. Howard Marshall, *The Gospel of Luke: A Commentary on the Greek Text* [Exeter: Paternoster Press, 1978], p. 85).

25. Amongst more than one hundred English translations discussed in Alan S. Duthie, *How To Choose Your Bible Wisely* (2nd edn; Carlisle/Swindon: Paternoster Press / Bible Society, 1995), Rieu's work is unaccountably omitted.

26. Douglas R. Hofstadter, *Le Ton beau de Marot: In Praise of the Music of Language* (New York: Basic Books, 1997).

(Greek)	(Rieu)	(New English Bible)	(Jerusalem Bible)	(Lattimore)
Καὶ εἶπεν Μαριάμ·	And Mary said:	And Mary said:	And Mary said:	Then Mary said:
Μεγαλύνει ἡ ψυχή μου τὸν κύριον, καὶ ἠγαλλίασεν τὸ πνεῦμά μου ἐπὶ τῷ θεῷ τῷ σωτῆρί μου, ὅτι ἐπέβλεψεν ἐπὶ τὴν ταπείνωσιν τῆς δούλης αὐτοῦ. ἰδοὺ γὰρ ἀπὸ τοῦ νῦν μακαριοῦσίν με πᾶσαι αἱ γενεαί, ὅτι ἐποίησέν μοι μεγάλα ὁ δυνατός· καὶ ἅγιον τὸ ὄνομα αὐτοῦ, καὶ τὸ ἔλεος αὐτοῦ εἰς γενεὰς καὶ γενεὰς τοῖς φοβουμένοις αὐτόν. Ἐποίησεν κράτος ἐν βραχίονι αὐτοῦ διεσκόρπισεν ὑπερηφάνους διανοίᾳ καρδίας αὐτῶν· καθεῖλεν δυνάστας ἀπὸ	'My soul magnifies the Lord, And my spirit has exulted in my saviour God; For he has looked upon his servant's lowliness— And all generations from to-day will call me happy. For the Mighty One has done great things for me, And his Name is holy. His mercy for those who fear him Stretches from generation to generation. He has wrought a victory with his arm: He has scattered the proud in the conceit of their hearts; He has dragged dynasts from their thrones and exalted the humble, Filled the hungry with good things	'Tell out my soul, the greatness of the Lord, rejoice, rejoice, my spirit, in God my saviour; so tenderly has he looked upon his servant, humble as she is. For from this day forth, all generations will count me blessed, so wonderfully has he dealt with me, the Lord, the Mighty One. His name is Holy; his mercy sure from generation to generation toward those who fear him; the deeds his own right arm has done disclose his might: the arrogant of heart and mind he has put to rout, he has brought down monarchs from their thrones,	'My soul proclaims the greatness of the Lord and my spirit exults in God my saviour; because he has looked upon his lowly handmaid. Yes, from this day forward all generations will call me blessed, for the Almighty has done great things for me. Holy is his name, and his mercy reaches from age to age for those who fear him. He has shown the power of his arm, He has routed the proud of heart. He has pulled down princes from their thrones and exalted the lowly. The hungry he has filled with good things, the rich	'My soul exalts the Lord, and my spirit rejoices in God my saviour, because he cast down his eyes to the low estate of his slave girl. Behold, after now all the generations will bless me; because the mighty one has done great things for me, and his name is holy; and his mercy is for generations and generations, for those who fear him. He has taken power into his arm, and scattered the proud in the imagination of their hearts. He has pulled down the dynasts from their thrones, and raised up the humble; he has filled the hungry with good things, and sent the rich away empty. He has reached out his hand to Israel his servant, through the memory

			of mercy; as he said to our fathers, to Abraham and his seed forever.'
θρόνων καὶ ὕψωσεν ταπεινούς, πεινῶντας ἐνέπλησεν ἀγαθῶν καὶ πλουτοῦντας ἐξαπέστειλεν κενούς. ἀντελάβετο Ἰσραὴλ παιδὸς αὐτοῦ, μνησθῆναι ἐλέους, καθὼς ἐλάλησεν πρὸς τοὺς πατέρας ἡμῶν, τῷ Ἀβραὰμ καὶ τῷ σπέρματι αὐτοῦ εἰς τὸν αἰῶνα.	and sent away the rich man empty; He has embraced his servant Israel, So that, as he told our fathers, His mercy may be kept in mind By Abraham and his sons for ever.'	but the humble have been lifted high. The hungry he has satisfied with good things, the rich sent empty away. He has ranged himself at the side of Israel his servant; firm in his promise to our forefathers, he has not forgotten to show mercy to Abraham and his children's children, for ever.'	sent empty away. He has come to the help of Israel his servant, mindful of his mercy —according to the promise he made to our ancestors— of his mercy to Abraham and to his descendants for ever.'

OTHERNESS AND EQUIVALENCE IN BIBLE TRANSLATION: A RESPONSE TO SIMON CRISP

Lénart J. de Regt

As we have heard, functional equivalence (FE) in Bible translation involves an attempt to reproduce for the reader of a translation the impact of the original text on its first readers. FE is based on a certain optimism about the process of translation and about the possibility of establishing the original meaning and impact of the text.

It is true that FE in Bible translation and the historical-critical approach are both optimistic about the possibility of discovering and expressing the original meaning of the biblical text. But this does not imply that FE is necessarily dependent on the historical-critical approach or its presuppositions if it is to achieve this purpose. Synchronic approaches to biblical texts have often presupposed access to the original meaning of the text as well, or at least to the meaning of the text in its final form. For example, analysis of the literary structure of a text can be based on the assumption that the structure as originally intended is recoverable. In any case, a certain optimism remains in synchronic as well as historical-critical approaches that the meaning of the text is recoverable through autonomous study of the Bible. A way of studying the Bible that indeed has its roots in the Reformation view that Scripture has to be self-interpreting, and is not to be controlled by church tradition or church hierarchy.

This point of view, that the Bible can be read and interpreted directly, like other texts, can indeed be linked to the view on the nature of language of which Dr Crisp gave a summary. But before one relates FE to this modern view of language, one should at least include non-cognitive functions that propositions can have according to a linguist such as Roman Jakobson, a different voice from the East in fact. Even if one would accept that propositions are building blocks of language, this does not imply that they are logical. Even '[i]f we analyze language from the standpoint of the information it carries, we cannot restrict the notion of information to the cognitive aspect of language'.[1] A proposition may be there to make or maintain *contact* between speaker and hearer. And the speaker can *express his or her attitude* to what she or he is speaking about, for example by means of interjections and particles. And when it comes to the poetic function of language, there can be focus on the message not just to refer to objects, but to the message for its own sake, on the (artful) choice of words, *how the message is framed*. To quote one nice example: 'The symmetry of three disyllabic verbs with an identical initial consonant and identical final vowel added splendor to the laconic victory message of Caesar: "Veni, vidi, vici"'.[2] By now, such functions of language are part of the view of language to which FE is related. FE has indeed and increasingly paid attention to the form and impact of the source text as well as the information content, for example in the area of metaphor, poetry and rhetorical features.

The optimism that, through exegesis, we can recover the original meaning of the biblical text is no longer widespread. But, as Dr Crisp has hinted, when translators retreat (partially) to formal correspondence or more literal renderings, this is not necessarily the answer. While formal correspondence in translation would perhaps be able to take better care of how the message was framed in the source text (its poetic function), it is harder to see how a literal translation could, for instance, render the speaker's or author's attitude to what the text speaks about, or how a literal translation could effectively differentiate between natural and elevated manners of speaking in such a way that this difference would still be clear in the receptor language.

Now, what about the implications for Bible translation of the Orthodox view of Scripture as a window onto the timeless reality? If already the source texts are (a gracious adjustment but) not an adequate expression of the reality and otherness of the divine, how much less can this reality be expressed by any translation, whether it is literally or functionally equivalent! In this light, even formal/literal correspondence of a translation with the source text does not give access to a single meaning; such a meaning can still not be recovered. But in so far as several intended meanings are involved, it is probably true that a translation with a high degree of formal correspondence to the source text will leave more room for finding some of these different meanings and interpretations in the same text. This will indeed leave more room for the otherness of the text in the translation as well.

1.   R. Jakobson, 'Closing Statement: Linguistics and Poetics', in Th.A. Sebeok, *Style in Language* (Cambridge, MA: MIT Press, 1964), pp. 350-77 (354).

2.   Jakobson, 'Closing Statement', p. 358.

The distancing effect of the past tense in Jonah's prayer in the belly of the great fish may serve as an example of the otherness of the Biblical text (including its translation). In their fascinating chapter on translating sacred and sensitive text, Hatim and Mason discuss this passage.

> 'It is at least superficially disconcerting to find Jonah referring to his present act of praying...in the past tense.' The way these quotations from the Psalms 'are incorporated into the...text, ...suggests that the use of this tense is marked, expectation-defying and therefore highly dynamic... What then are the intended effects? ...it serves to underscore the earnest supplication from Jonah in his present position of powerlessness, and yet still express his confidence that God will in fact deliver him'[3]

But, as my colleague was saying, more careful attention to the range of stylistic and rhetorical possibilities of the receptor language can also be effective in preserving a sense of this distance from the otherness of the text. In this way, FE translations could strongly impress this sense on the reader. If FE translations do this as well as giving expression to cognitive information, they will have a strong point as well. In such cases, FE translations would not be flat, but powerful and full of impact. And that too would contribute to the sense of distance between reader and divine reality.

3.   B. Hatim and I. Mason, *The Translator as Communicator* (London/New York: Routledge, 1997), pp. 124-25.

BETWEEN LYING AND BLASPHEMY OR ON TRANSLATING A
FOUR-LETTER WORD IN THE HEBREW BIBLE: CRITICAL
REFLECTIONS ON BIBLE TRANSLATION

Robert P. Carroll[†]

She who translates a biblical verse literally is a liar; but she who elaborates on it is a blasphemer.

adaptation of a saying of Rabbi Judah
(2nd century CE; *T. Meg.* 4.41)

The Bible is written for the sake of the reader who has been denied it... The people who wrote the Bible seem to have thought of God in a way much like Kafka's.

Franz Rosenzweig[1]

...inside or between languages, human communication equals translation. A study of translation is a study of language.

George Steiner[2]

You can't transport human meanings whole from one culture to another any more than you can transliterate a text.

Eva Hoffmann[3]

Biblical translation goes on forever as a task never to be undone but also never to be completed either. Translating is a way of life, whether it be of texts or cultures, travel or relocation of persons. Translating the Bible is also very much a Sisyphean task—no sooner done than requiring to be done again and again. Bible translators may therefore be likened to the

1. Martin Buber and Franz Rosenzweig, *Scripture and Translation* (trans. Lawrence Rosenwald with Everett Fox; Bloomington: Indiana University Press, 1994 [ET of *Die Schrift und ihre Verdeutschung*, 1936]), pp. 57, 219.

2. George Steiner, *After Babel: Aspects of Language and Translation* (Oxford: Oxford University Press, 3rd edn, 1993 [1975]), p. 47.

3. Eva Hoffmann, *Lost in Translation: A Life in a New Language* (London: Minerva, 1991), p. 175.

ancient Greek figure of Sisyphus, a creature doomed to repeat a task endlessly without hope of final completion of the task ever. Rather like painting the Forth Railway Bridge in the East of Scotland, no sooner has the Bible been translated but it is time to start all over again and (re)translate it again. That is one of the (many) reasons that there are so many translated versions of the Bible on the market today. Bible translation is of course also both an industry and a thriving commercial enterprise which will never shut down nor be out of work. However, in this paper I shall try to work somewhere in-between the Scylla and Charybdis of what Rabbi Judah has demarcated as lying (literalism) and blaspheming (expansion), while at the same time trying to tease out some of the issues involved in biblical translation and the larger sociopolitical and cultural questions that bear on the craft and industry of Bible translation in contemporary Western society.

My focus will be on that most famous of four-letter words in the Hebrew Bible, which is frequently represented by the Greek phrase *Tetragrammaton*: that is, the personal name of the deity in the text as represented by the consonantal Hebrew text Y-H-W-H (יהוה). It is unvocalized as such, though frequently represented in the Masoretic Text by means of that euphemistic circumlocution אדני, 'Lord', which combines the consonants of the written text (*Ketiv*) with the vowels of the vocalized reading (*Qere*) of the text and exchanges the personal for the politely innocuous translation of piety. This arrangement of Jewish piety has given rise in the past to the English form of the personal name of the deity as 'Jehovah' (a now obsolete form of the name, apart from its usage by members of the religious group known as Jehovah's Witnesses). Of course the word 'Lord' does not translate the Hebrew name יהוה in any sense whatsoever and is therefore quite confusing, because אדני is itself also a word which appears legitimately throughout the Hebrew Bible. To reduce two very distinctive words to doing the duty of only one of the words is a most curious maltreatment and distortion of language by translators. Piety violates philology! Yet, out of respect for Jewish people one tends to use the conventional transliteration of the four Hebrew consonants without benefit of speculative vocalization; but such a practice raises a number of issues about culture, religion, intellectual integrity and philology. I am not sure how far down these four, somewhat different, roads I would wish to go with this paper, but I imagine that any discussion period following this paper would be free to pursue such journeys as far as the discussants would wish to go. However, the central focus of this paper will be on the question of to what extent should readers and translators of the Bible ignore the personal name factor of the *Tetragrammaton* in favour of euphemized circumlocutions? Is this a fair and proper way to treat the business of translation or a complete dereliction of duty on the part of translators? If it is the latter, then what should translators do when they encounter the *Tetragrammaton* in the text? As part of my approach to answering—well, raising—these questions, I shall try to provide a far from comprehensive account of how English translations have solved or evaded the problem. The Hebrew Text itself has no such problem, only *the read (spoken) or interpreted text* (translation = interpretation) raises the issue in its most acute forms, so it is the practice of Bible reading and/or Bible translation-interpretation which problematizes the matter and which constitutes the core and focus of this paper.

Such a narrow focus for this paper should not be allowed to conceal the writer's hope that many of the larger issues and bigger questions involved in Bible translation and biblical interpretation will be given an airing—if not in this paper, then in the discussion period. The paper is aimed at generating a discussion more than it is designed to solve or resolve the fundamental question about the translation of the Bible's most famous and most prominent four-letter word. In a number of other places I have written in passing on issues involved in translating the Bible, so this paper should be grouped with all those publications as part of an ongoing project of reflecting on 'Bible translation and the cultural production of Bibles in Western culture and civilization' (see the Bibliography at the end of this volume under Carroll). Here my main focus must be on the question: if it is an illegitimate exercise just to transliterate words instead of translating them, what are the translators to do about translating the proper name of the divine in the Hebrew text? Even if I use the generic term 'god' in English—which of course does not even translate the *Tetragrammaton* at all!—I still have the cultural-intellectual-religious problems of using upper or lower case G/god in English, not to mention the Jewish conventions for writing the peculiar form of the word G-d in English! While it is quite normal practice to transliterate or find an approximation to a proper name in a professional translation task, such a normal activity here foregrounds the problem of vocalizing the consonantal form of the biblical divine name. What are good, reliable, accurate and honest translators to do given the parameters of the translational problem here?

The Problematics of Bible Translation

There are far too many fundamental problems involved in translating the Bible for me to attempt to delineate them here, but I do want to touch on a few because they have some bearing on the subject matter of this paper. Some of them arise because Bible translation is always carried on under specific constraints and circumstances that render the task something more (a great deal more?) than just a translation from one language into another language. What those constraints and circumstances may be will differ from time to time and culture to culture. In the first instance, the general category of 'sacred scriptures' applied to the Bible will inevitably shape (if not distort) the dynamics of the translational enterprise. It is not just a case of translating a foreign language (technically two languages because of the Aramaic portions of the Bible; three languages if Aramaic and the Greek of the New Testament are included in the process) into the receptor vernacular language. Where 'sacred scripture' is concerned many other factors come into play, of which 'magnification' is only one such factor:

> Magnification is the subtler form of treason. It can arise from a variety of motives. Through misjudgment or professional obligation, the translator may render an original which is slighter than his own natural powers (Baudelaire translating Thomas Hood's 'The Bridge of Sighs'). The source may have become numinous or canonic and later versions exalt it to an alien elevation. *This is certainly the case at many points in the Authorized Version.* In the Psalms, for example, the formulaic, literalist texture of the Hebrew idiom is frequently distorted to baroque magnificence. Or compare the King James's version of the Book of Job with that of M.H. Pope in the Anchor Bible in 1965.[4]

While I cannot speak for other linguistic cultural traditions and practices, I do know that where English Bibles are concerned getting out from under the malign shadow cast by the King James Bible (KJV, aka the Authorized Version, AV) is one of the most difficult tasks facing contemporary biblical translators (if and where they are aware of the problem).[5] So many versions are just revisions of the KJV (e.g. RSV) or modernized replications of it (e.g. NIV), so that when a genuinely original version appears in English (e.g. NEB; cf. REB) there is instantly a revolt against it. We are trapped in *the spider's web of traditional translations* and each new translation

---

4.   Steiner, *After Babel*, p. 401; my emphasis (RPC).
5.   On the KJV see Robert Carroll and Stephen Prickett (eds.), *The Bible: Authorized King James Version* (The World's Classics; Oxford: Oxford University Press, 1997).

attempts to be both innovative (original) and yet traditional because of the interpretive communities in which such Bibles have their place. I am not sure if this is part of the ongoing (continuing) quarrel (polemic) between Jerome and Augustine about the relationship of translation to original source or traditional interpretation,[6] but I am inclined to think that it is. Every translation of the Bible inevitably puts all subsequent translations in its debt, so that all previous translations tend to constitute the gravitational pull against which contemporary translations are forced to operate. In recent years I have noticed the tendency of individual translators seeking to provide their own translations as a way to escape from the invidious influence of such overpowering magisterial translations.[7] Parallel to this problem with English translations we may note the equivalent problem in the German language where much of what Martin Buber and Franz Rosen-zweig were trying to do with their translation of the Bible, *Die Schrift*, was to take the Bible out from under the overwhelming (deforming) influence of Martin Luther's German *Die Bibel*.[8] I fear not everybody who reads the Bible in translation is often aware of just how complex and complicated are matters relating to Bible translation; and when it comes to major biblical translations, the Prefaces to such translations do not always adver-tize or even refer to such matters. The politics and ideologies involved in Bible translation activities are fascinating, but I hope not to have to get involved with them in this paper. The technical aspects of Bible translation are complex enough without going into general ideological and cultural matters as well.

The one point where all these matters come together, making things so complicated that they cannot be avoided, is, in my judgment, the problems associated with translating the *Tetragrammaton* in the Hebrew Bible. I dislike thoroughly the euphemistic circumlocution 'the LORD' (the upper case letters distinguish the proper name YHWH from the respectful 'Lord' [אדני]), but if I were to go for the conventional critical representation

---

6. See Werner Schwartz, *Principles and Problems of Biblical Translation: Some Reformation Controversies and Their Background* (Cambridge: Cambridge University Press, 1955). See also Noorda and Rogerson in this volume.

7. See Robert Alter, *Genesis: Translation and Commentary* (New York: W.W. Norton, 1996); Sidney Brichto, *The Peoples Bible* (London: Sinclair–Stevenson, 2000); Everett Fox, *The Five Books of Moses: Genesis, Exodus, Leviticus, Numbers, Deuteronomy* (The Schocken Bible, 1; New York: Schocken Books, 1995), etc.

8. See especially Rosenzweig's essay, 'Scripture and Luther', in Buber and Rosen-zweig, *Scripture and Translation*, pp. 47-69.

of the consonantal text plus the Masoretic vowels—an abomination in itself?—I would give unnecessary offence to pious Jews. So what are intelligent, informed and learned non-Jews to do in this matter? That is where the problem becomes practical. As an academic I feel it is my duty to translate and read the Hebrew text as best I can; *and* I do not feel that it is part of my duty *as a scholar* to have to conform to the ideological or pious demands of religious communities which also happen to use such texts for non-academic purposes. But, of course, in the course of my academic work I also work with or encounter pious Jewish scholars and then the problem does become practical and acute. We may call this a social or ideo-cultural sidebar to the problem—a lemma of practical application—but I hear Jewish scholars strongly expressing their feelings on this point, so I am (have become) very conscious of the matter as a practical problem. At the same time, as a *child of the Enlightenment* I am also very conscious (even more so than with the piety issue) of violating a hard-earned and long established value of the Enlightenment. So what are scholars to do in this sensitive area? Advice may be freely offered by the responder and by others during the discussion period.

The Englishing of the Tetragrammaton

In the first instance I suppose the best approach I can use is to report on and record the practices of previous biblical translators who have worked on public translated versions of the Bible. Looking at how they have performed will not necessarily resolve any problems, but it may help to outline what some of the problems are. Everett Fox, in his stunning undertaking of translating the Pentateuch, does the right thing in my judgment: he simply transliterates the Hebrew four consonants and reproduces in his translation the *Tetragrammaton simpliciter* YHWH.[9] When he gets to the heart of the matter at Exod. 3.14-16, he follows suit and represents the text as 'EHYEH ASHER EHYEH/I will be-there howsoever I will be-there. And he said: Thus shall you say to the Children of Israel: EHYEH/I-WILL-BE-THERE sends me to you.'[10] In my judgment, that is not quite perfection in terms of representing the Hebrew text because it incorporates into the text something of Martin Buber's understanding of the text's sense of the meaning of the divine name as ER IST DA, 'he is there'.[11] But otherwise I think that is

9. Fox, *The Five Books of Moses*, p. 17.
10. Fox, *The Five Books of Moses*, p. 273.
11. Buber, *Die Schrift*, pp. 158-59; cf. Buber, *Moses* (The East and West Library; Oxford: Phaidon Press, 1946), pp. 39-55.

probably the best way to go, even if it does in some sense abandon the translator's duty to render into the receptor (or target) language all that is present in the original text. It does, however, illustrate nicely the principle of how each translation is heavily in debt to previous translations and I do wonder whether contemporary Jewish translations of the Bible can avoid being overinfluenced by the great work of Buber and Rosenzweig on *Die Schrift*?

The Jewish Publication Society's *Tanakh* follows fairly conventional practice with its LORD for YHWH[12] and at Exod. 3.14 reverts to transliterating the Hebrew 'Ehyeh-Asher-Ehyeh', but without the Buberian gloss. The only other critical remark I would want to venture here about these translations would be the quite obvious question: to what extent can a transliteration be regarded as a *successful* translation performance? Does it not look rather too much like a confession of failure or acknowledgment of defeat of the translational process? On the other hand, it must be acknowledged that the *Tetragrammaton* has a long history of being marked in the text as something special or something different: for example, some of the Qumran scrolls represent the *Tetragrammaton* as being written in the old archaic Phoenician (Canaanite) script, thus drawing attention to the word (and perhaps its pronunciation). It is as if the English text represented the word in Gothic letters, runes or Anglo-Saxon forms. Here substance, style, content all play a part in marking the word as special and different. So perhaps translators do have a duty to incorporate something of the history of the word's reception (*Rezeptionsgeschichte*) into their translated versions. That too would make an interesting discussion period topic, even though it may distract our attention from the more immediate task of translating the text *as stated*.

Of the making of English Bibles there is no end, and much study of the biblical translational enterprise is a weariness to the flesh. Part of what makes it such a wearying study is that so many translated Bibles copy each other in order to constitute *a tradition of translation*. That is, once a translation has been made the tendency is for revised editions to be produced, so that there is invariably and inevitably a family resemblance between Bibles and their revisions. Thus the tendency among revisions derived from the KJB is to render the *Tetragrammaton* as LORD, a practice also followed by the NEB and its revision the REB. The Introductions to the NEB and REB do, however, devote a paragraph each to explaining what is involved in the

---

12. Cf. Gen. 2.4; see also Alter, *Genesis*, p. 7.

Hebrew text at this point; at which point they also provide the conventional vocalization of YHWH in accordance with scholarly practice (or prejudice, if that is how you view it). The Introduction to the NEB does, however, draw attention to the fact that it has followed the ancient Protestant translation practice of using the vocalized form—Jehovah—at Exod. 3.15 (with a footnote indicating the Hebrew consonants and its probable pronunciation), a practice it describes as an 'incorrect but customary form'. The footnote at Exod. 3.14 is retained in the REB, but in the text 'Jehovah' has been dropped in favour of the translation, 'God answered, "I AM that I am. Tell them that I AM has sent you to them" '. This at least has the virtue of being a translated form, even though I would prefer the more focused translation of 'I will be...' as a better rendering of *'ehyeh*.

The RSV reads 'I AM WHO I AM' at 3.14 and its revision—the notion of a revision of a revision has, in my opinion, something of an infinite regression (or progression?) to it—the New Revised Standard Version (NRSV) leaves that unrevised. The RSV had a footnote at this point that indicated the possibility of an alternative translation of 'I WILL BE WHAT I WILL BE', and this footnote also is retained in the NRSV. To this day I remain unconvinced, where not baffled, by the tendencies of Englished Bibles to lapse into capital letters (screaming upper case letters!) at certain points in the text, as if the deity were deemed to express itself in upper case letters (cf. KJV at Rev. 17.5). I would regard this unjustifiable practice as having to do with what Steiner called 'magnification', where the status and category of 'sacred scripture' influences the translators. Yet it is a technique used so infrequently, that I suspect ideology and 'the heat of the moment-generated emotions' may account more especially for Rev. 17.5 than any rational account of translational processes would account for its usage here. Even so, I would still have expected the translators to have rendered *everything* throughout the Bible deemed to have been uttered by the deity in upper case letters, otherwise there is neither textual justification nor interpretative warrant whatsoever for the two examples from Exod. 3 and Rev. 17. But then, as is well known with English Bibles, many weird and wonderful things pass for translation which are more highly speculative of interpretation than is warranted of straightforward translations. Translated Bibles easily become palimpsests of translators' ideological prejudices and cultural holdings.

The NIV, which is a more up-to-date revision of the AV, designed for fundamentalists and church-going Christian folk of an evangelical persuasion—a version which I think has succeeded in replacing the KJV as currently the most popular English translation of the Bible on the market—has no surprises in store. In its Preface it acknowledges the common practice regarding the *Tetragrammaton*, but offers a few variations on other renderings of combinations of the *Tetragrammaton* with distinctive words (e.g. 'Lord of hosts' becomes in the NIV 'the LORD Almighty'). Such compound names of the deity always pose problems for translators, whether of ancient culture, signification, ambiguity or just nomenclature. Far too many different words are used in the Hebrew Bible to refer to the deity for modern English translations not to have problems rendering them into *suitable* English. A fundamental problem here has to do with ideological takes on the Bible. Scholars and historians know that the Bible comes to us out of a cultural background of, what for the want of a better word I shall call, 'polytheism': a world peopled with gods and goddesses, their families, kith and kin and all the extended relations such divine pantheons went in for in ancient times. Much of that background is, at times, foregrounded in the Bible by means of compound names for the deity and/or the many, many names of God in the Bible. But the translators of the Bible tend to belong to monist or monotheistic (or even Trinitarian) cultural backgrounds, so have a very strong tendency to translate the cultural world of the Bible into the 'equivalent' (as imagined) terms of their own cultural world. This ideological-cultural shift can make for major distortions in translation and raises yet again one of the most fundamental sets of questions about Bible translation. Should translators be translating the world of the text or the world of the translators? Or should they be seeking to fuse these two different and distinct horizons of differing cultures into the one translation? This set of questions could occupy a whole Workshop itself and not just one paper in a Workshop, but I shall put it down on the agenda for the discussion period arising from this paper.

The *Tetragrammaton* appears so frequently in the Hebrew text of the Bible that it would not be possible or profitable to scrutinize the whole Bible in order to observe the consistency (or otherwise) of translators in the matter of translating it. So instead of taking that line of approach I have just made use of Exod. 3.13-15 as a test case for observing the practices of different translators. Of course that particular pericope of the text poses many problems of interpretation as well as translation.[13] Yet it is a very important biblical text for seeking to understand the relationship between

---

13. See Robert P. Carroll, ' "Strange Fire": Abstract of Presence Absent in the Text. Meditations on Exodus 3 (for George Steiner on his 65th Birthday)', *JSOT* 61 (1994), pp. 39-58, for one route of approach to reading that difficult text.

the *Tetragrammaton* and meaning (if not usage). A very important but also a very strange story/text in the Bible. If the proper name/first person of the verb היה, *hyh*, 'to be' (the so-called imperfect/incomplete form of the verb: 'I will be') can be said to be a proper name, then how are translators to translate this strange word phenomenon? The actual name of the deity is represented throughout the Hebrew Bible as being 'in the third person' ('he will be'), as it were, and not in the first person (except for v. 14 of Exod. 3). So deep strangeness enters the text here, a strangeness not taken up into other biblical texts (apart perhaps from the strange 'hymns to Marduk' material influences in Isa. 40–48). Perhaps it is not part of the translators' task to deal with the larger questions of meaning and reference, style and substance posed by the text; and yet, I cannot help but feel that some attention needs to be given by translators to the range and boundaries of what is thought or imagined to be going on in the story of 'Moses at the burning bush' in Exod. 3. However the story is interpreted, then that interpretation ought to be the form in which the translation of the name/phrase is represented throughout all such translations (cf. Buber's ICH BIN DA rendering of Exod. 3.14 which, at least, has logic and symmetry on its side). Translation itself may be interpretation, but there is also a deep need for pre-translation interpretation too (*Deutungsbedürftigkeit*, to use Erich Auerbach's famous analytical term) prior to the formal act of translating the text. That becomes a necessity in order for translators to have some idea of the directions in which their translation should go. The fundamental question for translators before they start on the formal translating task must be: 'What is going on in this text?' My own approach to Exod. 3 favours a reading of the text as a piece of evasive wordplay,[14] which would see the divine response as not being a proper name but a dismissal of the enquiry of Moses: something along the lines of 'never you mind about my name, I shall be *there* if only you would get yourself *there* too; forget the name business and get yourself out of here and down to Egypt land, pronto!' But how then can translators possibly register such an evasive non-answer as the subject of subsequent sentences, where the noun/proper name YHWH represents someone called (named) YHWH, a character in the text of whom it is said that he speaks, command things and acts? An impossible task for translators, or a story which they spoil every time they fail to render the Exod. 3 narrative as setting them such an impossible task?

---

14. Cf. Fox, *The Five Books of Moses*, p. 270.

Attention to the texture—the warp and woof—of the text, in my judgment, undermines the translators' task of making *usable* sense of the text for foreign language readers. But why shouldn't translators of the Bible occasionally have to admit defeat, and concede the point that they find a specific piece of text untranslatable as to sense, nuance and opacity?[15] I wonder if it will ever prove possible for printed Bibles to be published containing acknowledgments of the defeat of translators at specific points in the translational processes? I think that would involve a considerable extension of the footnotes or marginalia, where translators might confess more freely to the hopelessly ambiguous state of a specific part of the text, with a range of possible translations or explanations of what the problems really are at these junctures of the text. Everett Fox's *Five Books* volume offers such an arrangement and is all the better as a book on Bible translation for it. This is especially the case because the commentary is interleaved with the translation, which itself has footnotes attached to it. Once the Shocken Bible is completed, it will be a magnificent project and will also afford enormous opportunities for readers to inform themselves, by means of the reading process, of much of what is involved in a proper translation of the Bible.

Time does not permit me to make this paper a more comprehensive study of the central problems of translating the most famous four-letter word in the Bible, the *Tetragrammaton*. Revised for publication this paper will show many and great improvements, but its first draft status will have to protect it from too many harsh criticisms. I have chosen the case of the problem of translating the *Tetragrammaton* because it illustrates many of the primal problems facing Bible translators; problems that cannot be avoided once the translation process is undertaken. Philology and piety come to the fore and confront each other at this point. Accuracy may need to give way to awe or awe concede the ground to accuracy, thus raising the permanent problems of the 'what' and 'why' of Bible translations. How should they be done, why should they be done and for whom and for what purpose should they be undertaken? Answers to all of these questions would take much more than a brief response and discussion session could ever afford.

15. On the opacity of texts, cf. Stephen Prickett, *Words and the Word: Language, Poetics and Biblical Interpretation* (Cambridge: Cambridge University Press, 1986).

Suggestions for Further Reading[16]

Barnstone, Willis, *The Poetics of Translation: History, Theory, Practice* (New Haven: Yale University Press, 1993).

Budick, Sandor, and Wolfgang Iser (eds.), *The Translatability of Cultures: Figurations of the Space Between* (Irvine Studies in the Humanities; Stanford: Stanford University Press, 1996).

Hargreaves, Cecil, *A Translator's Freedom: Modern English Bibles* (BibSem, 22; Sheffield: JSOT Press, 1993).

Kelly, Louis, *The True Interpreter: A History of Translation Theory and Practice in the West* (Oxford: Basil Blackwell, 1979).

Niranjana, Tejaswini, *Siting Translation: History, Post-Structuralism, and the Colonial Context* (Berkeley: University of California Press, 1992).

Venuti, Lawrence, *The Translator's Invisibility: A History of Translation* (Translation Studies; London: Routledge).

16. Editors' note: we have chosen to leave the list here as it is (items can also be found in the composite Bibliography at the end of this volume), since these books are not referred to within the essay itself.

'BETWEEN LYING AND BLASPHEMY':
RESPONDING TO ROBERT CARROLL

Athalya Brenner

Robert Carroll sent his paper to us by e-mail on 9 May 2000, just before going down to London. In the e-mail message to which the paper was attached he made it quite clear that the paper was a draft only, and that he intended to improve it by elaborating some of the points he mentioned in it. As you probably know by now, Robert Carroll died the next night in his sleep. His paper on Bible translations was the last paper he wrote, and he never got round to finishing it properly. If, however, you wish to learn more about his ideas on Bible translation, and particularly about devotee ideologies in such translations, let me refer you especially to two articles he published in 1996, both mentioned in the bibliography he supplied in his paper: 'He-Bibles and She-Bibles' in *Biblical Interpretation* 4, and 'Cultural Encroachment' in *Semeia* 76.[1] The articles' names are certainly worth noting and relevant to the present collection, even before tackling the articles themselves and the contribution to this volume.

When Robert's paper came through by e-mail we burst out laughing. Originally Robert was going to do a paper on the links between 'dynamic equivalence' translation and scriptural authority. There was never time to ask why he had changed his mind. His paper, when it came, was about the translation of the *Tetragrammaton*. I solemnly promise that, in my capacity as midwife for the workshop that—eventually—begat the present collection of essays,[2] I didn't put him up to it. But the result, of course, is of high

---

1.   R.P. Carroll, 'He-Bibles and She-Bibles: Reflections on the Violence Done to Texts by Productions of English Translations of the Bible', *BibInt* 4 (1996), pp. 257-269; and 'Cultural Encroachment and Bible Translation: Observations on Elements of Violence, Race and Class in the Production of Bibles in Translation', in Randall C. Bailey and Tina Pippin (eds.), *Race, Class, and the Politics of Bible Translation* (Semeia, 76; Atlanta: Scholars Press, 1996), pp. 39-53.

2.   Editors' note: For details about the Workshop and about the ongoing Dutch debate about translating the *Tetragrammaton*, see the Introduction to this volume.

relevance to the ongoing Dutch discussion, although Robert didn't know much—if anything at all—about this ongoing internal affair. So let us try to gather how Robert's analysis can illuminate this discussion.[3] My response, hopefully a mixture of critique *and* homage to Robert's erudition, intellectual integrity and good sense, will touch upon two areas: the citations presented at the beginning of the paper; and the points Robert himself earmarked for further discussion.

Robert was in the habit of constructing his papers, essays and lectures around quotations: these always indicated his *ad hoc* frame of reference, to be further substantiated or refuted as the case may be in the body of his emerging text. The quotations also reflect his own place, as he saw it, in a space/chain of transmitted knowledge. So what did he give us here? To begin with, a passage from *Tosefta Megillah*, dealing with the two ways of Bible translation, literal as against 'sense' (=often expansionist) translation. The grammatical gender of the Hebrew forms in the original, here quoted in English translation—pronouns, verb forms—all indicate a masculine subject:

> He who translates a biblical verse literally is a liar;
> but he who elaborates on it is a blasphemer.

But Robert changed the 'he's' and so on into 'she's'. By inverting the subject's gender—from masculine to feminine—a certain playfulness was achieved. The inversion points, lightly but decidedly, to the problems contemporary women, especially feminists, would have with the prevailing concepts of the Jewish (and Christian) god as authoritative father, husband and son. This would have its bearings on translation practices, as evidenced by the current Dutch debate. This debate, concerning the *Tetragrammaton*'s translation, is not only about inclusive language and *gender* authority—see Robert's quotation from Steiner about translation as language, as communication of ideas and norms ('A study of translation is a study of language'). It is also about authority in general, about a claimed knowledge of the capitalized Divine through translation practices—see the quotation from Rosenzweig ('The Bible is written for the sake of the reader who has been denied it'). And the undertaking is doomed to failure from the outset by the very nature of human language itself and the translation process itself—see the quotation from Hoffmann (her title is *Lost in Translation*)—even before other ideological issues are being considered.

---

3.   At the workshop Dr A. Hunter, Robert's colleague from Glasgow, graciously agreed to read the paper.

Robert was one of the most widely read persons one could ever hope to meet, with areas of interest ranging high and low and immediate and distant. In his last and latest visiting card he defined himself as 'scholar, speaker and cultural critic'. But, as he would have been quick to point out, he was no feminist (although some of his best friends are, and he promoted feminists in the workplace with all his might). He was also totally non-religious, a harsh critic of religious excess and other excessive ideologies. In fact, he himself busily deconstructed his own scholarly positions by being noisily excessive in defense of what he considered the best ideology of all, that is, freedom of speech and choice. You can say he was a pious believer in his own lack of piety and his own choices, allowing similar freedoms to others. For him, then, the power of ideology (including his own) was always present, always to be elucidated and critiqued, always to be respected as well. So he read religious literature, and dealt with it, and read feminist literature and foamed at the mouth against it—see his many articles on feminist protests against what was viewed as biblical/prophetic pornography.[4] And, emphatically, demanded to know of feminist Bible critics whether they view their own gendered concerns against contemporary social, moral and intellectual concerns in general.

To come back to his quotations, especially the first perverted one from the *Tosefta*. 'She who translates a biblical verse...' would hope to do so in a manner that would be agreeable to her, that would redress a balance not for antiquity but for her own time and place, as Mary Phil Korsak has done.[5] 'She who translates' would hope to substitute—not translate; this would seem to be an impossibility—for the Hebrew *Tetragrammaton* something that would suit her. And, in this context, this would be as much an elaboration as older and current renderings such as 'the Lord'. A direct if playful reminder, a warning to feminists hotly engaged in the *Tetragrammaton* debate, about joining the practices against which they claim to fight, when pitfalls of transliterating are many and recognized, hence this solution should be ruled out and previous translation traditions should perhaps be abandoned in the spirit of the times. On the other hand, this is

4. A wonderful example is his article, 'Desire under the Terebinths: On Pornographic Representation in the Prophets—A Response', in A. Brenner (ed.), *A Feminist Companion to the Latter Prophets* (Sheffield: Sheffield Academic Press, 1995), pp. 275-307.

5. See Korsak's article, 'Translating the Bible', in this volume, pp. 132-46.

also a reminder to no 'she who translates' that feminist opinions regarding the Bible's language for today should be heeded.

So where to start? Carroll suggests we start *not* with an ideology of authority—divine authority as perceived by the translator, canonical authority, etic secular authority as against any particular emic religious authority— but with an ideology of language and its authoritative role in human life. Is this a more complex way of suggesting we should deal with the Bible as with any other canonical literary work, a substitution of one kind of authority for another? Perhaps this is so. The gentle goading towards making a choice, a choice for scholarship as guiding principle rather than partisan ideology as such, is at the very least refreshing. It is ironic, one hopes even self-ironic and not without its downside, for since when are scholars free of personal ideologies? But, at the very least, considering the requirements of source and target languages universalizes partisan audience requirements for the duration of the translation process. Or, at any rate, ceding authority to language posits group ideologies and group interest in a broader context of what is 'correct' and possible; it brings other fundamental criteria into play, thus conceivably leading to a better chance for relative consent in the community of Bible consumers (readers).

Robert had the habit of writing in a circular rather than straight linear fashion. Often he would veer between general principles and a specific case study, going back and forth from one to the other. His case study in this unfinished paper is the translation of Yhwh, as influenced by the burning bush episode in Exod. 3, especially vv. 13-15. Let us therefore list his major concerns, the ones he was hoping will be discussed further after he had finished presenting his ideas.

1. In referring to the *Tetragrammaton*, as well as to other matters in Bible translations, what is the balance to be struck between piety/ ideology—of any kind—and philology?

2. In Western societies the Bible is a cultural commodity, a product. How does recognition of this factor influence translation practices and the use of translations?

3. In how far, if at all, should transliteration be accepted in Bible translation?

4. A cluster of issues concerns the mutual relations among translations (to distinguish from the relations between a translation and the original—Hebrew, Aramaic, Greek texts). The KJB is authoritative father to many English translations. Do we prefer it to the translation family of the NEB/REB? Do we prefer the latter? And

if so, why?[6] Should a translation state the original text, or to what extent and how should it nod and wink at least in the direction of the Bible translations' reception history? Here there is an opportunity to look both at Carroll's own paper and at John Rogerson's paper (pp. 17-30 in this volume).

At this point, let me add a question of my own to Robert's question. This question is addressed especially to the members of the Committee for the new Dutch translation. How can we define past, present and future links between Dutch translations in the light of the situation concerning English translations?

5. Coming back to Exod. 3 as a key for pre-interpretation and translation of the name Yhwh. As Robert asks, does anybody know—beyond reception history—what goes on in this text? Is it really, as generations of readers and translators agree, an *explanation*—successful or otherwise, enigmatic or otherwise—of the *Tetragrammaton*? Or, should we agree with Robert that the text of Exod. 3.13-15 is a monumental tease and send down, a 'What's in a name?' enigmatic, even humorous waiver, which would alter our perception as well as translation of Yhwh everywhere in the Hebrew Bible?

6. Finally, as Robert writes, notes appended to a translation represent a measure of defeat. Barring transliteration, yet recognizing the impossibility of the task of translation, would it make sense for the translator to squarely admit defeat in certain cases, hopefully not too many?

Robert Carroll touched on those and other questions in his paper, just touched on them. Unfortunately, he could not do more. But we, Bible translators and consumers, continue to ponder them.

---

6. For this cluster of issues/questions see the short case study in the 'Appendix' to Crisp's article, 'Icon of the Ineffable?' pp. 36-49 in this volume.

DOMESTICATING THE TRANSCENDENT.
THE AFRICAN TRANSFORMATION OF CHRISTIANITY: COMPARATIVE REFLECTIONS ON ETHNICITY AND RELIGIOUS MOBILIZATION IN AFRICA

Lamin Sanneh

Ethnicity and the Modern Missionary Movement

Through the modern missionary movement Africa was, ironically, offered a chance to answer the intellectual assault of the West, because the same missionary movement that identified itself with colonialism in terms of establishing schools, modern clinics and architecture, scientific agriculture, the emancipation of women, a bureaucratic state, town planning and modern means of transport and communication, also identified itself with indigenous societies by fostering the use of mother tongues in Bible translation and literacy. Let me present the subject in this way. The missionary sponsorship of Bible translation became the catalyst for profound changes and developments in language, culture and ethnicity, changes that invested ethnic identity with the materials for a reawakened sense of local identity.

Bible Translation and the Ethnic Cause

The sponsorship of indigenous languages for Bible translation became the exception, at least in unintended consequences if not in deliberate design, to the wholesale Western assault on the Africa of ethnic classification. In that sphere the Western encounter allowed the ground to be shifted to African languages as things of native origin for which Africans had only God and the ancestors to thank, and not the whites who gave the languages written form.

Accordingly, in the language projects of modern missions Europe confronted the native character of non-Western races in its irreducible profundity, in its core self-understanding, rather than as space to be filled with European speech forms and habits only. In that confrontation only two responses were possible for Europeans. One was for them to say that blacks were too different from Europeans to belong to the same category of homo sapiens, and may accordingly be excluded from the privilege of civilized company. The second was to say that, given this difference as a mark of human diversity, there was no basis for saying that one race was superior or inferior to another, but only that the human condition was deeply marked by variety and difference, as Herbert Spencer maintained, and that, given the uncontrived nature of the ethnic spirit, Africans might possess by that fact an advantage for the gospel that Europe had chosen to abandon. Both attitudes were prevalent, although the second was much truer to the facts and more attuned to field experience than the first. Consequently, the tribes and ethnic groups of Africa came to be furnished with the necessary cultural and linguistic apparatus for mother tongue development, and that gave them confidence not only in who they were but in what they were here for.

I have argued in *Translating the Message* (1989)[1] that the 'central and enduring character of Christian history is the rendering of God's eternal counsels into terms of everyday speech. By that path believers have come to stand before their God'. Bible translation has marked the history of Christianity from its very origins: the gospels are a translated version of the preaching and message of Jesus, and the epistles a further interpretation and application of that preaching and message. Christianity is unique in being promoted outside the language of the founder of the religion. Having abandoned the mother tongue of Jesus, Christians were freed to promote a Gentile religion, the religion of the uncircumcised and the non-Chosen People. Consequently, Christianity through Bible translation offered to the world a genuine share in the heritage of Jesus, however inferior in cultural attainment ethnic groups might be, or might be deemed to be. Similarly, with regard to those languages and cultures that had attained the highest levels of civilization and thus transcended tribal life, Christianity by virtue of its open policy on Bible translation would not surrender to them as an exclusive right the heritage of Jesus.

In Bible translation, hitherto taboo ethnic groups and their languages and cultures were effectively destigmatized while, at the same time, superior cultures were stripped of their right to constitute themselves into exclusive standards of access to God. In affirming weak and stigmatized languages and cultures, Bible translation bade fair to Western cultural prerequisites

---

1. Lamin Sanneh, *Translating the Message: The Missionary Impact on Culture* (American Society of Missiology, 13; Maryknoll, NY: Orbis Books, 1989), frontispiece.

for membership in the human family. Bible translation breathed new life into local languages and equipped local populations for participation in the emerging new world context. This action results from Bible translation being based on the idea that all languages are equal in terms of their value and right in mediating the truth of God; but that, by the same token, they are all equally inadequate in relation to that truth. No language can claim exclusive prerogative on the truth of God, just as, conversely, no language is intrinsically unworthy to be a language of faith and devotion.[2] The message of God and the language of ordinary human communication shared the same moral universe, though no human language in any combination is completely identical with that message. The quest for divine meaning is not exhausted by any one historical approximation, even though such approximations are inseparable from such quest or its results. Language is all we have to speak to God and to be spoken to. In the process, we learn that language is in fact God's gift to us.

As if to reinforce this theological point, Bible translation looked to the common forms of local expression in all their rich diversity and paradox, and by so doing enfranchised the language and speech of ordinary people rather than the elitist forms. There were corresponding implications for the affected societies and cultures. Where it happened, such indigenous social and cultural revival often set off mass social change.

Thus it was that indigenous religious and cultural categories received validation by their being adopted in translation. In few fields was this principle more important than in the matter of adopting the names of what were essentially ethnic deities as the God of Scripture, for in those names was contained not only the religious world view but the rules of property, social structure and personal identity. Almost everywhere in the mission field, missionaries and local agents had to confront three fundamental questions: 1) How else can we transmit the faith except in the language

2.   Such a favorable view of indigenous languages was not universally shared. Saul Bellow's famous attack on African languages as unworthy of great literary merit is a case in point. Some ethnographers expressed similar sentiments, as in the example of Sayers, who wrote of one Sierra Leonean language thus: 'Limba is a very fourth-rate language in which, so far as my experience goes, it is almost impossible to get any fine shades of meaning expressed'. E.F. Sayers, 'Notes on the Native Language Affinities in Sierra Leone', *Sierra Leone Studies*, old series 10 (1927). In contrast, speaking of vernacular Bible translation, Westermann remarks: 'No African languages have hitherto been found into which the Bible could not be translated'. D. Westermann, 'The Place and Function of the Vernacular in African Education', *International Review of Mission* (January1925), p. 28.

and experience of the ethnic groups to whom the message is being brought? 2) How may such ethnic groups connect with the message unless there is in the message itself a point of contact? 3) Finally, how best can we ascertain that contact point except through systematic attention to ethnic specificity as revealed in language, usage and culture? Even those missionaries who confined themselves deliberately to the development and technical side of mission could not escape entirely the repercussions of theological engagement with the local communities in which they lived. The striking mark of Christianity in its mission is its confidence that since God spoke to us all, then all human speech in its concrete ethnic diversity is hallowed for our ordinary as well as consecrated use, and so missionaries plunged into hitherto neglected languages and cultures to engage their moral potential for the message, and to bring that potential into public harmony with the values of choice and ethnic fulfillment. Through mother tongue translation, Christianity would crystallize, not into a cultural confectionery as such, but into a power that can make God sound as sweet music to ethnic ears.[3] It conforms to the insight of the incarnation, namely, that divinity is not a human loan word but humanity is the chosen language of divine self-expression.

The general principle of Christianity succeeding as ethnic fulfillment rather than as ethnic self-rejection has been well expressed by Professor Diedrich Westermann of Berlin, a former missionary to Africa. He argued that, in each people, the mental life has evolved to produce an individual shape and a proper mode of expression. He went on, giving a striking illustration of what today we would call *inculturation*:

> In this sense we speak of the soul of a people, and the most immediate, the most adequate exponent of the soul of a people is its language. By taking away a people's language we cripple or destroy its soul and kill its mental individuality... We do not want Christianity to appear in the eyes of the Natives as the religion of the white man, and the opinion to prevail that the African must become a pseudo-European in order to become a Christian, but we want to implant the Gospel deep into the soil of the African mind, so that it may grow there in its own African form, not as a gift of the white man but as the gift of God... If this is to be effected, the Gospel and the whole Christian education must take root in the mother soil of the vernacular. Only in this way will it enter into the African mind and become the

---

3. In his Preface to his Zulu dictionary, R.C.A. Samuelson, the interpreter to King Cetywayo, affirms, 'It is the mother-tongue which is sweet'. *The King Cetywayo Zulu-Dictionary* (Durban: The Commercial Printing Co., 1923).

medium of a new life—not of new forms of life—and of a regeneration of the people's soul... If the Christian Church in Africa is to be really African and really Christian, it must be built upon the basis of the indigenous peculiarities and gifts of the people, it must become part of the African genius, and these will for ever be embedded in the mother language. A people without a language and a tradition of its own is individually dead, it has become part of a mass instead of being a living personality... If the African is to keep and develop his own soul and is to become a separate personality, his education must not begin by inoculating him with a foreign civilization, but it must implant respect for the indigenous racial life, it must teach him to love his country and tribe as gifts given by God which are to be purified and brought to full growth by the new divine life. One of these gifts is the vernacular, it is the vessel in which the whole national life is contained and through which it finds expression.[4]

The Theological Dimension: Domesticating the Transcendent

The field dimension of Bible translation came to grips with this language issue and, in so doing, activated a profound religious process in African societies. James Green, the Church Missionary Society agent in South Africa, wrote that the issue concerning the word that the church should use to instruct the Zulu about God the Creator belongs directly to the task of theology. He did not wish to minimize questions of philology and other technical features of language work, but he was convinced that at the heart of the enterprise is the theological question: has God been known to the Zulus in former times and, if so, how can we ascertain that? To answer that question, the only reasonable course was to embrace the terms that the Zulus, in God's own providence, had been accustomed to employ. It was the Zulu frame that would shape what missionaries brought, or thought they were bringing, for in the Zulu way of receiving the message missionaries would awaken to the God who had preceded them among the Zulus. That was the first order of business. It was a necessary step. It had to be taken, and was taken willingly and without delay. Yet in taking that step, the missionary committed himself or herself to the next step, namely, the natural developments in the Zulu world view that Christian translation would have stimulated but which belonged with Zulu self-understanding, and therefore lay well beyond the power of the missionary to control. That further step many missionaries were unwilling to take, or allow to be taken, though there was little they could do to stop it.

4.   Westermann, 'Place and Function of the Vernacular', pp. 26-27, 28.

Green saw the problem clearly, and moved courageously to confront it. Thus he spoke of the phases of God's instruction of the human race:

> God revealed Himself to men by degrees; adding to that knowledge, from time to time, as they were able to receive the increase. We find, in addition, that God, in His ineffable love, when He began to raise fallen man to dwell in His Presence, humbled Himself to the level of man's ignorance, as witness the wording of the First Commandment. Those words, *'Thou shalt have none other gods but Me'*, would be received by those on whose ears they first fell, as admitting that there were other gods besides the Lord, God of Abraham, and of Isaac, and of Jacob.[5]

And further:

> The Hebrew *elohim* was a class-name covering many supernatural beings— the gods or goddesses of the nations, angels, shades of the departed—and also human representations of the divine, such as rulers and judges; for the Prophets *elohim* became the One and Only God,[6]

the Supreme Deity of monotheist religion. The Hebrew *elohim* was translated into the Greek *ho-theos*, and the sacred personal name Yahweh by *kurios*, 'Lord'. Paul, a Jew, employed *theos* when addressing both rustic Lycaonians and highly educated Athenians. It is unlikely these radically different audiences understood the same thing by the word. The Teutonic word *god* was, like *elohim*, a class-word, and meant a superhuman person who was worshiped as having power over nature and the fortunes of humanity. Christian usage, however, domesticated the word to express what became distinctive of Christianity. A similar process of reciprocal effect can be discerned in the process of the African domestication of the God of Christianity.

By seeking to penetrate ethnic cultures and societies with the message of the Bible, translators found a paradox of the need to reconcile opposites. Green concluded that, in the nature of the case, 'we must look into the heart and mind of the Zulu, ascertain the principal features in his character, and denote God in the Zulu tongue by a word related to that distinguishing characteristic'.[7] The task as Green described it would be very different from that of seeking to transmit the Western intellectual

5. James Green, *An Inquiry into the Principles which should Regulate the Selection of a Word to Denote 'God' in the Language of a Heathen Race; With Special Application to the Case of the Zulus*, pp. 4-5.

6. Edwin W. Smith (ed.), *African Ideas of God: A Symposium* (London: Edinburgh House Press, 1950), p. 34.

7. Green, *Inquiry*, p. 24.

tradition, since, as colonial governments insisted, that was viewed as beyond the ability of 'natives'. Consequently, Bible commentaries, Bible dictionaries and lexicons as the fruits of the Western intellectual tradition were left out of the work of translation, and in that ironic way African societies were shielded from Western intellectual domination. The only exception was in the field of theological training, where relatively few Africans were educated in the Western tradition of commentaries, exegesis and systematic thought. But even they would have to deal with the mass of Christian Africans weaned on the mother tongue.

As such scriptural translation pointed in a different direction, toward the discovery of Zulu ways of thought and patterns of life as the functioning frame for Christianity. Thus the sort of proficiency required for receiving the message had its roots in mother tongue affirmation, for:

> the law which holds the earth in its orbit and regulates the fall of a pin, is the same law which has directed the Greek to call God *theos* [and] has guided the Zulu to speak of Him as *Unkulunkulu*. And that law we must accept with its consequences.[8]

Scriptural translation turned the *ethnoi* into primary mother tongue agents, though many people—in addition—acquired literacy in Western languages that, in the case of English, did not remain unaffected.

A corresponding double effect attended the work of missionaries themselves, for by translating the Bible into the mother tongue, missionaries, with the assistance and leadership of local language experts, learnt the vernacular and so made the strategic shift from the familiar Western idiom to a totally new system. Thus Bible translation in its consequences affected ethnic sensibility, gave it material expression, moral affirmation and a historical vocation,[9] even if at the same time it mediated the spread of European cultural ideas. In so many places in Africa, from the Ashanti of Ghana, the Kaka of Cameroon, the Gikuyu of Kenya, to the Ndebele

8.   Green, *Inquiry*, p. 41.

9.   'The missions have realized from the beginning that if they wanted to reach the heart of the Africans and to influence their inner life, they could do so only through the medium of their own language, and they have kept to this principle; even where a considerable section of the people know a European language, Church work is with rare exceptions done in the vernacular, and it is characteristic that most African books and periodicals deal with religious subjects. Only in this way was it possible and will it be possible in the future to build up an indigenous African Church'. Diedrich Westermann, *The African To-day and To-morrow* (London: Oxford University Press for the International African Institute, 3rd edn, 1949), p. 124.

and Shona of Zimbabwe and the Zulu of South Africa, we find in Bible translation work this ethnic theme being taken up, not in a cruel design to foment inter-tribal bigotry, but in the critical historical effort to reclaim and refocus the race instinct. Thus, in his *Schism and Renewal in Africa* (1968), David Barrett described the many examples of Bible translation work and fellowship helping to break down inter-ethnic barriers and overcome the cumulative residue of tribal grudge.[10] It is that theme that John Taylor also was trying to give theological voice to in his suggestive book *Primal Vision* (1963), though he was cutting against the grain of prevailing ideas of evolutionary anthropology. Much Western thought was being diverted into empty speculation about the genesis of the idea of God. The theory that primitive religion is a rudimentary and false grasp of reality placed African religions in the camp of pagan polytheism. Education and cultural refinement were needed to dispel the illusion and, by stages of successive development, to upgrade native understanding of religion from polytheism to monotheism. Such theories are based on the view that religion is corelative with the stage of civilization people have attained, and they do not allow us to grasp fully the depth of the ethnic force in the domestication of Christianity, or, more precisely, of the God of Christianity.[11] 'The heathen in his blindness bows to wood and stone', intones a line from a famous missionary hymn; yet worship of God cannot be inspired by blindness, or, from an economic perspective, induced by hunger. At the heart of the African ethnic experience of God, says Hermann Baumann, the German ethnologist, stands a creative principle. It is that which distinguishes Africans from, say, the Polynesians.[12] And what is equally curious in the large historical literature on the subject is how

10. David Barrett, *Schism and Renewal in Africa* (Nairobi: Oxford University Press, 1968).

11. The following statement is typical of what is suggestive and at the same time revealing of the ethnic potential as well as of prevailing intellectual biases of the day: 'The genealogies in the Gospel linking Christ himself with the unnumbered myriad of the dead are a symbol of the unbroken cord with which God will finally draw Adam back to Paradise.' John V. Taylor, *The Primal Vision* (London: SCM Press, 1963), p. 171. Elsewhere Taylor draws on Greek examples to argue that Africans lack a sense of sin and guilt except where it is induced by external crisis and despair, and even there Africans would seek remedy in projecting their feelings (pp. 176-78). Cf. Hendrik Kraemer: 'Theology is the effort to reflect in a system of coherent thinking the religious apprehension of existence'. *The Christian Message in a Non-Christian World* (London: Edinburgh House Press, 1938), p. 111.

12. Smith (ed.), *African Ideas of God*, p. 6.

historians are still dominated by ethnicity and tribe as sub-categories of European race theory. So ethnicity and tribe are construed as colonial and missionary ploys of victimization, or, which is no better, as examples of negative agency, of primitive tribes acting from malice towards their neighbors. Thus, whether in victimization or in negative agency, the view persisted that what whites thought and intended had normative valence for what blacks did and practised, so that the connection of white history with black history is one of superimposition and capture. Edward Said has made this point brilliantly in his *Orientalism*.[13]

However, vernacular Bible translation offers a more complex picture. On the face of it, missions did impose a written form on oral cultures, and thereby interfered with internal morphological processes; yet, in the logic of the case, mother tongue literacy freed up mother tongue reserves for creative adaptation, as Gérard has shown.[14] Consequently, as students of culture we can profit from understanding the theological nature of the missionary engagement with non-Western cultures, because, where it was the case, in their systematic and successful cultivation of the mother tongue for translating the Scriptures, missionaries went right to the heart of living cultures. In this respect, James Green was convinced that in looking for the right Zulu concept to adopt for God, missionaries should resist their own scholastic bias and reject any rigidly abstract terms and, instead, settle on those terms that have within them the idea of personality. Our conception of God as infinite, unconditioned and absolute, though justified, should nevertheless not be allowed to obfuscate the idea of personality. Biblical theology, Green insisted, warranted having the paradox of these two contrasting conceptions of God, that is to say, the paradox of God as an unconditioned infinity and God as a personal deity. True knowledge of God demanded the concurrent validity of these two apparently contradictory ideas, so that what in strict logic could not be predicated of God as Spirit and Architect became in the reality of religious life a necessity. The scholastic tenor of the question—did human beings first believe in an infinite deity, and then by faith ascribe to such deity personality? Or did human beings first know God as the personal God, and then go on to acknowledge His infinity?—was resolved by the historical nature of biblical faith. From their field experience, missionaries were left in little doubt that Africans needed no convincing about the existence of God, contrary to prevailing

    13. Edward Said, *Orientalism* (New York: Pantheon Books, 1978).

    14. Albert S. Gérard, *Four African Literatures: Xhosa, Sotho, Zulu, Amharic* (Berkeley: University of California Press, 1971).

philosophical thought in Europe of the day. Edwin Smith recounts an anecdote about how Emil Ludwig, the eminent German biographer, found out at a social occasion that Smith was a missionary in Central Africa, and promptly took him aside to press him about African ideas of God. Finally Ludwig responded to Smith's hands-on account by indulging a stereotypical speculation, 'How can the untutored African conceive God?' Smith assured him of the facts of the case, that Africans, indeed, did not need persuading of God's existence. Ludwig protested, 'How can this be? Deity is a philosophical concept which savages are incapable of framing'.[15] The facts did not fit his theory, but Mephistopheles must have the last word.

The missionary movement enabled scholars to move away from abstract speculation about savages and to avail themselves of firsthand, detailed fieldwork on the subject. A working framework was produced that met the stringent standard of fitting with the facts on the ground. By pooling evidence over as wide an area and as diverse a number of cultures as possible, a consensus emerged: that, for Africans, God has personality with a personal name; God acts and speaks; is not a human being; is ultimate power and judge to whom they are accountable; and, what is more, is entitled to their faith and worship. This idea of God as having personality precludes the view of God as Cosmic Mana, as abstract power or natural potency represented by the notion of *force vitale*. Indeed, culture, not nature, is the decisive field of encounter with God. Thus breach of a grave interdiction, such as kin-murder, is deemed a moral dereliction and dooms the culprit to judgment and chastisement that only God, and not the chief, can inflict. However circuitous or delayed the path of retribution, however indirect the course, and whatever the standing of the clan or lineage of the offender, ultimately there can be no escape from God's justice. In other words, in grave sin God is the offended party. That is why oaths are taken in the name of a personal God, however often people may repair to the intermediary divinities otherwise. God is the great and eternal Someone who not only suffuses creation with the breath of life, and thus gives us healing plants and sacred streams, but also presides over our moral acts and actions as an all-purpose incarnate mystery.

This rock-like feature of transcendent Personality, at the core of African ideas of God, means that the whole debate about whether monotheism or polytheism was the first or final stage of religious development is not as illuminating as the discovery of the concrete terms by which the first dim

15. Smith (ed.), *African Ideas of God*, p. 1.

awareness of God is signaled to people, whether in Africa or among the ancient Hebrews. And we have, Green insisted, the warrant of the Bible for this view, because in it the divine is revealed as a person, not just as an idea.

The question about whether, in using personal attributes for God, we have not incurred too great a risk for any reasonable and proper notion of God's infinity, is at heart really a religious question. In other words, it was awe of the religious mind that prompted it to veer towards a sense of human inadequacy before divine transcendence, a human inability, for example, to unite infinity with personhood, to reconcile an incomprehensible transcendence with the human celebration of a personal God. Archbishop William Temple affirms:

> It is wonder that prompts the mind to examine its environment—and at first the elementary wonder how to make the best of it; but the inquiry ends in the wonder of awe, before that which, the more it is understood, by so much the more transcends our understanding.[16]

The same idea is repeated in Sir James Frazer's contention that 'The mind of man refuses to acquiesce in the phenomena of sense'.[17]

Modern philosophy, Green continued, took infinity as a principle of speculative thought, and in so doing sundered it from its religious roots in order to claim it as the perfection and crown of the system of human cognition. Thus philosophy of religion ended, as it began, in rootless speculation, speaking to the elite few of an abstraction, rather than to flesh-and-blood humanity of a progressive relationship founded on divine instruction. Thus, if we started from the religious roots of knowledge, we should see that the impulse to understanding was grounded in the encounter with a personal God, with a God who had spoken and acted and who, as the source of living and meaning, was graciously available to us in the habits and languages of human community, in fact in ethnic particularity, if you will. In philosophy it was the accepted custom to speak of God as the Supreme Being; in religion it was the living God. As long as we kept close to the soil, we would not split God between an abstract form

---

16. Cited in Smith (ed.), *African Ideas of God*, p. 31.

17. J.G. Frazer, *The Worship of Nature* (London: Macmillan, 1926), I, p. 1. Pauline thought is kin to this notion. God who made the heaven, the earth, the sea and everything in them, did not leave himself without a witness (Acts 14.15-17). Einstein made a different but related point by insisting that facts are according to the theory we bring to them.

and a personal deity. That was the spirit in which Green and his colleagues approached their work.

In the mission field this split, which has been such a fateful mark of modern Western thought, was not made, or not made with the same effect.[18] Green cited a remark on this point, to the effect that:

> All ancient religion, as distinguished from the primitive, laboured under the total inability of even conceiving the idea of the *worship of God*. It split and went to pieces upon that rock; acknowledging, in a speculative sense, one God, but not applying worship to Him. The local, the limited, the finite, was, as such, an object of worship; the Infinite, as such, was not. The one was personal; the other impersonal. Man stood in relation to the one; he could not place himself in relation to the other.[19]

In that formulation, the particular and the concrete merely functioned as idolatrous diversion, while the general and universal were emasculated of any specific content or power. That procedure sat poorly with experience and tradition, and so the question for religion at this point was how the conception of a universal God could be reconciled with worship of God in all the particularity and concreteness necessarily involved in worship as such, notably in the particularity and concreteness of language, symbol, ritual, esthetics, music, dance and art. It turns out, however, that these were not opposite conceptions but different levels of apprehending the real. The truth, of which ethnic particularity became a concrete hypostasis and a representation, was still capable at a different level of thought of more general, conceptual expression. It is a matter of the 'One and the Many', of the *one* God and the *many* attributes.

The theme is taken up in the perceptive defense of a converted traditional African diviner against missionary criticism. The diviner argued that the christological exclusiveness of the missionaries was not consistent

---

18. Westermann stressed this as one of the most important effects of education in the mother tongue. He writes: 'The teaching of the vernacular is by many considered as a waste of time; this may be true for the pure rationalist and for those who regard knowledge of a European language and education as two almost identical things. But if education in Africa means the full development of personality and of the organic growth of a new society, it cannot lose sight of the soil out of which the existing society has grown and the human values it has produced. The medium for studying and appreciating these things and for assigning them their due place in the new order of things is the Native language, and from this point of view it is one of the important means of education.' Westermann, *The African To-day and To-morrow*, p. 128.

19. Green, *Inquiry*, p. 10.

with the missionaries' own adoption of the expansive African name for God, to whom traditional Ifa divination has typically accorded many complementary attributes—such as the 'great Almighty one', the 'Child of God', the 'One who came whom we have put to death with cudgels causelessly', the 'One who is mightiest among the gods and prevailed to do on a certain occasion what they could not'.[20] For Africans, too, it is not good, not only for 'man', but also for divinity, to be alone (Gen. 2.18). A lot more was involved in domesticating the transcendent in African culture than missionaries realized at the time.

Thus could Johannes Christaller, the great missionary linguist, urge Africans, especially Christian Africans:

> not to despise the sparks of truth entrusted to and preserved by their own people, and let them not forget that by entering into their way of thinking and by acknowledging what is good and expounding what is wrong they will gain the more access to the hearts and minds of their less favoured countrymen.[21]

Thus, too, could Edwin Smith inveigh against foisting an artificial culture on Africans, for the African:

> cannot be treated as if he were a European who happened to be born black. He ought not to be regarded as if he were a building so badly constructed that it must be torn down, its foundations torn up and a new structure erected on its site, on a totally new plan and with entirely new materials.[22]

On the issue of colonial authorities imposing European languages such as English, Smith was cogent, saying, 'to insist upon an African abandoning his own tongue and to speak and think in a language so different as English, is like demanding that the various Italian peoples should learn Chinese in order to overcome their linguistic problem'.[23] Professor Diedrich Westermann, agreeing with Smith, appealed for mother tongue literacy:

> If the African is to keep and develop his own soul and is to become a separate personality, his education must not begin by inoculating him with a

---

20. Cited in J.F. Ade Ajayi, *Christian Missions in Nigeria, 1841–1891: The Making of a New Elite* (Evanston, IL: Northwestern University Press, 1969), p. 235.

21. Cited in J.B. Danquah, *The Akan Doctrine of God* (London: Lutterworth Press, 1944), p. 186.

22. Edwin W. Smith, *The Golden Stool: Some Aspects of the Conflict of Cultures in Modern Africa* (London: Holborn Publishing House, 1926), p. 295.

23. Smith, *The Golden Stool*, p. 303.

foreign civilization, but it must implant respect for the indigenous racial life, it must teach him to love his country and tribe as gifts given by God which are to be purified and brought to full growth by the new divine life. ... One of these gifts is the vernacular, it is the vessel in which the whole national life is contained and through which it finds expression.[24]

Both Westermann and Edwin Smith knew of the contrary policy adopted for India by Alexander Duff, and they were determined there would be no repeating of that in Africa.

As an intellectual matter, we are familiar with the dilemma that theology has rightly construed as the incompatibility of idolatry and worship of God, of self-moralization and trust in God. Yet we have not noticed, or not noticed to the same extent, the operative theology of Bible translation acting as a solvent on the race or ethnic problem by responding to its enduring yearning for messianic consolation and giving it the central figure of the New Testament, the figure of Nazareth, a tribal Jewish figure. In the historical record of the missionary encounter with African societies this Jesus, born of Mary in Bethlehem, this man who grew up in Hebrew society and culture and was marked with all the Jewish characteristics of time, space and blood, became the Africans' brother, example and savior. The cosmic Christ, by contrast, stripped of the inconveniences of his tribal Jewish heritage, equipped with standardized toneless gestures and refined in the astringent essence of rational formalism, never took root among the tribes. As Edward Wilmot Blyden noted:

> Voltaire, who denounced the god brought to his country, was condemned as an infidel. But he could not recognise in the Christ brought from Rome the Jesus of Nazareth, of Bethlehem, of Bethany, of the Mount of Beatitudes or the Sea of Galilee, and in the rush of patriotic impulse exclaimed, 'Dieu n'est pas Français'.[25]

Alexander Fraser reported, in *The Church Missionary Review* (February 1908), the objection of an Indian, Keshub Chunder Sen:

> that the Christ that we to-day preach in India is an English Christ, and Englishman, with the customs and manners of an Englishman about him, and the acceptance of whose message means denationalisation, and who, therefore, must raise hostility in every true son of India.[26]

24. Westermann, 'Place and Function of the Vernacular'.

25. Edward Wilmot Blyden, *The Three Needs of Liberia: A Lecture Delivered at Lower Buchanan, Grand Bassa Country, Liberia, January 26, 1908* (London: C.M. Phillips, 1908), p. 31.

26. Cited in Blyden, *The Three Needs of Liberia*, p. 31.

Thus could my adopted Creole grandmother, Cecilia Moore, for example, say of the Jesus of Nazareth, the Jewish Jesus, 'Na we yone', 'He is our own', but not of the cosmic Christ we study in philosophy of religion.

As Blyden insisted, Christ's cosmic transformation tribalized him for Europeans whose intellectual elites harmonized him with the Western philosophical ideal, thereby evading the inconvenient facts of their own history. The Western quest for the historical Jesus ended being a quest for the primacy of critical method, for what will conform to the West's rational scruples and cultural tastes. Accordingly, Jesus was constructed as a fictional character that reflected prevailing agendas.[27] New discoveries outside the accepted idiom were ruled out, and so was the possibility that an African Christianity, founded on mother tongue affirmation and expressed in ethnic accent, could rise to take its place in the universal human quest for transcendence. The courageous if forlorn career of Albert Schweitzer of Franco-German Alsace, latterly translated into Gabonese Lamberene, for example, is testimony of this. His creed of 'reverence for life' left little room for African ideas of God or for Africans themselves, whom he kept at arms' length though he lived among them. Schweitzer has become an icon of the West, an Enlightenment hero who forsook a lucrative, secure career in Europe for a life of danger and deprivation in the jungles of Africa. Yet the Western adulation of Schweitzer contrasts with African attitudes to him. He thus represents a strange controversy. Europeans honor him for not preaching to Africans, but Africans resent him for his aloofness, his condescension. Schweitzer did not believe in evangelizing Africans, only in doing good for them and being entitled to their gratitude. In his view, Africans lacked the cultural qualifications presupposed in Christianity, and it was the duty of Europeans to remedy that cultural deficiency without requiring Christianity. The race matter was thus transmuted into a cultural matter; but, even in that cultural guise, it was still a matter of race. Who would thus have suspected that the ideology of the cosmic Christ, and the Enlightenment dalliance with the historical Jesus, would create cultural barriers with African Christians? Or how Africans who flocked almost by herd instinct to

27. For a summary of such treatment see Charlotte Allen, *The Human Christ: The Search for the Historical Jesus* (New York: Free Press, 1998). Allen, for example, writes about Renan's *Life of Jesus*, that it was a wishful self-portrait. In Renan's hands Jesus was reduced to 'a matinee idol, handsome and languorous, with perfect manners and winning ways, whose attractiveness to women added a sexual frison to the traditional gospel stories'. See also the review in *The Wall Street Journal* (26 May 1998), p. A16.

the Jewish Jesus in preference to the Enlightenment Christ would end up paying their ethnic homage in mother tongue hymns, songs and prayers to the ruler of the universe?

Conclusion

In spite of serious political and cultural obstacles, African leadership remained crucial for the course and final outcome of Africa's encounter with the West in its colonial and missionary phase. Ultimately, mother tongue affirmation would complicate the logic of continued foreign over-lordship, an affirmation that Bible translation and literacy did a lot to advance. In Africa and elsewhere the boundaries of Christianity's cultural frontiers were expanded and deepened rather than being merely repeated on the European pattern, resulting in a shift of key and scale to local initiative, local enterprise and local paradigm. Western forms of the religion, being themselves transformations of an earlier commensurate vernacular process, were scrambled within the African setting by the process of reappropriation and adaptation.

Another issue relates to the liberating and empowering effects of Bible translation on the native idiom. We need not insist here on an original affinity between a translated and translatable Christianity, and the infinite series of complex indigenous adaptations and idioms arising from that. What remains a fact was the novel and empowering response on the ground, a response that the native idiom inscribed into the thoughts and habits of millions of people. The spectacle of a translated Bible, proceeding as divine oracle in the accents of native speech, being at the same time novel and patriotic, empowered victim and marginal populations. This kind of empowerment, of making the crucial connection with victim and marginal populations, I have called *antistructure*.[28]

28. See Lamin Sanneh, *Abolitionists Abroad: American Blacks and the Making of Modern West Africa* (Cambridge, MA, and London: Harvard University Press, 1999).

RESPONSE TO LAMIN SANNEH,
'DOMESTICATING THE TRANSCENDENT.
THE AFRICAN TRANSFORMATION OF CHRISTIANITY'

Theo Witvliet

First of all, I would like to thank Professor Sanneh for his clear and challenging analysis of developments and procedures in the context of African
Christianity that all too often have escaped our attention. His analysis transmits a nuanced picture of the history of the Western missionary enterprise,
because it elucidates a striking *paradox*. Although Christian missionaries
were part and parcel of the colonial assault on the history and culture of
Africans, they could nevertheless identify with African societies by promoting the use of the vernacular in Bible translation and thereby empowered
people with a new sense of identity.

A Dramatic Shift

This insight is all the more important when we realize that, for the last 50
years, there is a major shift going on in the history of Christianity.[1] On the
threshold of the twenty-first century, Christianity is moving away from
Europe and becoming more and more a religion of the Southern Hemi-
sphere. In the last hundred years, especially after the Second World War,
there has been a dramatic movement southward. At the beginning of the
twentieth century more than 70 per cent of the world's Christian population still was European. At the end of that century the European percen-
tage had diminished to 28 per cent of the total, while all over the world
about 43 per cent of the people who call themselves Christian are Africans
or Latin Americans. How is this extraordinary shift to be explained?

Of course, the reasons for the revival and growth of Christianity in

1. Cf. the interesting article by Dana L. Robert, 'Shifting Southward: Global Christianity Since 1945', *International Bulletin of Missionary Research* 24 (April 2000),
pp. 50-58.

countries of the 'Third World' are complex and diverse. But at least part of the answer to this question has to do, as Lamin Sanneh has shown convincingly, with the mother tongue projects of Bible translations. Translations are at the heart of the process called 'inculturation', the rooting of the gospel in a specific context. Reliance on a vernacular Bible has certainly stimulated grassroots leadership, involvement in local cultures and, especially in Latin American countries, the growth of basic communities in the 1970s and the 1980s.[2]

A very obvious form of African Christianity is the spirituality of so-called African Independent or African Initiated Churches—churches founded and led by African themselves that, today, not only exist in African countries, but also, for example, among African communities here in Amsterdam. Making use of Bible translations in their own language, prophetic African leaders (often women) interpret the Scriptures in line with their own traditional practices, by focusing, for instance, on healing body and spirit through prayer, laying on of hands and using holy water.

So in my opinion there is much evidence to support the thesis of Lamin Sanneh that missionary sponsorship of Bible translation became the catalyst for new developments in language, culture and ethnicity. Thanks to the use of mother tongue in spreading the Scriptures, Christianity has been able to take roots in African, Latin American and even in Asian local soil. Yes, also in Asia where Christianity is still a small minority in most places. The history of mission in Korea is a case in point. According to David Kwang-sun Suh, it was fortunate that in their translation of the Bible the Protestant missionaries did not use the Chinese signs that were fashionable among the educated but the language of ordinary people, the *minjung* ('mass of the people').[3] Translation, as a metaphor of inculturation, has been able to provide a reawakened sense of local identity. Reading the Bible in the vernacular meant that the biblical stories came to life in the historical experiences of the Korean common people, who suffered under Japanese domination.

Of course, in itself this phenomenon is not new in the history of

2. Cf. Carlos Mesters, 'The Use of the Bible in Christian Communities of the Common People', in Sergio Torres and John Eagleson (eds.), *The Challenge of Basic Christian Communities* (Maryknoll, NY: Orbis Books, 1981), pp. 197-210.

3. David Kwang-sun Suh, 'A Biographical Sketch of an Asian Theological Consultation', in Kim Yong-Bock (ed.), *Minjung Theology: People as the Subjects of History* (Singapore: Commission on Theological Concerns, Christian Conference of Asia, 1981), pp. 17-40.

Christianity. Also in Europe Bible translations had great impact on cultural and linguistic developments. A well-known example is Martin Luther's Bible translation into German. Wilhelm and Jacob Grimm, the famous collectors of fairy tales who were also the godfathers of German philology, expressed this beautifully. In 1846 they observed that Martin Luther was the one who breathed new life into the German language 'just as in this particular good year the sun makes the noble wine fiery and lovely'.[4] Undoubtedly they were thinking of his Bible translation, which in the course of history contributed much in providing the German people with a sense of cultural and ethnic identity.

But the difference between the European and the African situation is precisely the paradox mentioned above. European people were never deprived of their culture and history to the same degree as Africans in colonial and neocolonial times. In his theological reflection on this paradox, Lamin Sanneh invites us to revise our deeply rooted prejudices. If, in traditional African belief there is a God that acts and speaks, if there is—as John Mbiti assumes—One Supreme God,[5] then we are challenged to look carefully at a number of oppositions that by and large are still taken for granted. I am not thinking only of well-known oppositions like monotheism over against polytheism, civilized over against savage, enlightenment over against opacity (Africa as the 'dark continent'), development over against the primitive, culture over against nature. Theologically more subtle is the way the opposition of the concept of 'revelation' to that of 'nature' has been operational in reserving full knowledge of God for Western Christianity, whereas Africans only had 'natural' religion, if any religion at all. At most African people were granted 'sparks of truth', as in the case of the missionary linguist Johannes Christaller, quoted by Sanneh in his paper.[6] All those oppositions have created a hierarchical universe in which 'the truth' was very unequally divided among people and continents, although the Enlightenment view *formally* held all people to be equal. In his paper Sanneh has eloquently demonstrated this apparent contradiction by unmasking the 'doing good' of Enlightenment hero Albert Schweizer in Lambarene.

---

4. Wilhelm Grimm, 'Bericht über das deutsche Wörterbuch (1846)', in Jacob Grimm und Wilhelm Grimm, *Über das Deutsche, Schriften zur Zeit-, Rechts-, Sprach- und Literaturgeschichte* (Leipzig: Verlag Philipp Reclam jun., 1986), pp. 209-20 (209-10).

5. John Mbiti, *Concepts of God in Africa* (London: SPCK, 1970), p. xiii.

6. Cf. Sanneh, 'Domesticating the Transcendent', p. 83 in this volume.

The Particular and the Universal

There is in the contribution of Lamin Sanneh yet another antithesis that seems to bother him most. It is the opposition between the universal and the local. The *universal* stands for the ideals of modern philosophy, of the Enlightenment, of infinite transcendence, of the God of the philosophers who is infinite and impersonal, of the cosmic Christ. The *local* stands for the particularity and concreteness necessarily involved in worship: it stands for flesh-and-blood experience, for tradition, for the particular God of Abraham, Isaac and Jacob, for God as a person, for Jesus as a tribal Jewish figure.

In order to show how missionaries—at least some missionaries—dealt with this complex question, Sanneh quotes extensively from the writings of James Green. I regret that Sanneh does not reveal to us in how far his own theological position coincides with that of this Missionary Society agent in South Africa. But I presume that, at least, he feels some affinity with this kind of thinking.

The solution, proposed by Green, is that apparently God is revealing himself *in degrees*. It is a concept of the history of salvation, of the *Heils-geschichte*, whereby the implicit assumption is that one's own conceptual insight in the process of salvation is capable of having an overview that others do not possess in the same degree. In fact, it presupposes a hierarchy of possession of truth whereby the missionary himself and the tradition he belongs to are on top.

The concept that Green (and Sanneh?) maintains of the *one* God and the *many* representations is not as innocent as it seems. It presupposes a hierarchical universe that makes the missionary always the one who *gives*, never the one who *receives*. There is in my opinion less distance between Green and Albert Schweitzer than Sanneh seems to suggest. That Green uses the First Commandment, 'Thou shalt have none other gods but Me', in order to demonstrate that in the process of gradual revelation the Jews were only at the beginning (because they still believed that there were other gods), is not only unbiblical but also anti-Judaistic.

The concept of the 'One and the Many' leads Green to the conviction that 'the law'(!?) 'which holds the earth in its orbit and regulates the fall of a pin' is the same law that has directed the Greeks to call God *theos* and guided the Zulu to call him *Unculunkulu*.[7] The philosophical presupposition

---

7. Quoted by Sanneh, 'Domesticating the Transcendent', p. 81 of this volume.

here is that the abundant plurality of representations can be derived from one essence. This kind of thinking, which also prevails in what is nowadays called the 'theology of religions', is in fact the superficial offspring of a Western philosophy of identity. This idealistic tradition reached its zenith in the thinking of G.W.F. Hegel. Since modern times have shown all the extremes of radical evil (Kant: *das radikal Böse*) often committed in the name of 'God', this kind of 'innocent' thinking has been made completely obsolete. There is an irreducible plurality of religious representations, and there are also fundamental differences that cannot be covered by a unifying concept of oneness.

Curiously enough, the constraint of looking for 'logical' conceptual coherence has also seduced some African theologians who, apparently, had their theological education in the West, to use the term *preparatio evangelica*, 'preparation for the gospel', to describe the value of traditional African religions. In this way they try to harmonize a rationalized 'Christian' knowledge of God with a 'natural' African knowledge of divinity, this last being nothing more than a human potential which finds its realization in Christianity.[8] I do not think we must seek the solution to the problem of the universal and the particular in this direction.

I feel more comfortable when, at the end of his paper, Sanneh comes to speak of the enduring 'yearning for messianic consolation' by African people that suffer from 'anthropological' and 'structural' poverty, to use the terms of the late Engelbert Mveng.[9] With this yearning Africans flocked 'almost by herd instinct' to the Jewish Jesus in preference to the Enlightenment Christ. In this way they paid 'their ethnic homage in mother tongue hymns, songs and prayers to the ruler of the universe'.[10]

Here Sanneh leaves behind him the historical speculations about an alleged process of accumulative religious experience, based on a schematic salvation-historical way of thinking that cannot be completely detracted from the great diversity of biblical stories. 'Yearning for messianic consolation' stresses the eschatological dimension that lies beyond all human

8.   For a more extensive criticism on the *preparatio evangelica* thinking, see my book *A Place in the Sun: An Introduction to Liberation Theology in the Third World* (London; Maryknoll, NY: SCM Press/Orbis Books, 1985), pp. 95-96.

9.   See especially his lucid and passionate essay, 'Impoverishment and Liberation: A Theological Approach for Africa and the Third World', in R. Gibellini (ed.), *Paths of African Theology* (London: SCM Press; Maryknoll, NY: Orbis Books, 1994), pp. 154-65.

10.   Sanneh, 'Domesticating the Transcendent', pp. 84-85 of this volume.

concepts and understanding. Longing is the source from which history wells up, in the restless search for identity, for the fulfilment of the not-yet. Yearning and longing are not satisfied with a static conceptual scheme. It looks for the *totaliter aliter* of the unexpected and open-ended. As far as I can see, this approach is totally different from the theological insights of James Green. It does justice to the pneumatological and eschatological dynamics of the messianic kingdom as well as to the ambivalence and perplexity of everyday life experience.

Transmission of Tradition

From what Lamin Sanneh has told us in his paper, it becomes apparent that Bible translations are part and parcel of the transmission of religious traditions as a whole. However, as important as philological questions are, they do not suffice to determine the value and impact of a translation as such. Translations cannot be abstracted from their context. Always appearing *within* a specific tradition or at the crossroads of diverse cultural and religious traditions, they somehow take part in their vicissitudes. Therefore the famous question, Should a translation remain as close as possible to the original text or should it be adapted to the world view of the (modern) reader, is misleading and not very fruitful.

Every translation, however faithful to the sources, is a *commentary* on the original text *in a certain context*. That goes even for the *Verdeutschung* by Buber and Rosenzweig. Buber and Rosenzweig themselves were very much aware of this and used for their work the term 'commentary', in the Misdrashic sense. Living in the Republic of Weimar, they thought the time had come for a mating of the Jewish and the German spirit. As Klaus Reichert explains in a very instructive article, their purpose went in the direction of a two-culture theory. But they were not thinking along the lines of segregated Zionism or any brand of assimilated German Jewry. 'What they aimed at was to be Germans and Jews, with a capitalized AND.'[11] They sought 'to invent a language that is at one and the same time thoroughly Hebrew and the embodiment of a German that never existed, but might come into existence, be revealed, in the act of creation'.[12]

---

11. Klaus Reichert, ' "It Is Time": The Buber–Rosenzweig Bible Translation in Context', in S. Budick and W. Iser (eds.), *The Translatability of Cultures* (Stanford: Stanford University Press, 1996), pp. 169-85 (173-74).

12. Reichert, ' "It Is Time" ', p. 185, where he comments: 'Never has translation been more utopian, never it has been carried out with greater consequence'.

The habit of abstracting the debate about the value of translations from their context is probably due to a shriveled concept of the transmission of religious traditions. In Western Christian theology the transmission of tradition has been immensely rationalized. Tradition is reduced to the reception of certain texts, doctrines or moral codes: it is reduced to passively accepting certain truths. In reality, transmission of tradition is asking much creativity from the one who receives tradition. Every time tradition is transmitted, something new is created: there is always break and continuity, because the social and cultural situations in which traditions are transmitted are changing all the time. Transmission of religious tradition involves the particularity and concreteness of language, symbol, ritual, esthetics, music, dance and art. The continuity of tradition is never something *given*. It always has an open-ended dimension and is to be *discovered* again and again.

As they are part and parcel of the process of transmission, this also goes for translations. Let us remind ourselves that the German into which Luther translated was to a large extent *his own creation*. His translation meant forming:

> a new language out of the clumsy usage in the high German chancelleries by amalgamating it intertextually with the language actually spoken in everyday life, in the marketplace, in the nursery, by peasants an citizens, and forging it into a new literary medium.[13]

If it is true that translations are always part of a greater whole of cultural patterns, then, however carefully the philological and technical work has been done, they always remain vulnerable to manipulation. Although I do not doubt the overall positive picture Sanneh gave us, there is reason to believe that in Africa, as in all other continents, Bible translations into the vernacular have been operating in an *oppressive* way also. Writing from the perspective of African women, Mercy Amba Oduyoye, a theologian from Ghana with a long experience in the ecumenical movement, makes some pertinent remarks in this respect in her book *Daughters of Anowa*. She writes:

> Although the Christian heritage of the biblical, prophetic denunciation of oppression has served Africa well, oppressive strands of the same Bible do reinforce the traditional socio-cultural oppression of women. At this point,

13. Reichert, ' "It Is Time" ', pp. 169-70.

prophecy resumes its original character as a voice crying in the wilderness, ignored by the powerful and the respectable.[14]

But, if one does not want to remain in the wilderness, how is this situation to be changed? Mercy Amba Oduyoye urges African women to be critical and creative: 'We have to study the Bible ourselves with our own life experiences as the starting point'.[15] As the Bible speaks about a *living* God 'who has made all things new', Mercy Amba Oduyoye is very much aware that vital religious traditions always have to be 'invented' anew:

> As we review and record our own experiences of God, we begin to write a 'new book' of how God deals with today's world and its peoples. Nothing lies beyond the scope of this 'African Testament'.[16]

The question, however, remains: how do we know that this 'African Testament' is still in continuity with biblical Scriptures? The interaction between life experiences and the studying of the sources, as Mercy Amba Oduyoye suggests, is very important, but does not guarantee that this 'new book' remains open. Absolutism and exclusiveness can be avoided only if a third factor is taken into account. This factor I would label as 'cross-cultural communication'. Serious cross-cultural communication, as a permanent process of mutual learning, is—at least in my experience—the most efficient way to avoid the pitfalls of biblical fundamentalism on the one hand, and postmodern relativism on the other hand. Only if there is a willingness to put ourselves at stake by listening to interpretations and experiences from other cultures, as well as a mutual readiness to let the sources of Scriptures 'speak for themselves', is there a chance for a vital hermeneutical circulation. Otherwise, the hermeneutical enterprise has every risk of remaining a closed circle.

14. Mercy Amba Oduyoye, *Daughters of Anowa: African Women and Patriarchy* (Maryknoll: Orbis Books, 1995), pp. 175-76.

15. Oduyoye, *Daughters of Anowa*, p. 191.

16. Oduyoye, *Daughters of Anowa*, p. 191.

TRANSLATING THE BIBLE IN SOUTH AFRICA:
CHALLENGES TO RESPONSIBILITY AND CONTEXTUALITY[1]

Jeremy Punt

1. *Introduction*

Bible translation has a longer tradition, involves far more languages, is concerned with a greater variety of cultures and includes a wider range of literary types than any comparable translating activity. In fact, the Bible has almost always been read in translated format.[2] The range of the impact and the extent or width of the significance of the translations of the Bible on various aspects of the lives of people in Africa, and Southern Africa in particular, can hardly be underestimated.[3] It is often claimed that vernacular Bibles were primarily responsible for the spread of Christianity in Southern Africa, enabling Christian groups and 'churches' to develop and grow independently from established, mainline church formations. Granting the important influence of translated Bibles in the history of social developments in Africa and their valuable role in establishing indigenous churches,[4] the act of translation can, however, not be presented as mere

---

1.   Information for this paper supplied by the Information Manager of the Bible Society of South Africa, Mims Turley, and Dr D.H. Odendaal, minister in the URCSA, on the New Xhosa Bible is gratefully acknowledged.

2.   J.C. Trebolle Barrera, *The Jewish Bible and the Christian Bible: An Introduction to the History of the Bible* (trans. W.G.E. Watson; Leiden: E.J. Brill, 1998), p. 124.

3.   E.g. 'There is no doubt that the Bible is the most influential, most widely translated and the most widely read set of documents in contemporary Africa.' J.N.K. Mugambi, 'The Bible and Ecumenism in African Christianity', in H.W. Kinoti and J.M. Waliggo (eds.), *The Bible in African Christianity: Essays in Biblical Theology* (African Christianity Series; Nairobi: Acton, 1997), pp. 68-85 (78). Cf. Sanneh in this volume.

4.   'Translating the Bible into these African languages has meant, among other things, putting it right into the heart of African cultures'. J.S. Mbiti, 'The Bible in African Culture', in R. Gibellini (ed.), *Paths of African Theology* (London: SCM Press, 1994), pp. 27-39 (27).

pious benevolence of spreading The Message or offering Africa's indigenous people equal access to Christianity's sacred scriptures.

As much as every translator is a traitor, according to the Italian saying,
and therefore unable to do equal justice to both the original and the
translated script, translation work involves more than finding linguistic
equivalents for ancient documents and their texts.[5] This is already true of
the Greek translation of the Hebrew Bible which was produced in the
second and third centuries BCE in North Africa, and which became the
Bible of the early Christian church. The claim that the Septuagint or LXX
translators experienced no dissonance between the two interests of
'accentuation of the integrity of the text and the translation of it', but
recognized that the process of translation will inevitably involve choices
of interpretation,[6] highlights rather than dissolves the tension.[7]

With recent developments in linguistic theory there is increasing awareness that the relationship between words and their meanings is complex,
multivalent and contextually situated. To put it rather crudely, meanings are
expressed by words, and it is not words that *have* meanings. Words are in
any case not to be considered the basic unit of meaning, since meanings of
words are codetermined by their relationships to other words and sentences,
which form their context. In short, the notion of logico-grammatical paral-
lelism as tool for translation is no longer considered appropriate, due to the
influence of structural linguistics, the recognition of the conventionality of

---

5.   Cf. Whang's reference to the Korean sayings that 'translation is a creation' and
'translation is a rebellion', in his 'To Whom is a Translator Responsible—Reader or
Author?', in S.E. Porter and R.S. Hess (eds.), *Translating the Bible: Problems and Prospects* (JSNTSup, 173; Sheffield: Sheffield Academic Press, 1999), pp. 46-62 (49); also
W.R. Tate, *Biblical Interpretation: An Integrated Approach* (Peabody, MA: Hendrickson, 1991), pp. 148-52; A.C. Thiselton, 'Semantics and New Testament Interpretation',
in I.H. Marshall (ed.), *New Testament Interpretation: Essays on Principles and Methods*
(Exeter: Paternoster Press, 1979), pp. 75-104. Various ways of dealing with the cultural
conditioning of the translator are proposed by E.R. Wendland, *The Cultural Factor in
Bible Translation: A Study of Communicating the Word of God in a Central African
Cultural Context* (UBS Monograph Series, 2; London: UBS, 1987), pp. 193-206.

6.   M. Müller, '*Hebraica Sive Graeca Veritas*: The Jewish Bible at the Time of the
New Testament and the Christian Bible', *SJOT* 3/2 (1989), pp. 55-71 (65).

7.   Other indicators that the ancients were quite aware of the problems involved in
translation can e.g. be found in the prologue to Ben Sira, and the Gemara of the
Babylonian Talmud: 'If one translates a verse literally, he [sic] is a liar; if he adds
thereto, he is a blasphemer and a libeller.' Cited in Trebolle Barrera, *Jewish and Christian Bible*, p. 121; also Carroll and Brenner in this volume.

language, and the influence of transformational generative grammar.[8] And so it is increasingly realized that 'translation is a creative task, and not merely a mechanical one'.[9]

Translations have a human face, as they are always done by specific people fully clothed in their ideological accoutrements, attached to certain institutions with their ideological programmes and politics, for (and, in some cases, in association with) the intended readers unfamiliar with the original Hebrew, Aramaic and Greek languages of the Christian Bible. Differences in the world views of translators, and between contemporary translators and the original authors, foreground the socio-political or ideological nature of Bible translation. These considerations introduce issues, among others, related to the authority and the ownership of the Bible. Or, in other words, Bible translation issues go beyond the 'what' and the 'how' of translation theories and methodologies,[10] and also require us to think about *who* translates, *for whom*, and *why*? Of course, the perceived primary aim of Bible translation might not be identified similarly by academics, clergy, church folk and others who read or have an interest in the Bible.

In this paper, a brief account of the current position regarding Bible translation in South Africa, set against the broader continent, will be followed by a discussion of two recent, new translations of the Bible in South Africa. This discussion, in turn, will introduce the challenges of responsibility and

8.   The concept of transformational generative grammar is strongly connected to Noam Chomsky, and illuminates the arbitrariness of surface grammar. However, transformational approaches to translation can mistakenly contribute to a mere cognitive approach to the attempt to arrive at semantic equivalence, and foster the now untenable notion of a universal grammar of objects, events, abstracts and relations. Cf. Thiselton, 'Semantics', pp. 95-97.

9.   Thiselton, 'Semantics', pp. 78, 96.

10.   For such concerns in Bible translation in Africa, cf., e.g., P.C. Stine and E.R. Wendland (eds.), *Bridging the Gap: African Traditional Religion and Bible Translation* (UBS Monograph Series, 4; New York: UBS, 1990); E.R. Wendland, *Language, Society, and Translation: With Special Reference to the Style and Structure of Segments of Direct Speech in the Scriptures* (Cape Town: Bible Society of South Africa, 1985), on sociolinguistics and Bible translation; and Wendland, *Cultural Factor*, on intercultural communication and Bible translation. Translation is often defined as 'reproducing in the receptor language the closest natural equivalent of the source-language message, first in terms of meaning, and secondly in terms of style'. E.A. Nida and C.R. Taber, *The Theory and Practice of Translation* (Helps for Translators, 8; Leiden: E.J. Brill, repr. 1974), p. 12. Cf. Crisp and de Regt in this volume.

contextuality posed by Bible translations in Africa, as related to interpretation, the ownership and status of the Bible, and the significance of interpretive traditions.

Status Report on Bible Translation in South Africa

Since the middle of the fifteenth century and with the advent of the printing press, the Bible or sections of it have been translated into 2,212 languages. By the 1970s the Bible had been translated into 1,500 languages, which accounted for 97 per cent of the world's population at the time. The estimated 2,500 to 3,500 remaining languages represent less than 3 per cent of the world's population.[11] According to statistics supplied by the United Bible Society, by the end of 1999 the complete Bible was available in 366 languages, different 'testaments' in 928 languages and at least one book of the Bible in some further 918 languages. The three continents where the majority of Bible translations are to be found are Africa with 624 languages, Asia with 574 languages and the Americas with 456 languages.

These statistics put Bible translation activity on the African continent ahead when compared to the rest of the world, even when the figures are considered proportional to the languages of the continent.[12]

Bible Translation on the African Continent
Nowhere else is the world of the Bible as real or as alive as it is in Africa today.[13]

Nothing less than the first translation of Scripture connects Bible translation and the African continent. The Hebrew Bible in Greek, known as the Septuagint, came into existence on African soil in Alexandria somewhere during the latter half of the third century (c 280–260) BCE, ostensibly commissioned by Ptolemy Philadelphus. And indeed, the disappearance of

11. Nida and Taber, *Theory and Practice*, p. 175.
12. Cf. J.S. Mbiti, *Bible and Theology in African Christianity* (Nairobi: Oxford University Press, 1986), p. 23; Y. Schaaf, *On Their Way Rejoicing: The History and the Role of the Bible in Africa* (trans. P. Ellingworth; African Challenge Series, 5; Carlisle: Paternoster Press, 1994), pp. 132-44.
13. Mbiti, 'Bible in African Culture', p. 38. 'Even to those with little religious inclinations [sic], the Bible has proved to be important in its existential reflection on life and the human condition.' Z. Nthamburi and D. Waruta, 'Biblical Hermeneutics in African Instituted Churches', in Kinoti and Waliggo (eds.), *The Bible in African Christianity*, p. 49.

Christianity from Roman North Africa some centuries later is primarily attributed to the dominance of Latin as official and even exclusive 'church' language,[14] as much as the prominence of Christianity in the East is related to its embrace of local languages such as Syriac, Coptic, Ethiopian, Armenian and Greek.[15] The translation of the Bible into contemporary African languages, however, is a relatively recent phenomenon,[16] going back to the Christian missions of roughly the last two centuries.

The importance of the Bible in Africa is not in doubt, whether its translation is sometimes questioned and its reception contested, or while biblical hermeneutics on the continent is variegated, disputed and often in flux. The importance of 'translation' in and for African Christianity is often presented as being about more than a mechanical and technical discipline. It is also a metaphor for the inculturation of the gospel,[17]

---

14.   Schaaf, *On Their Way Rejoicing*, pp. 14-17. L. Sanneh, *Translating the Message: The Missionary Impact on Culture* (American Society of Missiology, 13; Maryknoll, NY: Orbis Books, 1989), p. 69, claims that 'The failure to produce a Punic version of the Bible was an ill omen for the church in North Africa'. E.A. Obeng, 'The Use of Biblical Critical Methods in Rooting the Scriptures in Africa', in Kinoti and Waliggo (eds.), *The Bible in African Christianity*, pp. 8-24 (24 n. 23), adds that Christianity's disappearance from Northern Africa was due to doctrinal controversies which divided and weakened it, and the prevailing perception *that as a religion it was elitist*. For the former one thinks of, e.g., Donatism, Montanism, Arianism; on the latter, see also Schaaf, *On Their Way Rejoicing*, pp. 16-17, arguing that the Berber peoples were largely excluded from Christianity during its early years.

15.   R. Gibellini, 'African Theologians Wonder...and Make Some Proposals', in Gibellini (ed.), *Paths of African Theology*, pp. 1-8 (2; referring to Teissier).

16.   Of course, not counting the Old Latin version from Carthage in the third century, or the Sahidic (Upper Egypt Coptic) Bible from the end of that century, or soon thereafter the Bohairic and Bashmuric Bibles. The Ethiopian Bible, in Ge'ez, might be dated as early as the fourth century: Schaaf, *On Their Way Rejoicing*, pp. 12, 14, 21. For a taxonomy of translations first published by 1885, and for a more recent picture, see Schaaf, *On Their Way Rejoicing*, pp. 91-93 and pp. 132-44.

17.   On this theme, cf., e.g., S.B. Bevans, *Models of Contextual Theology* (Faith and Cultures Series; Maryknoll, NY: Orbis Books, 1992), esp. pp. 30-46, and R.J. Schreiter, *Constructing Local Theologies* (Maryknoll, NY: Orbis Books, 1985), esp. pp. 6-9; in Africa, also K. Bediako, 'Epilogue', in Schaaf, *On Their Way Rejoicing*, pp. 243-54 (246-47). Maluleke, however, criticizes Sanneh and Bediako for their insistence on the 'translatability' of Christianity and, as he sees it, their respective attempts, within that framework, to disconnect African Christianity from Western colonialism and imperialism, and their reactions to the African intellectual critique on Christianity; see his 'Black and African Theologies in the New World Order: A Time to Drink from Our Own Wells', *JTSA* 96 (1996), pp. 3-19 (esp. 3-8).

characterized by the incarnational quality of Christianity that reached its zenith in the human form ascribed to Jesus Christ.[18] The vernacular Bible is generally the primary purveyor of Christianity, since 'the process of translating the Bible submitted the Christian faith to the terms of the local culture.[19] This is conspicuous in the influence of translated Bibles in contributing to the formation of local or indigenous churches'[20] theologies, as well as to social and cultural development in Africa.[21] The process of vernacular translation regularly initiated the first detailed inventory of local language and culture,[22] and had far reaching consequences and—in

18. Sanneh, *Translating the Message*, p. 3.

19. Nthamburi and Waruta, 'Biblical Hermeneutics', p. 42.

20. Surveys show that the incidence of founding new, independent churches was higher among communities in possession of vernacular Bibles; see Bediako 'Epilogue', p. 246; H.J.B. Combrink, 'Translating or Transforming—Receiving Matthew in Africa', *Scriptura* 58 (1996), pp. 273-84 (282). It often includes the notion that the vernacular Bible is 'proof' that the local people's God was all along the God of the Bible, and that 'they embody God's revelation and truth' through the translation; cf. Nthamburi and Waruta, 'Biblical Hermeneutics', p. 43; cf. Mbiti, *Bible and Theology*, pp. 29-31. In one example, the translation of the Christian Testament into Gikuyu in 1926 coincided with the conflict between Christian missionaries and Gikuyu Christians about traditions and customs, e.g. polygamy, dance and female circumcision, and resulted in the founding of the Akurinu church in 1927. Cf. N. Ndungu, 'The Bible in an African Independent Church', in Kinoti and Waliggo (eds.), *The Bible in African Christianity*, pp. 58-67 (60).

21. Cf. D.L. Whiteman, 'Bible Translation and Social and Cultural Development', in P.C. Stine (ed.), *Bible Translation and the Spread of the Church: The Last 200 Years* (Studies in Christian Mission, 2; Leiden: E.J. Brill, 1992), pp. 120-44 (134-36), who, while recognizing the need for more research in this regard, contends that vernacular Scripture contributes to the development of (especially) people of the Two-Thirds World, through strengthening their self-respect and dignity, expanding their life-worlds, contributing to literacy and promoting a new sense of identity; cf. also Mbiti, *Bible and Theology*, pp. 26-27. Cf. also A.F. Walls on the Septuagint translation's contribution to the Platonic and Stoic debates on the nature of law, reality and the Greek *logos* idea in his 'The Translation Principle in Christian History', in Stine (ed.), *Bible Translation*, pp. 24-39 (29).

22. Mbiti, *Bible and Theology*, p. 24; cf. E.A. Dahunsi, 'The Problem of Translating the Bible into African Languages', in E. Mveng and R.J.Z. Werblowsky (eds.), *Proceedings: The Jerusalem Conference on Black Africa and the Bible, April 24–30, 1972* (Jerusalem, 1972), pp. 117-20. This is, however, not unlike the early years of Christianity, where translated Bibles would present those on the frontier zones of the Roman Empire with the first literary corpus of their future reservoir of national literature; examples include the Armenian, Ethiopic and Old Slavonic translations; cf. Trebolle Barrera, *Jewish and Christian Bible*, p. 125. Constantine–Cyril's translation

subversive contradiction to the often dominant Western paradigm of the missionary translators—providing the root for nationalism.[23]

Vernacular Bibles, although the 'real engine of mission',[24] have led to the transmission of authority in both the mainline and 'independent' churches in Africa. Whereas in the past, before translations were available, authority was often related to the historical centres of missions and churches, access to vernacular Bibles relocated such authority to Africa.[25] The importance of translated Bibles in Africa should be related to the oft-heard argument that the Bible is considered by African theologians not only the primary 'source and norm of all Christian knowledge and the evidence of the divine will toward all humanity', but also the launching pad, a 'diving board'[26] or 'jumping pad'[27] from which African theologians initiate their efforts. It is peculiar, then, that the importance of the translation of the Bible into the African vernaculars often goes unaccounted for in theologizing in Africa.[28]

Bible translation in Africa extends beyond the religious realm since the translated Bible generally marks the first foray of a language into the

of the Roman Mass into Slavonic in the 9th century led to the creation of the Cyrillic alphabet; cf. Sanneh, *Translating the Message*, p. 73. For an optimistic view of Christianity's contribution to the development of the vernacular, cf. Sanneh, *Translating the Message*, pp. 51-53 and in this volume.

23.   L. Sanneh, 'Gospel and Culture: Ramifying Effects of Scriptural Translation', in Stine (ed.), *Bible Translation*, pp. 1-23 (16-17). He argues in *Translating the Message*, p. 106, 'An important difference, however, is that mission furnished nationalism with the resources necessary to its rise and success, whereas colonialism came upon it as a conspiracy'. Elsewhere Sanneh is more cautious in detaching mission from colonialism, reminding his readers that the growth of new Christian churches after African states' 20th-century independence indicates how colonialism inhibited the spread of the gospel; cf, e.g. in *Translating the Message*, p. 112.

24.   Livingstone, cf. Sanneh, *Translating the Message*, p. 114.

25.   Mbiti, *Bible and Theology*, pp. 40-42.

26.   E. Martey, *African Theology: Inculturation and Liberation* (Maryknoll, NY: Orbis Books, 1993), pp. 71-72.

27.   D.N. Wambudta, 'Hermeneutics and the Search for Theologia Africana', *ATJ* 9/2 (1980), pp. 29-39 (33).

28.   However, cf., e.g., K. Bediako, 'Understanding African Theology in the 20th Century', *Bulletin for Contextual Theology in Southern Africa & Africa* 3/2 (1996), pp. 1-11. (6-8); Combrink, 'Translating or Transforming', pp. 273-84; Mbiti, *Bible and Theology*, pp. 22-45; J. Parratt, 'African Theology and Biblical Hermeneutics', *ATJ* 12/2 (1983), pp. 88-94 (88); and, J.S. Ukpong, 'Rereading the Bible with African Eyes', *JTSA* 91 (1995), pp. 3-14 (3).

literary world. This reality is interpreted in different ways. On the one hand it is suggested that the translated Bible becomes the vehicle through which a language is moulded in a literary sense, simultaneously enriching the language through neologisms and new concepts and expressions.[29] Such 'imported' terminology often becomes part of the vernacular to such an extent that when newer translations use more contemporary and 'politically correct' terminology, they are viewed with suspicion. However, these very elements often end up disabling the traditional conceptual framework manifested in that language.[30] It is, on the other hand, felt that literalist 'transliteration' hardly contributes to presenting a meaningful translation, especially when foreign terms and expressions dominate. Meanwhile, negative perceptions surround some Bible translations in Africa, because local Christians are often not included in the translation activity.[31]

Bible translation is important in Africa among the cultural and linguistic variety and richness of the continent, and serves to make the Bible available to greater numbers of its people. However, amid the largely foreign-funded Bible translation activities in Africa—a condition which is exacerbated by African governments that do not seem to see the need for

---

29. Mbiti, 'Bible in African Culture', p. 28. Cf. also Nthamburi and Waruta, 'Biblical Hermeneutics', pp. 42-43, who add that literacy itself was encouraged, with the ability to read often being a requirement for baptism.

30. Cf. also the so-called 'union literary language', a syncretistic mix of different dialects, Schaaf, *On Their Way Rejoicing*, p. 109; cf. below on the Xhosa Bible. A related problem is that biblical terms are often translated with words and concepts that operate in the context of traditional African religious experience, see K.A. van der Jagt, 'Equivalence of Religious Terms across Cultures: Some Problems in Translating the Bible in the Turkana Language', in Stine (ed.), *Bible Translation*, pp. 131-53. In the extension of this argument is sometimes found the propagation of Africa's 'primal religions' as *prepaeratio Evangelica* (Bediako, 'Epilogue', pp. 247-51), which inevitably but ironically leaves very little of these religio-cultural frameworks intact. It is not so consoling, then, to argue that the translatability of Christianity is a countermeasure against cultural idolatry or romanticism, as Sanneh does in *Translating the Message*, p. 112—the boon of Christianity's translatability may also be its bane of an imposing hegemony. Indeed, the pluralism that follows in the wake of translatability ('the source of the success of Christianity across cultures', Sanneh, *Translating the Message*, p. 51) too often fits into the Christian master (imperialist) narrative. Cf. Sanneh and Witvliet in this volume.

31. Related concerns emerge regularly throughout e.g. Kinoti and Waliggo, *The Bible in African Christianity*, esp. pp. 1-2. Cf. Obeng, 'Use of Biblical Critical Methods', p. 21. Schaaf's optimism that 'now almost all translators are Africans' (*On Their Way Rejoicing*, p. 142) might not be wholly appropriate.

investing in this—'foreignness' in Bible translation seems set to remain an abiding feature of many translations in the foreseeable future.[32]

Africa's Oral Context

The strides made in translating the Bible into African languages is not necessarily counteracted by the high illiteracy rate characteristic of the continent. The emphasis on the oral context[33] of much of African life need not mitigate against making the Bible available on wider scale in Africa. Reclaiming the Bible in African Christianity today assumes many forms, ranging from the claim that the conceptual framework of Hebrew is closely aligned with those of African languages in general,[34] to the more widespread demand that the African cultural context should be acknowledged as analogous to the setting portrayed in the Bible, in particular that of the Hebrew Bible. The oral context of the first century is evoked with the claim that 'on the African scene the Bible relives a large part of its original setting with regard to the channels of communication and uses of language'.[35] With the Bible being used widely in church and church-related meetings, in groups and often in educational institutions, and with large portions of biblical material consigned to memory,[36] the oral Bible is indeed carried around widely over Africa, and perhaps more effectively than would have been the case if these were to have taken place in literary format.[37]

32.   Cf. Obeng, 'Use of Biblical Critical Methods', pp. 19-21.

33.   Which, ironically, sits well with the truism of modern linguistics, namely that the spoken word has priority over the written word. Cf. S.E. Porter, 'The Contemporary English Version and the Ideology of Translation', in Porter and Hess (eds.), *Translating the Bible*, pp. 18-45 (22, n. 15).

34.   C. Rabin, 'The Uniqueness of Bible Translation', in Mveng and Werblowsky (eds.), *Proceedings*, pp. 108-16 (115); P.K. Turkson, 'De Taal van de Bijbel en Afrika', *Wereld en Zending* 23/3 (1994), pp. 74-80.

35.   Mbiti, 'Bible in African Culture', p. 30.

36.   Cf. Ndungu, 'The Bible in an African Independent Church', p. 62; Mbiti, *Bible and Theology*, p. 43.

37.   In Africa oral traditions would rank among the 'hidden transcripts' (Scott) or the 'little traditions' (Meeks; Horsley; and others) which are often as emancipatory on one level as ambiguous on others. Cf. J. Éla, 'Christianity and Liberation in Africa', in Gibellini (ed.), *Paths of African Theology*, pp. 136-53 (144-50), for a strong plea on the need to 'translate' the gospel into an agenda for the transformation of life and society in Africa, from the perspective of those on the margins.

In the effort to translate the Bible into the remaining African languages, and since moral values entrenched in African culture were commonly transmitted through means such as song and dance, storytelling, proverbs and drama, these mediums might prove equally suitable as avenues for making Scripture available *and* alive on the African continent.[38] At the same time, massive literacy campaigns often use translated Bibles as their means of instruction, and not always without resistance.[39]

Bible Translation in South Africa

In South Africa a complete translation of the (66-book Protestant) Bible is available in 10 of the 11 official languages, while South Ndebele speakers have access to the Christian Testament in their own language. Translation work on the Hebrew Bible in South Ndebele was started in January 1999. Revised or new translations of Bibles in South Africa's languages have led to the new Afrikaans translation in 1983, the new Venda Bible in 1998 and the new Xhosa translation in 1996. Two Bible books (Genesis and Mark) have recently been translated and are published as part of the Afrikaans Bible for deaf people.

Two 'New' Indigenous Translations in South Africa: Xhosa and Afrikaans

Vernacular translations of the Bible in Southern Africa are nothing new,[40] but the two recent new translations of the Bible in Afrikaans and Xhosa illustrate both the value as well as many of the problems related to and misconceptions about indigenous, vernacular translations. Generally, the Bible-reading public nurtures the traditional and thus popular notion that one neutral, 'correct' biblical translation is possible and therefore mandatory, concluding that its production in the end largely depends on necessary effort and study on the side of the translators.

New translations of sacred and valued texts are bound to call forth reactions, if only for the reason that people tend to become so well acquainted with the older and established version that a new translation

---

38.   Obeng, 'Use of Biblical Critical Methods', p. 21. Cf. C.H.J. Van der Merwe, 'n Konkordante Vertaling van die Bybel in Afrikaans. Is dit Hoegenaamd Verantwoordbaar, en Hoe sal Dit Lyk?', *Nederduits Gereformeerde Teologiese Tydskrif* 40/3-4 (1999), pp. 293-303 (301).

39.   Schaaf, *On Their Way Rejoicing*, pp. 147-54.

40.   See Schaaf, *On Their Way Rejoicing*, esp. pp. 92-93, 113, 121.

fails to provide the same inspiration. In addition to a general human reaction against change and renewal, a new translation of sacred Scripture challenges the canonical status of previous translations, which were supported by certain dogmatic presuppositions and views of Scripture, and even the mysticism that surrounds words and expressions which are often no longer understood in the particular language.

The New Xhosa Translation

The first complete Xhosa Bible in one volume was translated by Weslyan missionaries and published by 1864, after all the books of the Bible had been translated into Xhosa by 1859. Various revisions of this version, in 1889 and 1892, proved unpopular among Xhosa speakers and led to a new revision of the 1864 edition in 1902. A so-called 'Union Version' was published in 1927, prepared by a committee that included various church leaders and Xhosa speakers; and further corrected editions were required because of attempts to standardize Xhosa orthography. In 1975 the Xhosa Bible was transcribed in the Revised Standard Orthography, and became the ninth edition of the union version. During the same year another translation project was started, which led to the new Xhosa Bible launched at a publication ceremony in King William's Town on 9 June 1996. Although the new Xhosa Bible (NXB) was not intended to replace the union version, the former has until now proved to be quite unpopular.

The NXB translation is largely based on the New International Version (NIV) and the Good News Bible (GNB), although the result was verified against the original texts, as in the *Biblia Hebraica Stuttgartensia* (BHS) and Nestle-Aland's 26th edition of the Christian Testament. The translation style can be broadly described as dynamic equivalent,[41] which differed from the previous version's more ideolectical approach. The NXB, in

---

41. Dynamic equivalence in translation can 'be defined in terms of the degree to which the receptors of the message in the receptor language respond to it in substantially the same manner as the receptors in the source language', according to Nida and Taber, *Theory and Practice*, p. 24—'dynamic' was subsequently replaced with 'functional' since the equivalence surpasses the notion of impact or appeal, focusing rather on sociosemiotic and sociolinguistic function. While D.A. Carson, 'New Bible Translations: An Assessment and Prospect', in H.C. Kee (ed.), *The Bible in the Twenty-First Century* (American Bible Society Symposium Papers; Harrisburg: Trinity Press International, 1993), pp. 37-67 (38, 41), applauds the apparent victory of dynamic equivalence in Bible translation practice, the sentiment is not shared by all as evidenced by, e.g., L. Greenspoon, 'Response', in Kee (ed.), *The Bible in the Twenty-First Century*, pp. 68-75 (68).

contrast to the more inclusive approach of the older version, reflects one Xhosa dialect, namely Pondo;[42] and, although the intended effect was probably a newer Xhosa, the result is perceived as an antiquated version of Xhosa which is not always properly understood by Xhosa speakers. The NXB therefore differs from the previous version in almost all respects: linguistic, grammatical and lexicographical.

Various positive factors often mentioned about the new translation range from recognition of formal aspects, such as a clearer paragraph layout, to grammatical issues. For example, the division of the typically long Pauline sentences into smaller units has found general appreciation, as the units are now easier to understand.

Certain interpretative choices of the NXB are causing, perhaps unexpected by its translators, discontent amongst its users. In the NXB it was decided to translate the *names* of the different books of the Bible; for example, Exodus became *Mfuduko*. Other familiar metaphors and words were also changed, with the well-known if mistaken Yehovah[43] being changed to *Ndikhoyo*. The term for 'apostles' is no longer recognizable in *Abafundi*, creating vast problems for the independent African churches for whom the term *abapostile* partly determined their theological and social identity. Page numbering was changed so that the Christian Testament starts afresh at p. 1, which caused confusion since in the past page numbers were often used for referencing.[44]

On the whole the NXB, which was translated at a huge cost, has not yet succeeded in even approaching the popularity of the older version which will—for the foreseeable future—remain the official Bible in Xhosa.

The New Afrikaans Translation
In 1983, at the height of the hermeneutical methodological emphasis—methodolomania—amid South African biblical scholars and during some

42. With which, apparently, the project leader, Oosthuysen, and probably also the co-translators, Mbenenge and Nkuhlu, were more familiar.

43. Cf. also Sanneh, *Translating the Message*, pp. 171-72, on the attempts of the early missionaries in Southern Africa to agree on an indigenous name for God, and where the Methodists' reluctance to use the Zulu 'uNkulunkulu' led to the creation of 'uJehova'.

44. Cf., e.g., the letter from the presbytery of Monti of the Uniting Reformed Church in Southern Africa, addressed to the general secretary of the Bible Society of South Africa on the new Xhosa translation. The presbytery expressed its 'regret' that this translation 'apparently does not answer the needs of the Xhosa-speaking community of the Eastern Cape'.

of the darkest years of Apartheid,[45] the new Afrikaans translation of the Bible was published. Replacing the 1933 (revised in 1953) Hebrew Bible based on Kittel's text and the Christian Testament based on the *textus receptus*, the text of BHS and the third edition of the United Bible Societies (1975),[46] respectively, were used for the new translation. The preface of the New Afrikaans Bible entitled, *Aan die Leser* ('To the Reader'), declares the following as its goal:

> The goal was a translation which takes the results of scientific research into account, but which stays as close as possible to the original text; a respectable translation through which Afrikaans–speakers are addressed outside and inside the church, in worship services and in household use, in our present circumstances and time.[47]

The New Afrikaans Bible was widely hailed both as academically responsible according to the highest academic and methodological standards, and

45.   K.D. Payle, 'The Afrikaans Bible Translation: A Translation for *All* Afrikaans Speakers?', *Nederduits Gereformeerde Teologiese Tydskrif* 39/1-2 (1998), pp. 122-301 (122-24), argues that since Afrikaans was instrumental in the creation, promotion and sustenance of Afrikaner nationalism during South Africa's Apartheid years, the new Afrikaans translation is inevitably accompanied by cultural and political baggage from the circumstances in which it originated. Payle, however, neglects to recognize that with the clear option for a dynamic equivalent translation which at least in theory requires (more) thoroughgoing interpretation in order to render as understandable a translated text as possible, the New Afrikaans Bible was even more prone—if not always overtly—to the political whims of its translaters than the earlier, 1933 (1953) concordant OAB. For the 1933 version's influence on the emancipation and national consciousness of the Afrikaner, cf. Schaaf, *On Their Way Rejoicing*, p. 113.

46.   With the Greek text similar to that of the 26th edition of Nestle and Aland. The transmission of the original documents of the Bible is contested; see e.g., D.J. Doughty, 'Pauline Paradigms and Pauline Authenticity', *JHC* 1 (1994), pp. 94-128 (also http.// www.depts.drew.edu/ihc/doughty.html); B.D. Ehrman, *The Orthodox Corruption of Scripture: The Effects of Early Christian Christological Controversies on the Text of the New Testament* (Oxford: Oxford University Press, 1993); M. Simonetti, *Biblical Interpretation in the Early Church: An Historical Introduction to Patristic Exegesis* (trans. J.A. Hughes; Edinburgh: T. & T. Clark, 1994). For an overview of this debate on the 'original' text in the context of Bible translating, cf. K.D. Clarke, 'Original Text or Canonical Text? Questioning the Shape of the New Testament Text We Translate', in Porter and Hess (eds.), *Translating the Bible*, pp. 281-322.

47.   Die doel was 'n vertaling wat rekening hou met die resultate van wetenskaplike ondersoek, maar wat so getrou moontlik aan die grondteks bly; 'n waardige vertaling waardeur Afrikaanssprekendes aangespreek word, buite en binne die kerk, in die erediens en in huislike gebruik, in ons teenwoordige situasie en tyd.

as providing a relevant, colloquial and inclusive Afrikaans rendering of the Bible.

The first Afrikaans translation of the Bible appeared in 1933[48] and, not without initial resistance, took over from the *Statenvertaling* which was widely used in Afrikaans-speaking churches and communities. The 1933 translation followed the *Statenvertaling* in using the *textus receptus* that Desiderius Erasmus of Rotterdam edited in 1515–16. The value of the *textus receptus* was severely compromised by the quality of the manuscripts Erasmus had available to him and the great hurry with which the text was completed. Also, the first edition was marred by many typographical errors.[49] The decision to use the *textus receptus* for the 1933 translation, although older and more reliable manuscripts were available, was an attempt to secure acceptance for the Afrikaans translation.

The New Afrikaans Bible translators claimed that their product was the result of scientific research, staying as close as possible to the original manuscripts, an attempt to provide a translation of the Bible in clear, understandable and respectable Afrikaans. The intended audience of the is clearly the 'ordinary' Afrikaans-speaking reader of the Bible. In the minutes of the committee that worked on the, it is recorded that a dynamic translation[50] is required, in understandable Afrikaans that avoids 'theological-technical, traditional-ecclesiastical concepts, pomposity and literalness'. The translation committee included language advisors.[51] Contrary to these intentions, it is sometimes argued that a certain amount of conservatism and traditionalism remained in the New Afrikaans Bible.[52]

---

48. Nine years after Afrikaans became an official language in South Africa.

49. The *textus receptus* nevertheless formed the basis of all leading Protestant translations prior to 1881, and was defended with a ferocity which amounted to superstition; cf. B.M. Metzger, *The Text of the New Testament: Its Transmission, Corruption, and Restoration* (Oxford: Clarendon Press, 2nd edn, 1968), pp. 98-102 (269).

50. J.P. Louw, 'Die Nuwe Afrikaanse Bybelvertaling: Kritiese Evaluering—Nuwe Testament', in J.P. Louw, W. Vosloo and V.N. Webb (eds.), *Die Taal van die Bybel en die Predikant* (Universiteit van Pretoria Teologiese Studies, 1; Pretoria: Nederduits Gereformeerde Kerk Boekhandel, 1986), pp. 1-11 (3, 11) argues that the New Afrikaans Bible is better characterized as being semi-dynamic, almost a functional translation. A functional translation attempts to balance the value of the formal aspects of the text with its content, giving attention to stylistic and structural functions of language and providing additional socio-historical footnotes on the biblical context.

51. J.P. Oberholzer, 'Die Afrikaanse Bybelvertaling 1983—Enkele Aantekeninge', *Hervormde Teologiese Studies* 40/1 (1984), pp. 82-91 (83-84).

52. Louw, 'Nuwe Afrikaanse Bybelvertaling', pp. 6-7, 10.

It was widely observed that the New Afrikaans Bible should not be seen as a replacement of, but should be used in conjunction with, the OAB—based on the argument that two different translation techniques were used, a dynamic equivalent in contrast to a concordant-literal translation.[53] The New Afrikaans Bible is promoted not as a revision of the OAB, but as another Afrikaans version[54] of the Bible: 'the difference is not so much in difference of meaning as in the way it was accomplished'.[55] Functional equivalent translation was developed against the background of the understanding of the Bible primarily as missionary tool.[56] The strong emphasis on evangelization appears in die final paragraph of the Preface: 'The new translation is offered with a prayer that it may serve to carry the Word of God into the hearts and lives of everyone speaking Afrikaans.'[57]

The New Afrikaans Bible is promoted as a conduit[58] for carrying the Word of God into the hearts and lives of Afrikaans-speaking people.

Resistance to the New Afrikaans Bible was typical of reactions to revised or new Bible translations,[59] with every one in three Afrikaans Bibles sold for example during 1997 still being the OAB. People often feel such allegiance to and even identify to such an extent with a particular translation, that any revision of it or contender for assuming its role is perceived as an affront to the Bible's inspiration,[60] canonicity and authority.

---

53.   Translation is often described and classified with reference to three techniques: formal equivalent or concordant (mechanical, word-for-word translation), ideolectical (reflecting the stylistic peculiarity of the text, its moulding, sphere, style and power of statement *both* dynamically *and* faithfully), and dynamic equivalent (emphasis on the intelligibility and impact of the translation in the receptor language). Nida and Taber, *Theory and Practice*, pp. 28-31, list some implications of prioritizing the 'heard language' over the 'written language'.

54.   But may the close alignment to the OAB accorded to the New Afrikaans Bible also be more ideologically inclined, with the purpose of securing recognition for the latter?

55.   Oberholzer, 'Afrikaanse Bybelvertaling 1983', p. 91.

56.   Van der Merwe, ''n Konkordante Vertaling', p. 298.

57.   'Die nuwe vertaling word aangebied met die bede dat dit mag dien om die Woord van God in te dra in die hart en lewe van almal wat Afrikaans praat'.

58.   The sentence is ambiguous, and can be understood in the sense that the New Afikaans Bible *is* the Word of God.

59.   And there are still many attempts to ameliorate adverse sentiments towards the New Afikaans Bible, e.g. P.A. Verhoef, 'Bekendstelling van die Verwysingbybel', *NGTT* 40/1-2 (1999), pp. 162-67 (165).

60.   It is interesting that inspiration is often claimed for the Bible in its various translated forms. C.D. Allert, 'Is a Translation Inspired? The Problems of Verbal

The functional equivalent translation style of the New Afrikaans Bible is seen as inhibiting independent study and reading of the Bible as a culturally conditioned text, foreign to our day and age, by people without sufficient knowledge of the original languages.[61]

Are concordant or ideolectic translations, even if some ambiguity remains, perhaps not more appropriate in South Africa? Should this option be considered, it will necessarily entail a broader understanding of the notion of 'concordance', avoiding dated and discredited theories of verbal correspondence, notions of a universal humanity and therefore language patterns, and the belief that a single simplistic yet comprehensive Bible translation can be accomplished.[62] Concordance will have to include semantic, text-linguistic, sociolinguistic and pragmatic correspondence.[63] On the other hand, paraphrased and easily readable translations have their role to play, as well. In short, it might become more important in the future to produce client-based translations,[64] instead of employing a kind of 'jack-of-all-trades' or 'mixed grill' approach to translations. The latter often leads only to strong or thick notions of canonization, inspiration and the like being attached to such projects.

Inspiration for Translation and a Proposed Solution', in Porter and Hess (eds.), *Translating the Bible*, pp. 85-113 (esp. 111-12), shows the untenability of ascribing inspiration—in the sense of direct, verbal communication from God—to both the original texts and their translations, and proposes 'a balanced understanding of the definition of inspiration based on the wider use of the concept'. Cf. also D.C. Aricheia, 'Theology and Translation: The Implications of Certain Theological Issues to the Translation Task', in Stine (ed.), *Bible Translation*, pp. 40-67 (55-62); B.W.R. Pearson, 'Remainderless Translations? Implications of the Tradition Concerning the Translation of the LXX for Modern Translation Theory', in Porter and Hess (eds.), *Translating the Bible*, pp. 63-84, esp. 72-79. Cf. Noorda in this volume.

61. Van der Merwe, ''n Konkordante Vertaling', p. 293.

62. Cf. E.A. Nida, 'Breakthroughs in Bible Translating', in Kee (ed.), *The Bible in the Twenty-First Century*, pp. 195-208 (199-204), on what he calls 'language universals'. The theories that a word has a basic meaning related to its origin, and that the dominant order of syntax in a given language can readily be determined and transposed into another language, are no longer tenable; cf. Van der Merwe, ''n Konkordante Vertaling', p. 299 and see Crisp in this volume.

63. Van der Merwe, ''n Konkordante Vertaling', pp. 298-301.

64. Probably going beyond the three translations varieties proposed by Nida and Taber, *Theory and Practice*, p. 31: a traditional translation for liturgical purposes, a literary type for the well-educated constituency, and the 'common' or 'popular' language translation for the 'common people'.

Emerging Issues of Bible Translation in the Third Millennium

Translation and Interpretation

> [T]he fact that the Bible is intended to be understood does not necessarily mean that all of it can be understood without studying or instruction.[65]

For all its importance, it is necessary to move beyond the dictum that translation is necessarily interpretation. Access to a translated Bible burdens its readers with the hermeneutical question, a responsibility previously shouldered by either the academy, or the church, or society at large, through for example the visual arts. And so Fasholé-Luke argues that, following the availability of Bible translation in the vernaculars, 'the vast majority of Africans' have an 'uncritical approach to Scripture'.[66] But regardless of approach, it is true that Bible translations involves both inculturation and hermeneutics, with the Bible often becoming the fountainhead of presenting the Christian faith in the context of the local culture.[67] The contextualization of Christianity through a vernacular Bible simultaneously required its readers to discern the meaning of the texts, and therefore 'biblical hermeneutics becomes an ongoing process within the locally founded Churches'.[68]

Translations are of course not neutral events,[69] but in Africa they are

65. Whang, 'To Whom is a Translator Responsible?', p. 58.

66. E.W. Fasholé-Luke, 'The Quest for African Christian Theology', *JRT* 32/2 (1975), pp. 69-89 (78). This is confirmed by various authors, e.g. Mugambi, 'The Bible and Ecumenism', pp. 78-82; Obeng, 'Use of Biblical Critical Methods', pp. 14-19. As elsewhere there is hardly consensus on hermeneutical method in Africa, cf. L. Magessa, 'From Privatized to Popular Biblical Hermeneutics in Africa', in Kinoti and Waliggo (eds.), *The Bible in African Christianity*, pp. 25-39 (30-31); Mugambi, 'The Bible and Ecumenism', pp. 80-82; Nthamburi and Waruta, 'Biblical Hermeneutics', pp. 50-51; Obeng, 'Use of Biblical Critical Methods', pp. 21-23. For literal hermeneutics in the Black Diaspora, cf. G.L.O.R. Yorke, 'The Bible and the Black Diaspora', in Kinoti and Waliggo (eds.), *The Bible in African Christianity*, pp. 145-64 (149-52).

67. Sanneh, 'Gospel and Culture', pp. 1-23 (also pp. 200-207), builds an elaborate argument to deal with the apparent contradiction between admitting to the universal nature of Christianity while avowing its particularist—or cultural—expression. Paul is cited as representative of *the* Christian position of culture: 'Christian life is indelibly marked by the stamp of culture, while Christian sources also instruct a penultimate status for culture.' So, theologically speaking, 'the cultural signs and symbols which *differentiate* them in their respective particularities *unite* them in relation to God'.

68. Nthamburi and Waruta, 'Biblical Hermeneutics', pp. 42-43.

69. Cf. P. Ellingworth, 'Exegetical Presuppositions in Translation', *BT* 33/3 (1982), pp. 317-23.

generally linked to an evangelizing thrust. Bible translations in Africa are therefore, on the one hand, ideologically laden in the sense of being (at least in part) purposefully directed at and incorporated in such processes of evangelization.[70] But, on the other hand, Bible translation engenders hermeneutical independence because people can now access the Bible in a local language. With the translated Bible contributing to the establishment of local, indigenous churches, it also ensures continuous hermeneutical efforts to glean biblical meanings. The translation is therefore hardly the end or culmination of the process to interpret the meaning of Christianity in a particular culture, but rather the initiating event towards ongoing contextualization. However, with the emphasis on functional equivalent translations where interpretative choices come ready made, the danger of imposing contemporary yet foreign world views of interpreters on local African communities or transposing African religious concepts onto biblical texts, is a very real one. But then again, this is also the case where a more or less concordant translation, set in its first-century, Middle Eastern culture and values, is made!

Populist readings are as much susceptible to the danger of selecting their overt or subliminal canon within the canon, supported by a 'totemized' selection (Sugirtharajah) of texts. Today we may accept such selective or 'advocacy' interpretative approaches (Schüssler Fiorenza) as unavoidable, aware that every interpreter is inevitably biased and compromised in one way or another, representing a particular interpretative community; we may even welcome a specific advocacy stance. Translators, however, generally do not have the luxury of deciding *a priori* to deal with selected portions from the Bible, although they are equally confronted with inevitable interpretative choices. The choice, at popular level, for a particular translation creates one of the biggest problems regarding translations, and is exacerbated since receptors of a translation often tend to inscribe it with notions of divine inspiration as soon as their identity becomes interrelated to the texts.[71]

---

70. Not only in Africa, of course; cf. Pearson, 'Remainderless Translations?', p. 81; Walls, 'Translation Principle', pp. 24-39, draws an analogy between translation and conversion. Carson, 'New Bible Translations', pp. 57-60, surmises that Bible translation's missionary involvement puts the emphasis on simplicity and clarity.

71. The receptors of the LXX presumed the need for and supported the idea that this document was inspired—theologians and apologists used the notion of the inspiration of the LXX to advance their own agendas. Pearson, 'Remainderless Translations?', p. 80.

Translation is clearly not peripheral to interpretation, providing the preliminary phase of interpretation;[72] but, in fact, interpretation often precedes translation,[73] so that the latter becomes the goal of interpretation.[74] Any attempt to sever the hermeneutical moment from the linguistic function of translation is doomed to result in an idealized and hegemonic script. It is nowadays accepted that biblical interpretation is neither objective nor neutral, displaying in often subtle ways the political ideology (or ideologies), interests and sentiments of the interpreter. If biblical interpretation is always accompanied by pre-understanding, biblical translation can also never be presupposition-less; or take place without pre-understanding. If biblical interpretation is political, biblical translation is political too, and in a twofold sense. Not only are translations equally politically informed regardless of the frequent claims to being faithful to the source text, using objective methodologies grounded in proper research and so on, but translations are often not subjected to the same scrutiny as is the case with interpretation.

More generally, translations can obfuscate or even misinterpret meaning, with regard to both formal and dynamic equivalent translations. When it comes to the translation of so-called technical terms such as 'grace' or 'righteousness' the choices made by translators in dynamic equivalent translations are often precarious.[75] In addition, Nida's notion of dynamic—later formulated as functional—equivalence needs to be criticized, as he perpetuates the Romanticist idea that the intention or meaning of the original author(s) can be determined.[76] For all the appreciation for a functional-equivalent translation as the 'best way to translate the most meaning to the largest possible audience', Nida's theory feeds into the notion of an inspired, remainderless translation.[77] And with his emphasis on contrasting

72.   Cf. H. Conzelmann and A. Lindemann, *Interpreting the New Testament: An Introduction to the Principles and Methods of New Testament Exegesis* (trans. S.S. Schatzmann; Peabody, MA: Hendrickson, 1988), p. 36.

73.   Acknowledgment of the multiplicity of meaning and the impossibility of translation neutrality does not require translational ambiguity, as Whang, 'To Whom is a Translator Responsible?', pp. 54-55, suggests. His is a preference for the original and authorial intention rather than concern for contemporary readers.

74.   I.H. Marshall, 'Introduction', in Marshall (ed.), *New Testament Interpretation: Essays on Principles and Methods* (Exeter: Paternoster Press, 1979), pp. 11-18 (12).

75.   Cf. Porter, 'The Contemporary English Version', pp. 42-45.

76.   Whang, 'To Whom is a Translator Responsible?', pp. 46-62, criticizes Nida's theory, but at the same time privileges the notion of the intention of the author (esp. pp. 49, 54).

77.   Pearson, 'Remainderless Translations?', pp. 83-84.

the form with the content of the text, Nida similarly fails to account for the influence of textual form and expression on meaning.

The difficulty of translating the Bible into another language requires attention to the language's traditional concepts.[78] In fact, to some extent translation is not so much a linguistic as a cultural exercise—cultural transposition[79]—epitomised by the absence of a term for 'religion' in many African cultures, since it is simply part and parcel of African cultures.[80] The challenge is therefore to mediate between two positions. On the one hand, the contemporizing tendency induced by a translated Bible is to no longer be alert to the differences between the biblical time, cultures and languages, and ours. On the other hand, to archaize (Caird) the Bible by viewing its texts as static, impenetrable and consigned to ancient times, is hardly an alternative to pursue. Should a balance not perhaps be sought rather in a more ideolectic translation accompanied by commentary and notes? Considering the close interaction between translation and interpretation and that relationship's underlying ideology, the question on how to evaluate the adequacy of a particular translation is still very much at hand.

Translation and Ownership of the Bible
The New Afrikaans Bible is an example of a contemporary translation which, in its use of the receptor language, fails to account for the use of Afrikaans in Black and Coloured communities in South Africa. The New Afrikaans Bible, for all its claims to the contrary, represents the interests of and was fomented in the ideology of Afrikaner nationalism. Its translators were all white, male, belonging to the (South African) Dutch Reformed Church and therefore representative of a minority among Afrikaans speakers.[81] Apart from sustaining a superior White Afrikaner myth, it simultaneously disempowers other communities that have at least an equal claim to the proprietorship of the language. Ironically, the successful propagation of

---

78.   For the danger of leaving 'life world' or 'culture' out of consideration in making translations, cf. also L.J. Luzbetak, 'Contextual Translation: The Role of Cultural Anthropology', in Stine (ed.), *Bible Translation*, pp. 108-19. Wendland, *Cultural Factor*, pp. 26-38, wants to respect the source text by decrying 'transculturation' as its complete adaptation to the receptors' sociocultural environment, and to the receptor text with insisting on the proper 'contextualization' of the source text.

79.   J. de Waard, 'Vertalen: Een culturele transpositie', *Wereld en Zending* 19/3 (1990), pp. 254-58.

80.   Cf. Stine and Wendland, *Bridging the Gap*, pp. vii-x.

81.   Payle, 'Afrikaans Bible Translation', pp. 122-29.

the historical myth that Afrikaans is the exclusive language of White Afri-kaners is encountered in the struggle slogan that Afrikaans is 'the language of the oppressor'.[82] Moreover, the New Afrikaans Bible may yet become a rallying point for a certain version of Afrikaner nationalism, in an appar-ently desperate attempt of some to avoid inclusion in building a (new) South African identity and consciousness. The discussion over the public use of Afrikaans, as in the New Afrikaans Bible, must be set in the context of what is referred to in some circles of South Africa's Afrikaner community as the 'Third Language War'. With other nationalist elements such as the flag and anthem falling away in the aftermath of the changes since 1994 in South Africa, Afrikaner nationalism is desperately clinging to its carrier language.

For different reasons altogether the ownership of the Bible is contested in South Africa's Xhosa-speaking communities, where the NXB is seen by some as a conspiracy against African Independent (Initiated) Churches (AICs). With the ongoing dis-ease between mainline churches and the AICs, the NXB's failure to retain the vernacular metaphors, words and expressions that often circumscribe the main tenets of these groups,[83] is regarded by many as an attempt to divorce them from the Bible and drain one of their most important knowledge resources.[84] There should be no doubt, whatever amount of revisionist missionary historiography is prac-ticed, that Christian missions in Africa (as elsewhere) were closely linked to the colonialist endeavour. This is not to deny missionaries' often valu-able contributions made to indigenous peoples and languages on certain terrains, but to acknowledge their imperialist motives and hegemonic corollaries, and the lasting influences and suspicions the latter created.

82.   An important part of nationalism is the rewriting or reinventing of history to suit the purposes of the group, and so a reconstructed history becomes 'historical reality'. Cf. Payle, 'Afrikaans Bible Translation', p. 123.

83.   'Abapostile' (apostles), 'Zion' and other terminology which were differently translated in the NXB, were used literally in the theologizing of AICs. At least two thousand churches in South Africa have, in one form or another, 'Zion' in their name. Cf. further in E. Isichei, *A History of Christianity in Africa: From Antiquity to the Present* (Grand Rapids; Laurenceville: Eerdmans, Africa World Press, 1995), pp. 313-17.

84.   One considerable difference between the New Afrikaans Bible and the NXB relates to the promotion of these translations. Unlike with the New Afrikaans Bible, very little publicity was given to the NXB, and this contributes to its pariah status in the larger Xhosa community of South Africa. Ministers to Xhosa–speaking communities are of the opinion that better publicity, vigorous advertising, workshops and discussions on the NXB might contribute to changing people's perceptions about this translation.

Over time and due to historical exigencies, translations were often accorded such autonomous and superior status tantamount to inscribing them with divine authority, and so exceeded recourse to either the original texts[85] of the Bible or subsequent, new and revised translations. Jerome's Latin translation of the Bible, completed early in the fifth century, became the Bible of the church for the next millennium.[86] Following various revisions and in an amended format, the ('divulgated') Vulgate was pronounced the official biblical text of the Roman Catholic Church by the Council of Trent in 1546. Another example is the Dutch *Statenvertaling* of 1637, long considered the most important if not the only acceptable version of the Bible—inscribed with divine authority—in the Netherlands and even elsewhere such as South Africa. Both the Vulgate and *Statenvertaling* are examples of translations achieving what amounted to canonical status.[87]

On the other hand, one of the most important results of vernacular translations in Africa was the loosening of the controlling grip of the missionaries and their societies.[88] But such claims are undermined when the close supervisory role of the United Bible Societies (UBS) in the translation projects they are involved in, is considered.[89] The UBS would insist, for

85. In the course of history, authority often related more to theological considerations than the idea of originality, as seen in respectively the preference of Catholicism for the Latin Vulgate, traditional Judaism for the Masoretic Text, and Protestantism for the *textus receptus*. Cf. Clarke, 'Original Text or Canonical Text?', p. 291.

86. Not without initial hiccups, as Jerome was accused among other things, of Judaizing the Bible because he used the Masoretic Text of the Hebrew Bible and not that of the LXX. Van der Merwe, '"n Konkordante Vertaling', p. 294; cf. Trebolle Barrera, *Jewish and Christian Bible*, pp. 353-57. Cf. Noorda and Rogerson in this volume.

87. And, of course, the KJV of 1605 (1611), which found almost immediate and wide acceptance, partly due to the support by the British monarch and partly because of it relatively superior translation quality; cf. Van der Merwe, '"n Konkordante Vertaling', pp. 294-95. For the general trend of identifying a particular translation with the 'Word of God', cf. Aricheia, 'Theology and Translation', p. 50; Porter, 'The Contemporary English Version', p. 34. Cf. Rogerson.

88. Bediako, 'Epilogue', p. 246.

89. In a recent article which praises the UBS for its effort towards indigenizing Bible translation, it is lamented by M. Kanyoro, 'Indigenizing Translation', *BT* 42/2A (1991), pp. 47-56 (56), that '[t]ranslation work is still predominantly in the hands of the West and true communion is an idea which has perhaps not yet fully come true'. This is despite E.A. Nida's claim that in 90% of UBS translation projects, the translators are nationals and the missionaries resource persons; see his 'Trends in Bible Translating within the United Bible Societies: An Historical Perspective', *BT* 42/2A (1991), pp. 2-4 (4).

example, on having one of their consultants on the translation team and that their 'recommended and supplied' commentaries be consulted.[90] The ideological influence of translation agencies is not lessened when it is claimed that some represent the 'extreme right wing Protestant missionary society'.[91] Amid the difficulty of decisively proving or disproving such claims, the perception that outside agencies peddle a particular ideology in their involvement with Bible translation in Africa is often determinative for the evaluation and acceptance of such translations by their intended receptors.

In Bible translation the voice of the marginalized in society is often effectively obliterated, and their liminal existence entrenched. On the African continent, it is worth remembering, two broad theological 'traditions' exist: one concerned with the vindication of traditional religions and traditions, and the other relating primarily to contemporary social and political realities. African and Black Theology may be soulmates (Tutu), but the latter's voice is generally not heard in Bible translation activities. Beyond theological configurations, the global village's influence requires of Bible translators to rethink the implications of gender issues, terminology used for people with a homosexual orientation, who are physically challenged, and so on, for their work.

Translation and the Status of the Bible: Commodity, Fetish and Icon
The Bible has, bar a few exceptions, traditionally been viewed as 'symbol of the Word of God' rather than the literal Word of God itself.[92] Recently, however, the symbolic nature of the Bible has been expanded to include a variety of different understandings of it. Acknowledging the change in people's perception of the nature and role of the Bible (and its status) for their lives, requires us to ask about the role of Bible translation in this change.

In a world soaked in global capitalism, the Bible has become another commodity, 'a material-cultural object in the capitalist period of Western civilization, especially in relation to the commodity culture of the consumerist society in which we in the West all live now'.[93] Add to this the

90. Cf. Nida and Taber, *Theory and Practice*, pp. 174-86.
91. E.g. Isichei, *History of Christianity in Africa*, p. 336, on the Wycliffe Bible translators; Schaaf, *On Their Way Rejoicing*, p. 198 (cf. p. 233), questions their translation policy of focusing on the Christian Testament.
92. S.M. Schneiders, *The Revelatory Text: Interpreting the New Testament as Sacred Scripture* (San Francisco: Harper, 1991), pp. 27-43.
93. R.P. Carroll, 'Lower Case Bibles: Commodity Culture and the Bible', in

professional study of the Bible, providing tenure to scholars of the Bible and having students pay fees for courses on it, and it is easy to show up the Bible as merchandise on the global capital market. And of course, the Bible as commodity should not, in the light of the fears of churches or other communities of faith regarding the imperative to safeguard the *ganz andere* ('totally different') status of the Bible, be seen as necessarily or totally something pernicious. The commodity status of the Bible is exactly the point where it becomes popularized and available also to the marginalized of society, and importantly, when it slips from the firm academic, ecclesiastical and other forms of control over its texts.[94]

On the other end of the spectrum of translating and appropriating the Bible, it becomes a fetish. A major complicatory factor for the adequate use of the Bible is the practice of venerating it, leading to either magical or idolatrous practices.[95] As a 'great code' (Frye) which has become a fetish, the Bible needs to be recoded, as indeed has already started to happen globally.[96] The 'manmade' (sic) quality of the Bible also reappears when it is no longer treated as fetish.[97] Such is the nature of treating the book as sacred object, that it is attributed magical qualities. In this context, appropriate caution is required when quoting and using statistics on Bibles sold, possessed, and so on, for determining its real value and role in Africa, because of the widespread 'magical' use of the Bible.[98] The mere possession or touching of the book, is considered beneficial.[99]

J.C. Exum and S.D. Moore (eds.), *Biblical Studies/Cultural Studies: The Third Sheffield Colloquium* (JSOTSup, 266; GCT, 7; Sheffield: Sheffield Academic Press, 1998), pp. 46-69 (47).

94. However, the close link between Bible and community, or constituency, might see an increase in the preferred choice for a particular translation, as Carson, 'New Bible Translations', pp. 57, 60-63, suggests, leading to increasing 'compartmentalization'.

95. Schneiders, *Revelatory Text*, p. 43.

96. Kwok Pui–Lan, 'On Color-Coding Jesus: An Interview with Kwok Pui-Lan', in R.S. Sugirtharajah (ed.), *The Postcolonial Bible* (BibPostcol, 1; Sheffield: Sheffield Academic Press, 1998), pp. 176-88 (186-87).

97. E. Schüssler Fiorenza, 'Introduction: Transforming the Legacy of *The Women's Bible*', in E. Schüssler Fiorenza (ed.), *Searching the Scriptures*. I. *A Feminist Introduction* (London: SCM Press, 1993), pp. 1-24 (4).

98. J.M. Waliggo, 'Bible and Catechism in Uganda', in Kinoti and Waliggo (eds.), *The Bible in African Christianity*, pp. 179-95.

99. D.L. Whiteman, 'Bible Translation and Social and Cultural Development', in Shine (ed.), *Bible Translation*, pp. 120-44 (137); Ndungu, 'The Bible in an African Independent Church', pp. 62-63; cf. Yorke, 'The Bible and the Black Diaspora', pp. 149-52, for such use of the Bible in the Black Diaspora.

It is somewhere between these positions that the Bible is accorded an iconic character—when the sacred myth turns sacred image[100]— and where perhaps the biggest challenge is presented to biblical translators and interpreters today.[101] The iconic nature of the Bible relates not only to what it is believed to prescribe but also to proscribe. This presents a double jeopardy that consists of inscribing the social marginalization of groups such as women and the poor, as well as the construction of a powerful patriarchal and kyriarchal ideology.[102]

Translation and the History of Interpretation

> They [sc translator and contemporary reader] cannot read the text without the knowledge they obtained through the development of history.[103]

In acknowledging the importance of reception studies for interpreting biblical texts, a certain ambiguity, however, remains. Although it is acknowledged that 'we stand inescapably in the shadow of those who have gone before us',[104] that shadow can have a positive as well as a negative effect on interpretation. Interpretative strategies developed by earlier interpretative communities often become 'foundational' in the sense of providing the setting against which subsequent readings are evaluated and the basis on which others are built.[105] When a particular interpretative approach

---

100. D.A. Lee, 'Touching the Sacred Text: The Bible as Icon in Feminist Reading', *Pacifica* 11/3 (1998), pp. 249-64 (256).

101. For the danger of bible idolatry or bibliolatry, cf. Lee, 'Touching the Sacred Text', p. 259. Cf. also my earlier argument on the danger of bibliology which easily turns into biliolatry, in J. Punt, 'The Bible, its Status and African Christian Theologies: Foundational Document or Stumbling Block?', *Religion & Theology* 5/3 (1998), pp. 265-310 (269, 272-74).

102. Lee, 'Touching the Sacred Text', pp. 260-61, wants to retain the notion of the Bible as icon, and cautions against iconophobia, pleading for a healthy balance between iconoclasm and iconophilia in developing 'a feminist poetics of sacred reading' (cf. pp. 263-64). For a different sense of the Bible as 'cultural icon' (in US politics) which approaches the notion of fetish, that is where authority transcends interpretation, cf. J.A. Glancy, 'House Readings and Field Readings: The Discourse of Slavery and Biblical/ Cultural Studies', in Exum and Moore (eds.), *Biblical Studies/Cultural Studies*, pp. 460- 77 (461, 476).

103. Whang, 'To Whom is a Translator Responsible?', p. 57.

104. M. Bockmuehl, 'A Commentator's Approach to the "Effective History" of Philippians', *JSNT* 60 (1995), pp. 57-88 (59).

105. V.L. Wimbush, 'The Bible and African Americans: An Outline of an Interpretive

becomes an exclusive or overpowering tradition for how to read a text, it is no less than interpretative imperialism and exclusivism. It is not out of place to refer in this regard also to a history or tradition of translation.[106]

Interpretative traditions are unavoidably part of translation activity, as soon as one accepts the reciprocal relationship between translation and interpretation. In the case of the NXB where the translation was based on the NIV and GNB translations of the original,[107] it is in a double sense prone to the danger of inevitable distortions of the original text's meaning, or more positively, runs the risk of being twice removed from the source text's particular significance. And the NXB now also has to contend with the accompanying hermeneutical tradition of those English translations.

The difference in the status and roles attributed to the Bible, especially concerning its de-sacralization, can also be understood in light of recent theorizing of the entanglement of textual traditions in the discourse of power. In this regard, Scott has argued for a distinction between hidden and public transcripts.[108] This distinction recognizes and emphasizes the relationship between power relations and discursive traditions. The relationship between power and discourse is in sharpest relief where divergence between public transcript and hidden transcripts is greatest. As much as the Bible, both in terms of texts selected as canon and the texts themselves, is a public transcript, a hermeneutic of suspicion and a subversive reading strategy seem in order. The biblical texts are the written records of society's powerful,[109] as

History', in C.H. Felder (ed.), *Stony the Road We Trod: African American Biblical Interpretation* (Minneapolis: Fortress Press, 1991), pp. 81-97 (84).

106. This refers to more than translation theory. Cf. Porter, 'The Contemporary English Version', pp. 18-45, who argues that the one characteristic of the Contemporary English Version (CEV) is the attempt by its authors not to have the CEV digress too much from the earlier King James and Authorized Versions, aligning itself with this 'grand tradition of traditional Bible translation'. Cf. also Noorda in this volume

107. Not exceptional as far as Bible translations in Africa are concerned; cf. Wendland, *Language, Society, and Translation*, esp. p. 41; Wendland, *Cultural Factor*, esp. pp. 17-19.

108. Public transcript is 'a shorthand way of describing the open interaction between subordinates and those who dominate' and 'where it is not positively misleading, is unlikely to tell the whole story about power relations'. Hidden transcript 'characterises discourse that takes place 'offstage', beyond direct observation by powerholders'. J.C. Scott, *Domination and the Arts of Resistance: Hidden Transcripts* (New Haven: Yale University Press, 1990), pp. 2-4.

109. The contention of those who argue like S.B. Thistlethwaite, 'Every Two Minutes: Battered Women and Feminist Interpretation', in L.M. Russell (ed.), *Feminist Interpretation of the Bible* (Philadelphia: Westminster Press, 1985), pp. 96-107 (100),

evidenced in their literacy and control over the production and selection of its texts.

Reference to the cultural, spatial and temporal distance between the original texts and contemporary translators and readers should not presuppose an empty divide. Especially in the case of the temporal element, history is not merely an empty gap, but is filled with a history of translation and interpretation[110] that can at once be an impediment to and an opportunity for contemporary understanding. It is therefore not only the biblical texts, or the canonical format, but also the accompanying interpretative traditions that come up for scrutiny.[111] In biblical scholarship examples of competing interpretative traditions in the Bible have been identified. Horsley[112] refers to the Bible's 'great' and 'little traditions'[113] with regard to the official Jerusalem tradition and the popular Galilean tradition during the time of Jesus; and, on the other hand, to contemporary scholarly and popular readings of the historical Jesus.[114] He explains how

that the Bible was 'written from the perspective of the powerless', cannot be sustained without further qualification.

110. S.E. Fowl, 'The New Testament, Theology, and Ethics', in J.B. Green (ed.), *Hearing the New Testament: Strategies for Interpretation* (Grand Rapids: Eerdmans, 1995), pp. 394-410 (401-402).

111. Some have been largely displaced, cf., e.g., the Hamitic interpretation of the curse of Canaan (Gen. 9); cf., e.g., D.H. Aaron, 'Early Rabbinic Exegesis on Noah's Son Ham and the So-Called "Hamitic Myth"', *JAAR* 63/4 (1995), pp. 721-59; G. Usry and C.S. Keener, *Black Man's Religion: Can Christianity Be Afrocentric?* (Downers Grove, IL: IVP, 1996), pp. 70-82.

112. R.A. Horsley, 'Historians and Jesus: Scripts in the Official and Popular Traditions', *Bulletin for Contextual Theology* 3/1 (1996), pp. 4-7.

113. For 'great and little traditions', see W.A. Meeks, 'A Hermeneutics of Social Embodiment', *HTR* 79/1-3 (1986), pp. 176-86. In similar vein and as part of her argument on different opinions regarding slavery in the US, Glancy, 'House Readings', pp. 460-77, introduces an important distinction between 'house' and 'field' readings.

114. The reading practices of ordinary readers should, therefore, *not* be romanticized; cf. above (n. 54) on the uncritical approach of the majority of African Bible readers. This kind of approach to Scripture often mitigates against the notion of 'popular readings' being, according to J.A. Draper, 'Great and Little Traditions: Challenges to the Dominant Western Paradigm of Biblical Interpretation', *Bulletin for Contextual Theology* 3/1 (1996), pp. 1-2 (2), *necessarily* innovative and liberatory, and challenging the 'great tradition' of the particular (oppressive) society. At times these popular readings rather achieve the opposite, which is to affirm the oppressive status quo, not only, but at times especially, because of the influence of particular (established) traditions or histories of interpretation. It is also a problem that describing 'great' and 'little' traditions,

these two sets of reading strategies or performances are at odds with one another, and often in conflict, too.

In the modern world interpretative traditions are powerful tools for controlling the meaning of texts, especially by 'professional middle-class culture and sensibilities'.[115] It has to be remembered that the available history of translation and interpretation, especially in so far as this is available today in written form, represents the interests and thoughts of the powerful of church and society: 'those who have won and not those who have lost in the course of history'. This means that the history of the translation and interpretation of the Bible can easily function as:

> nothing but a legitimation of successful historical processes or, even more cynically, nothing but a secondary hermeneutical legitimation of secondary biblical legitimations, which have been used in the history of the church to justify the acts of the rulers of the church, or, sometimes, of the rulers of the world.[116]

Eventually it has to be asked whether Bible translations are representative of the centre or whether the voices on the margins can be heard in their texts? Hardly any serious scholar will today contend that the Bible as we know it is the result of an organic, neutral or even essentially divinely inspired process. Vernacular Bibles are for the largest part indicative of the trend in Christianity to conflate religious language with the ordinary life-worlds of people,[117] but caution is in order on this point. Clearly the whole of what is often rather blithely referred to as 'the Bible' is—to generalize—the result of an intricate political process, from the oral traditions through the manuscripts, versions and selections through the construction of canon(s) through the development, maintenance and transformations of translations and interpretative traditions to the comparatively elaborate modern transla-tion and interpretation venture imposed on the Bible. To maintain the inno-cence of the choices made throughout the historical development of the

both earlier and contemporary, entails a vast amount of generalization, that their con-struction is once again dependent upon scholars involved in their own even greater traditions, and that they are often presented as relatively self-contained constructs.

115. L. Cormie, 'Revolutions in Reading the Bible', in D. Jobling, P.L. Day and G.T. Sheppard (eds.), *The Bible and the Politics of Exegesis* (Cleveland: Pilgrim, 1991), pp. 173-93 (190). Or as Horsley puts it: 'biblical scholarship only discerns the reality of the literate elite', 'Historians and Jesus', p. 5.

116. U. Luz, *Matthew in History: Interpretation, Influence, and Effects* (Minneapolis: Fortress Press, 1994), p. 64.

117. Sanneh, 'Gospel and Culture', p. 2.

biblical canon and as continued in its translation and interpretation today, seems naive.[118] Bible translations are political, and reflect the sentiments of those in control in church and society.[119]

It has become increasingly obvious and more important to account for the inseparable ties that bind texts, their translations and interpretations, and their historical consequences together. Texts and their interpretations simply do not exist in a historical void, but create historical effects, influence history. The inverse is equally true: historical circumstances and contexts give rise to new appropriations and interpretations of Scripture. Naturally, at any given point it is fairly difficult to tell exactly where a certain interpretation is the result of particular circumstances, as much as it is a trying matter to indicate which texts or interpretations thereof led to specific historical effects. Put bluntly, does history create texts, or do texts create history? Moreover, because (textual or interpretative) cause and (historical) effect often mix in some sort of reciprocality, the clear identification of these two elements as such also becomes difficult to distinguish.

How is the Bible (to be) translated and interpreted today and which or whose political concerns and interests are reflected in the resultant translations? Are the traditions of translation and interpretation that envelop the Bible recognized and accounted for, and are they addressed?

Conclusion

> Thus the most difficult problem facing Bible translators is that of cultural,
> theological and ethnic hegemony.[120]

Christianity is one of the few religions worldwide that does not insist that its sacred Scriptures should be read in the original language(s).[121] There is

---

118. Cf. Witvliet's Response to Sanneh in this volume.

119. E.g. although much is often made of the enrichment of a vernacular language by Bible translation, contributing to its orthography, vocabulary and even conceptual framework (cf. Sanneh in this volume), it is interesting to note the reluctance to incorporate, for example, inclusive language since it is—simply!—not considered 'as a translational possibility'; Aricheia 'Theology and Translation', p. 66. For a different if guarded opinion, cf. Ellingworth, 'Scope of Inclusive Language', de Waard, 'Vertalen', p. 258, refers in this regard to the ideologically determined interpretation of 'militant feminism'; Carson, 'New Bible Translations', pp. 53, 63, is bluntly neutral.

120. P. Perkins, 'Response', in Kee (ed.), *The Bible in the Twenty-First Century*, pp. 84-88 (88).

121. 'God's eternal counsels are compatible with ordinary, everyday speech' rather than being elitist and secret oracles, Sanneh, 'Gospel and Culture', p. 1. Walls,

also, in general, a move away from 'translationese',[122] in the sense of concordant translations that set stock by formal fidelity, but which are at times accompanied by unfaithfulness to the content and—the difficult to trace—impact of the original. However, accounting for the broader setting of translating activity in terms of the accompanying questions of responsibility and in terms of the concern for translational contextuality, is often still neglected in Bible translation in South Africa.

The current debate on the influence of Bible translations needs to proceed beyond interpretative matters, semantic eccentricities of ancient languages and methodological, literary concerns.[123] The increasing realization of the discursive power of language, on the one hand, and the recognition of the connection or relationship between religion and human (social and individual) identity, on the other hand—and the links between these two—require our attention for the involvement of (translated) Bibles to foster and maintain certain world views. Clearly Bible translations are never, regardless of explicit claims in this regard (cf. the New Afrikaans Bible), theologically, socio–culturally or politically isolated or neutral. And when it comes to the public use of the Bible, allowing and encouraging different translations as well as their interactive use might prove more sustainable and helpful than the tempting impulse to make an exclusive—canonizing—choice.

Has the perennial problem in Bible translation, namely to be faithful to the source text while providing an effective translation in the receptor language, both in meaning and form or style, not shifted somewhat? Although still a major concern, is the urgency of political responsibility in Bible translation not at least a matter of equal gravity, and is it not all too often neglected?

New Bible translations have almost without exception been the cause of serious discontent and even violent reaction in the church and society. It

'Translation Principle', pp. 24-25 (also Bediako, 'Epilogue', p. 246; Sanneh, *Translating the Message*, esp. pp. 211-38), contrasts in this respect Christianity with Hinduism, Judaism and Islam on the basis of a theological principle, namely the incarnation which mandates *and* requires continuous translation. Cf. further Aricheia, 'Theology and Translation', p. 50, on the translatability of Scripture in different religions.

122. Nida and Taber, *Theory and Practice*, p. 13.

123. Although M.N. Getui, 'The Bible as Tool for Ecumenism', in Kinoti and Waliggo (eds.), *The Bible in African Christianity*, pp. 86-97, sets up an agenda for ongoing and sustainable Bible translation in Africa, she fails to probe the ideological setting of such work.

may be that Bible translators are no longer killed, the fate that a Tyndale had to suffer in the sixteenth century for translating the Bible into the English vernacular. Nowadays it is rather Bible translations, through its enshrined kyriarchal, heterosexist and other disempowering ideologies, which have the power to consign people to marginalized status, to be perceived as second-rate human beings. The abiding danger of Bible translation is that it might perpetuate the imperialist interests of the political, ecclesial and other powerful groups in the church, academy and society—ultimately under the facade, constructed or otherwise, of innocent and neutral translations.

TRANSLATION, INTERPRETATION AND IDEOLOGY:
A RESPONSE TO JEREMY PUNT

Wim J.C. Weren

In my reaction to Jeremy Punt's lecture, first of all I would like to express my admiration for the many activities displayed on the African continent in the field of translating the Bible. The speaker has nicely reminded us of the fact that Africa has a long, albeit not uninterrupted tradition of translations. Important old translations such as the Septuagint, the Old Latin Version and the Sahidic and Bohairic Bibles came into existence on African soil. In the past two centuries the translations that were in use in Africa had been produced by Western missionaries, with their Western exegetical and theological paradigms. The unrivalled value of those paradigms was proudly recommended by the Western world and tacitly accepted by the native peoples. Nowadays, we are in a completely different situation. On the African continent, authoritative translations from the past are about to be replaced by translations in African languages, translated by African exegetes and linguists and intended for African readers. This process, which fits very well in a worldwide struggle for inculturation and ongoing contextualization, can only be applauded. These developments also have their repercussions upon Bible translating activities in Europe and America. More than in the past we are aware of the fact that the Western models are deeply rooted in their own restricted political, historical, cultural and geographical contexts and that they cannot be transposed to other parts of the world straight away. Therefore, it is with a certain modesty that I venture to make some comments on Jeremy Punt's lecture.

Dr Punt strongly emphasized the fundamental interconnectedness of translation and interpretation. I am in heartfelt agreement with this view. Both the Greek term ἑρμηνεύειν and the Latin word *interpretari* have a double meaning. The first meaning is 'to interpret', the second is 'to translate'.[1] Every translator is an interpreter too, and every translation is the

---

1.   W. Bauer, *Griechisch–Deutsches Wörterbuch zu den Schriften des Neuen Testa-*

expression of a particular understanding of the original text. Every translation offers only an approximate rendition of what can be read in its original, because a complete semantic reproduction of the source text is an impossible ideal. The original text will never be fully captured by any translation. As soon as the translation has been made, it can be confronted with the original text. The race would soon be run if it were clear and beyond doubt what the source text should really read like, but that's exactly where the shoe pinches. Many words, sentences and texts are not quite unequivocal. In the original text we find words and expressions whose meanings are ambiguous and cannot be determined in a crystal-clear way; or for which suitable equivalents in the receptor's language are missing. Is a translator permitted, in such cases, to create more clarity than is offered by the original? Or do we encounter the translator's skill when the somewhat vague character of the source text is still visible in the translation?

Jeremy Punt's reflections about these problems are stimulating. The New Xhosa Bible (1996) and the New Afrikaans Bible (1983) are at the background of his reflections. But, unfortunately, he has not offered us any concrete examples. I would like to fill this gap by an analysis of one short passage. My choice is the text of Mt. 1.18-25 in the New Afrikaans Bible.

Die geboorte van Jesus Christus
(Luke 2.1-7)

18 Hier volg nou die geskiedenis van die geboorte van Jesus Christus. Toe sy moeder Maria nog aan Josef verloof was, het dit geblyk dat sy swanger is sonder dat hulle gemeenskap gehad het. Die swangerskap het van die Heilige Gees gekom. 19 Haar verloofde, Josef, wat aan die wet van Moses getrou was maar haar tog nie in die openbaar tot skande wou maak nie, het hom voorgeneem om die verlowing stilweg te verbreek. 20 Terwyl hy dit in gedagte gehad het, het daar 'n engel van die Here in 'n droom aan hom verskyn en gesê: 'Josef seun van Dawid, moenie bang wees om met Maria te trou nie, want wat in haar verwek is, kom van die Heilige Gees. 21 Sy sal 'n Seun in die wêreld bring, en jy moet Hom Jesus noem, want dit is Hy wat sy volk van hulle sondes sal verlos'.

22 Dit het alles gebeur sodat die woord wat die Here deur sy profeet gesê het, vervul sou word:

23 'Die maagd sal swanger word
en 'n Seun in die wêreld bring,
en hulle sal Hom Immanuel noem.'

Die naam betekent God by ons.

24 Toe Josef uit die slaap wakker word, het hy gemaak soos die engel van die Here hom beveel het en met haar getrou. 25 Hy het egter nie met haar omgang gehad voordat sy haar Seun in die wêreld gebring het nie. En Josef het Hom Jesus genoem.

Matthew 1.18-25 in the New Afrikaans Bible

1. The pericope has been provided with a heading by the translators: *Die geboorte van Jesus Christus* ('The Birth of Jesus Christ'); and with a reference to Lk. 2.1-7, a text supposed to be parallel to Matthew's text. Such a heading is the result of an interpretative choice, and has a direct influence upon the way in which the reader might understand the passage. In this case, the choice is far from satisfactory. The present heading exclusively focuses upon an event which Matthew's text only mentions in 1.25 and 2.1—each time by means of a subordinate clause. The translators have neglected the fact that almost the entire story told in our passage is situated in the time before Jesus' birth, and that we come across motifs that are of more importance, such as the naming of Mary's child.

The formulation of the heading corresponds to the translation of γένεσις in 1.18a ('birth'). This translation can be severely criticized as well. The Greek word γένεσις implies far more than someone's birth; it also points to his coming into being, his origin or descent.[2] Here we have the origin of Jesus Christ. His origin is also discussed in 1.1-17 (see γένεσις in 1.1) but that passage, Jesus' genealogy, is concluded by the mysterious remark that he is truly Mary's child, yet not the child of Joseph, her husband. This intriguing fact is elaborated upon in 1.18-25, and here it becomes clear that Jesus' roots go far deeper than his human descent: his origin is in the unfathomable depths of God.

2. In the Greek text we find a number of words with regard to procreation, pregnancy, birth and marriage: γένεσις (v. 18), μνηστεύω (v. 18), μήτηρ (v. 18), συνέρχομαι (v. 18), ἐν γαστρί ἔχω (vv. 18, 23), ἀνήρ (v. 19), ἀπολύω (v. 19), παραλαμβάνω + γυνή (vv. 20, 24), γεννάω (v. 20), τίκτω + υἱός (vv. 21, 23, 25), καλέω + ὄνομα (vv. 21, 23, 25), παρθένος (v. 23), γινώσκω (v. 25). From this series, γεννάω ('to father'), συνέρχομαι and γινώσκω ('to have sexual intercourse') are translated excellently. The New Afrikaans Bible does justice to the fact that συνέρχομαι has

---

2. W. Weren, *Windows on Jesus: Methods in Gospel Exegesis* (London: SCM Press, 1999), p. 220.

sexual connotations, just like the Latin *convenire* of the Vulgate and the word *co-ire*.

I am, however, far less satisfied with the rendition of terms that apply to the liaison between Mary and Joseph. In the New Afrikaans Bible, Mary is engaged (*verloof*) to Joseph; Joseph, ὁ ἀνήρ αὐτῆς, is her fiancé (in 1.16—where ἀνήρ is also to be found—he was depicted as being Mary's husband!), and intends to break off the engagement. And yet, after the intervention of an angel, he does marry her. In this rendering we are confronted with the phenomenon of transculturation: customs and institutions from antiquity are adapted to customs and institutions we are familiar with.

In the Greek text of Mt. 1.18-25 it is supposed that readers are familiar with Jewish marriage customs in the first century CE. The story relates that Mary was already betrothed to Joseph when she became pregnant, but the young couple was not as yet living together in the same house. In that intervening period Mary definitely was Joseph's wife and, inversely, Joseph definitely was her husband, as is clearly indicated in the text (1.16, 19, 20, 24). Since Joseph knows it is impossible that he is the biological father of Mary's child, he ponders over breaking off the marriage, already sealed in a juridical sense, and over sending his wife away, according to the conventions of his time.

The New Afrikaans Bible translators have wrestled with the problem of how to express, in Afrikaans, the regulations referred to in Matthew's story. They decided to make a distinction between engagement and marriage; but, is an engagement before getting married the common practice in South Africa today? Is this really a fitting example of inculturation? And yet, if this were the case, we still have the fact that these terms are actually inaccurate, because in the Jewish context of the first century of the Christian Era a distinction between engagement and marriage did not exist. That is why the text says that Joseph decided to send his wife away or to divorce her. Being the husband, he is fully justified in taking legal action; and is only wrestling with the problem of what to do now that his wife is being pregnant: should he repudiate her in public, or quietly put an end to the relationship that had been legally sealed earlier? In many respects, Matthew's description of the relationship between husband and wife is offensive for many present-day readers. Translators are inclined to create a more softened picture, but I would like to remain as close as possible to the original. In doing so, it is not my intention to stress that the ancient customs ought to be imposed on people living many centuries later and in quite different contexts. No, my intention is to stress that the Bible is a book originating in the far past and situated in particular socio-political contexts that have their own ideological views, and those may be outdated and not valid for all eternity.

3. According to the Greek text, Joseph was a δίκαιος. In the New Afrikaans Bible, this characterization has been changed into someone who was faithful to the Law of Moses (*aan die wet van Moses getrou was*). This translation is a fine representation of the obvious meaning of δίκαιος in this literary context. However, it is a pity that δίκαιος or the plural of this word in other passages of Matthew has not been translated in the same way. In the New Africaans Bible we find *mense wat op die regte pad is* (9.13; 'people who are on the right way'), *'n goeie mens* (10.41; 'an upright human being'), *die gelowiges* (13.43; the believers) and *die wat die wil van God gedoen het* (25.37, 46; 'those who have done the will of God'). These formulations do not make it clear that δίκαιος refers to allegiance to the Torah. This notion has faded, and δίκαιος in those instances mainly refers to general or Christian ethical qualifications.

4. Matthew 1.18 and 1.20 provide us with a further explanation of Mary's pregnancy. In both cases, the text refers to the creative, life-spending force of…? Well, of whom actually?

Here the translators are compelled to make an interpretative choice. Like almost all other translations known to me, the New Africaans Bible testifies to the traditional view that the text here deals with the Holy Spirit. From the fact that *Heilige Gees* has been written with two reverential capitals, it appears that the New Africaans Bible translators have understood πνεῦμα ἅγιον as the name of a divine person. They also use these capitals in the case of *Here* ('Lord'; vv. 20, 22, 24), *Seun* ('Son'; vv. 21, 23, 25) and when personal nouns occur that refer to Jesus (vv. 21, 23, 25).

These capitals create a semantic clarity that, in the Greek text, is not at all present. Matthew's text shows considerable ambiguity. According to 1.18, Mary is pregnant 'from a holy spirit' (no capitals and no definite article); in 1.20 these words return but in a different order: 'from a spirit, which is holy'. In the latter case the emphasis is clearly upon 'holy'. And that is the information Joseph needs. An angel informs him of the fact that he must relinquish his idea that someone else has caused Mary's pregnancy. Neither did his wife commit adultery nor was she the victim of rape. No, what is fathered in her is the fruit of a mysterious interplay between Mary and the creative vigour of God himself or herself. The translation 'from a holy spirit' acknowledges the fact that there is no definite article in the Greek text. Moreover, this translation clearly fits the context. Consequently, translating 'from a holy spirit' has good testimonials. Yet, nearly all translators prefer the interpretation first mentioned: the Holy Spirit (in capitals). Influenced by the later developed Trinitarian doctrine, they create more clarity than is offered by the Greek text.

5. By using small but telling signals translators give evidence of their way of understanding the text, an understanding that they want to convey to the readers of their translation. By inserting inverted commas they indicate which parts of the text—according to them—do belong to direct speech, and which parts do not. A divergent typeface is often used in the case of words or clauses that are derived from the Old Testament. By starting new paragraphs, the translators express their view upon the structure of the text. All these choices must rely upon a sound analysis of the Greek text.

Regarding these issues, the New Afrikaans Bible deserves to be praised. Let us look at the following points.

- The quotation from Isa. 7.14 has been made visible by using indentations and inverted commas. That Mt. 1.23 is in fact a combination of quotations from Isa. 7.14 and 8.8, is made clear in an explanatory note.
- The literal agreements between the quotation and the surrounding text ('to become pregnant', 'to bear a son', 'to give the name') are faithfully rendered in the New Afrikaans Bible. This enables the reader to ask the exciting question, whether the whole story should be understood as a kind of Midrash on the quotation from Isaiah.
- Matthew 1.22-23 is rightly printed as a narrator's text and not as the continuation of the words spoken by the angel (character's text). In these two verses the narrator interrupts his story for a closer reflection, and informs his readers that the whole story should be perceived as the fulfilment of Scripture. The narrator's commentary is placed in the centre of the passage and not at the end, as elsewhere in Matthew.
- The New Afrikaans Bible clarifies the structure of Mt 1.18-25 through indentations at the beginning of a new paragraph. The proposed structure of the text cannot be improved. Verse 18a is understood as an introductory sentence, as a heading for the story. Three parts (vv. 18b-21; vv. 22-23; vv. 24-25) follow this

heading. A new paragraph at the beginning of v. 22 indicates that here the story is interrupted for a short commentary, given by the narrator.

I will now conclude my response with three questions for further discussion.

1. By presenting this example, I have tried to show that interpretation is a characteristic of every translation. My first questions would be, Should every interpretation be allowed? Which criteria could be applied to separate the corn from the chaff?

2. Is offering an abundance of interpretative information better or worse than offering too small a portion of such information?

3. What exactly is the difference between interpretation and ideology? Isn't the Bible, which is the result of varying cultural contexts, full of ideologies itself? And, if so, which ideologies from the Bible ought to be embraced, or even promoted, and which should be contested?

TRANSLATING THE BIBLE:
BIBLE TRANSLATIONS AND GENDER ISSUES

Mary Phil Korsak

Introduction

The purpose of the paper is twofold. First, it aims to provide some insights into different approaches to Bible translation in the English language. Second, it attempts to bring to the fore issues of embedded patriarchal ideology and authority in biblical writings and translations. Broadly speaking, the history of the Bible itself is the history of texts created and revised in patriarchal settings, promoting male images and values and demoting female images and values.[1] Most biblical texts are the work of men, not of women. Most Bible translations are done by men, not by women. Different versions therefore are presented and examined here to see to what extent they accentuate or mitigate an androcentric bias which is characteristic of the source texts.

The paper begins with a brief evocation of the Revised Standard Version, the most illustrious of English translations, whose history goes back to the seventeenth century. By way of contrast, two twentieth-century English translations, the New English Bible and *The Holy Bible* by Ronald Knox,[2] are then introduced. To situate my own experience as a Bible translator, there follows a brief survey of the changes taking place today in the field of literary translation with particular reference to the UK. Against this background I present my work on a new English version of Hebrew Genesis, entitled *At the Start... Genesis Made New*.[3] The quotations in the paper are mainly taken from the book of Genesis.

---

1.   Asphodel Long, *In a Chariot Drawn by Lions* (London: The Women's Press, 1992).
2.   Ronald Knox, *The Holy Bible* (London: Burns and Oates, 1949).
3.   Mary Phil Korsak, *At the Start... Genesis Made New: A Translation of the Hebrew Text* (European Series Louvain Cahiers Number 124; Louvain: European Association for the Promotion of Poetry, 1992; New York: Doubleday, 1993).

The Revised Standard Version

The history of REV is familiar. It is a cultural as well as a religious monument. Its forerunners appeared in Shakespeare's time, when the English language had attained a glorious peak. Shakespeare died in 1616. The Authorised or King James Version (AV; KJV) was published in 1611. The language of that period provided an excellent medium for translating the Bible. Moreover, early versions were the work of outstanding Hebrew scholars who, in the context of the Protestant Reformation, paid for their initiative with their lives. Their translations, in the form of many revised versions, have come down as a legacy to the present day. Consequently the Standard Version has acquired a hallowed character, and any changes are strictly censured. For example, potential revisions of the American Standard Version (ASV) in the 1940's were discussed extensively by committees of scholars and reviewers, and modifications were determined by a two-thirds majority vote. Furthermore, the RSV has exercised an influence on the English language and English literature down the centuries. Any cultured person, for instance, understands what is implied by 'Vanity of vanities…' (Qoh. 1.2) just as they do by 'A rose by any other name…'[4] Moreover, the RSV has come to be considered an authority in its own right. It has popular as well as scholarly backing.

> Mucking about with the Bible is a predictable way to make people upset and angry. Many feel an instinctive protectiveness about their familiar translation, as though they were preserving God's original words. Biblical translation is a subject on which everyone has a view and most people feel natural experts.[5]

By 'the Bible' people understand 'the Bible in English'. Even those who make a stand against the embedded ideologies of RSV kow-tow to its greatness. For instance, the translation entitled *The New Testament and Psalms: An Inclusive Version*, which seeks to eliminate 'differences of gender, race and physical disability',[6] does so not by retranslating the Bible but by adapting the New Revised Standard Version (NRSV), replacing 'those metaphors which can be considered sexist, racist or offensive in any way' by metaphors that are judged inoffensive.

---

4. William Shakespeare, *Romeo and Juliet*, Act 2, Scene 1.
5. Margaret Hebblethewaite, *Fresh Beginnings* (Review of 'At the Start…Genesis Made New'; *The Tablet*, 5 March 1994).
6. *The New Testament and Psalms: An Inclusive Version* ('General Introduction'; New York: Oxford University Press, 1995), p. viii.

The New English Bible, and The Holy Bible *by Ronald Knox*

Two other English versions are quoted along with the RSV. The New English Bible (NEB) is a translation 'in current English undertaken by the major Christian bodies (other than Roman Catholic) of the British Isles. It is not a revision of the Authorised Version, nor is it intended to replace it' (NEB cover flap). Its horizon is ecumenical. The years of work invested by scholarly committees justify its claim to authority. Its style ensures that it is readily accessible to contemporary readers. The first edition was published in 1961. In contrast, *The Holy Bible* by Ronald Knox is the work of one scholar, a Roman Catholic clergyman. The Knox translation appeared in the 1950s. (The first book, *Genesis*, was published in 1949.) Formerly, the translation known as the Douai Version was a favourite in the Roman Catholic Church. This version also went back to the seventeenth century: it was used by the 'papists' under the Elizabethan persecution. *The Holy Bible* then has something in common with the NEB: both versions break with the ancient tradition of venerable predecessors, adopting a free style in order to reach out to contemporary readers.

Literary Translation on the Threshold of the Twenty-first Century

A jump is now made to the world of literary translation and the changes taking place there. As recently as the 1960s and the 1970s, the translator appeared as a modest figure, hidden, anonymous, hard-working, unrecognized, at the service of the source text and subordinate to the original writer. By contrast, today, on the threshold of the 21st century, translators' voices are growing more assertive—and this despite the disadvantages of globalization, highly developed technology, bigger publishing houses and the pressure of economic forces as a distinct threat to the art of translation.[7] This change has been promoted over the last 20 years by the development of 'Translation Studies' in academic circles, which has fostered the recognition that literary translation involves *research*, that it is itself an art form: it is claimed that the translator creates *a new text, a new language*.[8]

---

7.   'The tendency within these external forces is to downgrade the artistry to want the translator to be a compliant cog helping turn the wheels of a vast machine more virtual by the day.' Peter Bush, *The Art of Translation* (The British Council Literary Translation Exhibition, www.literarytranslation.com, 1999).

8.   'Translators…have to research the text…other translations and critical interpretations, and then make a radically different move. They must create in their

Personally, I feel at home with this perspective. Through work done on biblical texts, I have come to regard myself as a translator cum poet. Bible translation implies a creative and artistic endeavour.

Translating the Hebrew Genesis

The translator's work is marked by her affinity with and perception of the source text. The translator who wrestles with Hebrew Genesis cannot fail to be moved by the power of the book, by its primitive strength, by its popular character, which is 'rough and tender, naive and wise'. The words are Etty Hillesum's.[9] My perception of the Bible as poetry is comforted by the vision of an artist like Chagall, who wrote, 'Since my youth I have been fascinated by the Bible. It has always appeared to me, and still does, as one of the greatest sources of poetry of all time.'[10] In poetry, because form and meaning are inextricably intertwined, the repetition of words, the use of metaphor and analogy, which are formal characteristics of writing, not only contribute to the reader's aesthetic enjoyment but also play a significant role in the transmission of meaning. To illustrate what is involved, it is necessary to broach some technical aspects of the translator's task.

At the Start... Genesis Made New is based on the principle of one English word for one Hebrew word, an approach adopted already in the nineteenth century by Julia E. Smith.[11] This means searching for an

language a new text, a new language that will develop through many drafts and re-writings in a constant to-ing and fro-ing in relation to a…text of which they will have to cultivate different versions. Although the translator pursues many paths of meaning, his or her art reaches to create a rich and ambiguous language.' Peter Bush, Art of Translation (The British Council Literary Translation Exhibition on the Internet, www.literarytranslation.com, 1999).

9.   Etty Hillesum, *Journal 1941–1943* (French trans. P. Noble; Paris: Edition du Seuil, 1988), p. 155.

10.   'Depuis ma première jeunesse, j'ai été captivé par la Bible. Il m'a toujours semblé et il me semble encore que c'est la plus grande source de poésie de tous les temps. Depuis lors j'ai cherché ce reflet dans la vie et dans l'Art. La Bible est comme une résonance de la nature et ce secret j'ai essayé de le transmettre.' Marc Chagall, *Le Message Biblique*, quoted in the Cimiez Museum in Nice.

11.   'I soon gave my attention to the Hebrew… and wrote it out word for word… endeavouring to put the same English word for the same Hebrew or Greek word, everywhere, while King James's translators have wholly differed from this rule; but it appeared to us to give a much clearer understanding of the text.' Julia E. Smith, *The Holy Bible: Containing the Old and New Testaments: Translated Literally from the Original Tongues* (Hartford: American Publishing Company, 1876), p. 1.

English word that can systematically carry the weight of particular Hebrew word, a painstaking task which implies a deal of the lexical research. What has just been said is clarified by an example.

Many words have a variety of meanings. Hebrew שָׂפָה, for instance, means 'lip', 'language' and 'shore'. In the normal run, a translator would consider these three distinct meanings essential and opt for 'lip', 'language' or 'shore' according to context. The translator who applies the above principle, on the contrary, examines the possibility of using one English word in all three cases. Her research leads along several paths. 'Lip' is 'lip' when it refers to a speech organ (as everyone will agree), but is it possible to use the word 'lip' for 'language' and 'lip' for 'shore'? To answer these questions, it is necessary to examine all the biblical contexts in which שָׂפָה occurs and to check lexicons, dictionaries and thesaurus. In the case of 'lip' for 'language', English has the following usage, 'Don't give me any of your lip', meaning 'talk' or 'language', the connotation being 'saucy talk or language'. The *Oxford English Dictionary* also gives 'lip' for 'language' as an archaism inherited from Bible translations! Furthermore, an analogy springs to mind: another speech organ: 'tongue' is commonly used to mean 'language'. So 'lip' for 'language' has possibilities. It then becomes a question of weighing up losses and gains before making a final choice. To summarize the gains: colloquial and archaic usage suggest that 'lip' for 'language', though not current, is comprehensible. Furthermore, 'lip' for 'language' has the potential value of analogy and metaphor.

This technical explanation reveals something of the cards the translator has in hand, but what matters at the end of the day is the effect on the reader. To allow the reader to make comparisons, here are the renderings of Gen. 11.7 in the 'Tower of Babel' story from *At the Start... Genesis Made New* (*ATS*), The RSV, NEB and *The Holy Bible* (HB):

> Come we will go down and make their *lip* babble there
> so that no man shall hear the *lip* of his companion (*ATS*).

> Come, let us go down, and there confuse their *language*, that they may not understand one another's *speech* (RSV).

> Come, let us go down there and confuse their *speech*, so that they will not understand *what they say* to one another (NEB).

A similar principle is adopted in E. Fox's translation, *In the Beginning* (New York: Schocken Books, 1983).

> It would be well to go down and throw confusion into the *speech* they use
> there, so that they will not be able to understand each other (HB) (both
> *language* or *speech* understood).

It is worth noting that the last three versions quoted not only translate
the meaning of שָׂפָה according to context, but also translate the same word
by English variants: 'language/speech' (RSV); 'speech/what they say'
(NEB); 'language'/no translation (HB). Avoiding repetition is one of the
rules of good prose-writing, the inference being that these versions are
intended first and foremost for reading. *At the Start*, on the contrary,
deliberately transmits repetitions that are an integral part of the Hebrew
text. By so doing it intends to foster the text's potential for memorization
and recitation, in keeping with Hebrew tradition.

Returning now to 'lip' for 'shore'. Here also analogies are to be found:
'the lip of the sea' is comparable to current phrases such as 'the arm of the
river', 'the foot of the mountain', 'the head of the stream'. The metaphors
in these phrases suggest an anthropomorphic perception of the natural
environment. Such phrases, however, are overfamiliar, and the primitive
and poetic personalization of nature they originally conveyed is no longer
perceived. It is argued here that the coining of a new phrase, 'the lip of the
sea', can reinvigorate the language by heightening awareness of these
anthropomorphic metaphors. Thus, by echoing ancient Hebrew usage,
poetic connotations in the English language are renewed. These subtleties,
which are vital for the translator poet, may appear fastidious but it is
thanks to innumerable details of this kind that an overall impression is
made upon the reader. To illustrate, here is Gen. 22.17 from the different
versions:

> Yes, Bless! I will bless you
> Increase! I will increase your seed
> like the stars of the skies
> like the sand on the sea's *lip* (*ATS*).

> I will indeed bless you, and I will multiply your descendants as the stars of
> heaven and as the sand which is on the *seashore* (RSV).

> I will bless you abundantly and greatly multiply your descendants until they
> are as numerous as the stars in the sky and the grains of sand on the *sea-
> shore* (NEB).
> More and more I will bless thee, more and more will I give increase to thy
> posterity, till they are as countless as the stars in heaven or the sand by the
> *sea shore* (HB).

The first quotation above shows how the translator who sets out to *restore* Hebrew vocabulary through the medium of English finds herself inventing *a new language*, a poetic language, which, when developed in many details, can convey a fresh perception of the book of Genesis.

A glance at the above quotations suffices for other differences between the versions to leap from the page. More of this below. To continue discussion of lexical choices, *At the Start... Genesis Made New* echoes Hebrew word patterns, which underscore the meaning of the Hebrew text. To give an example, הָאָדָם and הָאֲדָמָה form an etymological pair. They are therefore translated by an etymological pair: 'the groundling' and 'the ground'. The message that comes across is as follows: 'the groundling' is to serve 'the ground' (2.5); 'the groundling' is formed from the soil of 'the ground' (2.7); 'the groundling' will return to 'the ground' at death (3.17-19). This contrasts with the RSV reading: 'man' is to till 'the ground' (2.5); 'man' is formed of dust of 'the ground' (2.7); 'Adam' will return to 'the ground' at death (3.17-19).

Besides maintaining lexical links, *At the Start... Genesis Made New* preserves the lexical distinctions of the Hebrew text. To illustrate, another pair of words, אִישׁ/אִשָּׁה, is introduced. First, the relation between the two words is noted: אִישׁ is linked by assonance to אִשָּׁה Second, the distinction between הָאָדָם and אִישׁ, 'man' is noted. All three words, הָאָדָם, אִשָּׁה and אִישׁ, occur in vv. 2.22-23, which are here quoted from *At the Start... Genesis Made New* and RSV respectively:

> YHWH Elohim built the side
> he had taken from the groundling (הָאָדָם) into wo-man(אִשָּׁה)
> he brought her to the groundling (הָאָדָם)
> The groundling ((הָאָדָם) said
> > This one this time
> > is bone from my bones
> > flesh from my flesh
> > This one shall be called wo-man (אִשָּׁה)
> > for from man (אִישׁ)
> she has been taken this one (*ATS*).

> and the rib which the Lord God had taken from the man (הָאָדָם) he made into a woman (אִשָּׁה) and brought her to the man (הָאָדָם). Then the man (הָאָדָם) said,
> > This at last is bone of my bones
> > and flesh of my flesh;
> > she shall be called Woman (אִשָּׁה),
> because she was taken out of Man (אִישׁ) (RSV).

The verbal distinctions made here have meaningful implications. In *At the Start... Genesis Made New, the groundling,* הָאָדָם, is understood to be a generic that refers to man and woman, sometimes man with woman. It signifies the human being as related to the ground. The word *man*, like אִישׁ, is reserved for man (the male) in relation to woman, אִשָּׁה. Consequently, in this version the word 'man' (the male) occurs only three times in the Garden of Eden story (Gen. 2.22, 23; 3.6). The above quotation shows man and woman issuing from the human 'groundling'. In RSV, on the other hand, where 'man/the man' (sometimes without, sometimes with an article) translates both הָאָדָם and אִישׁ, the word 'man' occurs 22 times (variant 'husband' twice) in the same story. Where 'man' without the article signifies a generic, 'the man' signifies 'the male'. The above quotation tells that a woman is made from the rib of 'the man' (the male). NEB makes the same choices as RSV here. Knox, on the other hand, has several words for הָאָדָם: 'human' (2.5); 'man/the man' (2.7, 9); 'Adam' (2.19) and 'husband' (3.6, 16). The words 'human' and 'man' have generic value. The words 'the man', 'Adam' and 'husband' signify the male. Here is *The Holy Bible* rendering of the same verses:

> This rib, which he had taken out of Adam, the Lord God formed into a woman; and when he brought her to Adam, Adam said, Here, at last, is bone that comes from mine, flesh that comes from mine; it shall be called Woman, this thing that was taken out of Man.

In summary, the above exposition of different principles guiding the translator's lexical choices reveals significant consequences for gender issues.

Returning to technicalities, it has been shown that a poetic rendering seeks to transmit formal characteristics of the source text such as verbal repetition, word links and lexical difference. To these must be added Hebrew wordplay. Wordplay is found, notably, in naming verses. In Gen. 11.9, for example, the Hebrew name 'Babel' is explained by the Hebrew verb בלל. בבל/בלל is rendered as follows in the different versions:

> So they called its name *Babel*
> for there YHWH made the lip of all the earth *babble* (*ATS*).

> Therefore its name was called *Babel*, because there the Lord *confused* the language of all the earth (RSV).

> That is why it is called *Babel*, because the Lord there made a *babble* of the language of all the world (NEB).

> That is why it was called Babel, *Confusion*, because it was there that the
> Lord *confused* the whole world's speech (HB).

The quotations show that the three contemporary versions transmit
Hebrew wordplay in naming verses, whereas RSV does not. (Sometimes
the RSV adds an explanatory footnote.) A second naming verse illustrates
how the loss of wordplay can involve a loss of meaning. Gen. 3.20
contains the Hebrew wordplay חוה/חי. Here are the two versions that
reflect the wordplay, followed by the reading of RSV:

> The groundling called his woman's name *Life* (Eve)[12]
> for she is the mother of all that *lives* (*ATS*).

> The name which Adam gave his wife was Eve, *Life*, because she was the
> mother of all *living* men (HB).

> The man called his wife's name *Eve*, because she is the mother of all *living*
> (RSV).

NEB follows RSV here also. Both have a footnote: 'That is *Life*' (NEB);
'The name in Hebrew resembles the word for *living*' (RSV). However,
because it has been so long omitted from the texts and probably also
because of all the negative commentary aimed at Eve, the meaning of this
name has generally been forgotten. In the Hebrew text, a person's name is
linked to their identity. A name is associated with power. If Eve were
known as 'Life', her reputation would not have suffered as it has done.
The meaningless name Eve has left her defenceless.

Passing to more general considerations, the above quotations illustrate
how *At the Start... Genesis Made New* follows the Hebrew text closely,
seeking to preserve the clarity of its concrete vocabulary and metaphorical
usage and reflecting its brevity. Furthermore, rhythmic lines in English
echo the spoken rhythms of the Hebrew. For this reason, the English text
is laid out in an original free verse form. Other choices concern names. On
the one hand, in order to reflect the original culture of the source text,
divine names keep their Hebrew character. For example, Hebrew אלהים is
transliterated as 'Elohim' (cf. 'Allah' for the Koran); the consonants of the
Tetragrammaton are transliterated as *Y.H.W.H.* These names have rich
religious and cultural connotations. On the other hand, to facilitate reading
in English, as a general principle, familiar English-sounding names are
used in the case of human characters. For the same reason, traditional

---

12. The Septuagint renders the wordplay: *Zōe/zōntōn*. The Vulgate, however,
names the woman 'Eva', probably because Eva sounds like חוה.

forms of the English tense system are used, despite the fact that the Hebrew has perfect and imperfect verb forms and no tense system.

It is difficult to communicate the flavour of a translation by giving a few isolated examples. Some academics assign *At the Start... Genesis Made New* to the field of *ethnopoetics*. In his preface to the translation David Moody, Professor of English and American Literature at York University, notes that this version conveys:

> the essential remoteness of the ethos of YHWH and his people from the English-speaking world of today... It brings home to us its distance and difference, and so enables us to find a valid relation to it as readers from another time, another world.[13]

Yes, I have tried to render the content, form and music of the Hebrew text. While recognizing that it is impossible to pin down the original, I hope that the poetic quality of the translation will ensure its appeal among cultured readers, that it will be read aloud, that it will sing out, that the new form will permit the reader to connect to the essential. The translation does not intend to convey any explicit ideology. It avoids footnotes that tell the reader how and what to read. It seeks especially, but not exclusively, to interest the secularized, offering them, as David Moody puts it, 'a new experience of the book hitherto known as *Genesis*'.

Patriarchal Ideology and the Bible

The first part of this paper has looked at different approaches to Bible translation and, in the process, broached some gender issues. To further discussion of the latter, a definition of patriarchal ideology is now proposed. An ideology can be defined as a set of ideas that serves to promote power, covering up a truth that threatens to destabilize that power. In the case of the Bible a specific meaning, likely to serve a prevailing ideology, is attributed to a text to the exclusion of other different interpretations. This paper argues that it is possible to discern ideological influences in translated Bibles, which serve the cause of patriarchy at the expense of womankind. This view was defended as early as the nineteenth century by American E. Cady Stanton. In 1895, in her introduction to *The Woman's Bible*, Stanton wrote:

> From the inauguration of the movement for woman's emancipation the Bible has been used to hold her in the 'divinely ordained sphere' prescribed

---

13. David Moody, Foreword, to *At the Start... Genesis Made New*, pp. xi-xiii.

in the Old and New Testaments… When in the early part of the Nineteenth Century, women began to protest against their civil and political degradation, they were referred to the Bible for an answer.[14]

The accusations made here by Stanton are not to be explained away as feminist imaginings. On the contrary, substantial evidence of the abuse of women, which finds justification in the Bible, is supplied by nineteenth-century American jurisprudence. The following example is taken from a divorce case in Joyner v. Joyner 1862:

> Unto the woman it is said: 'Thy desire shall be to thy husband and he shall rule over thee': Genesis 3,16. It follows that the law gives the husband power to use such a degree of force as is necessary to make the wife behave herself and know her place.[15]

While these legal assertions may appear ludicrous to us in a different day and age, religious beliefs and cultural reception concerning the status of woman have not changed all that much since Stanton's time. Her claim that 'The Bible teaches that woman brought sin and death into the world, that she precipitated the fall of the race, that she was arraigned before the judgement seat of Heaven, tried, condemned and sentenced', is still part of official religious teaching, though the terms used today may be less dramatic. This view remains deeply ingrained in our cultural heritage. The outstanding American Bible scholar, Robert Alter, for instance, presents

---

14. E. Cady Stanton, *The Woman's Bible*, 'Introduction' (1895), p. 7.

15. 'The wife must be subject to her husband. Every man must govern his household, and if by reason of an unruly temper, or an unbridled tongue, the wife persistently treats her husband with disrespect, and he submits to it, he not only loses all sense of self-respect, but loses the respect of other members of his family, without which he cannot expect to govern them, and forfeits the respect of his neighbours. Such have been the incidents of the marriage relation from the beginning of the human race. Unto the woman it is said: "Thy desire shall be to thy husband and he shall rule over thee": Gen 3,16. It follows that the law gives the husband power to use such a degree of force as is necessary to make the wife behave herself and know her place.' It is sufficient for our purpose to state that there may be circumstances which will mitigate, excuse and so far justify the husband in striking the wife 'with a horse-whip on one occasion and with a switch on another, leaving several bruises on the person', so as not to give her the right to abandon him, and claim to be divorced'. *Joyner* v. *Joyner*, 59 N.C. 322 1862. Quoted by Dr K. Lee at the Coolidge Colloquium, Cambridge, MA, 1994. Under the heading 'Lawmaking and Precedent: How Judges and Lawyers Reason from Prior Cases', Lee cites cases where women file a petition for divorce on grounds of assault and battery.

one view of Eve as 'man's subservient helpmate, whose weakness and blandishments will bring such woe into the world'.[16]

Genesis 3.16
The line quoted in the case *Joyner v. Joyner* is found in an updated form in RSV. It is of particular interest for this paper because it provides a biblical view of the man–woman relationship. Here is v. 3.16 in its entirety:

> To the woman he said,
> I will greatly multiply your pain in childbearing;
> in pain you shall bring forth children,
> *yet your desire shall be for your husband,*
> *and he shall rule over you* (RSV).

The immediate context of the verse is as follows: after the eating of the forbidden fruit, the Deity solemnly addresses the serpent, then the woman, then Adam. Verse 3.16 covers all that is said to the woman. This verse can be broken down into the constituent parts: 1-4. 1) The Deity speaks to the woman of increased labour and pregnancies; 2) of her labour and giving birth, 3) of woman's desire for her man; and in 4) announces that he (the husband) shall rule her (the woman). The first three pronouncements concern woman's birth-giving capacity and her sexual desire. Feminist Bible scholars[17] argue (I think fairly) that the fourth pronouncement about the husband's ruling belongs to the same context. Attention is drawn to this point. In contrast, as illustrated for example in *Joyner v. Joyner*, a man's power to rule over woman has generally been considered to apply much further afield.

In the line, 'yet your desire shall be for your husband and he shall rule over you', two words, 'desire' and 'rule' merit particular examination. The first word, Hebrew תשׁוקה, 'desire', occurs only three times in the Hebrew Bible. The second occurrence is in Gen. 4.7, where the same two words— 'desire' and 'rule'—are again found together. In this (obscure) verse God tells Cain that sin's 'desire is for you, but you must master it' (RSV). The third occurrence is in Song 7.11, where the context is also that of man–woman relationship. For this reason, it is worth digressing to look at Song 7.11. Here is the RSV rendering:

---

16. Robert Alter, *The Art of Biblical Narrative* (New York: Basic Books, 1981), p. 146.
17. For a feminist perspective: Carol Meyers, *Discovering Eve: Ancient Israelite Women in Context* (New York: Oxford University Press, 1988); and Phyllis Trible, 'Depatriarchalizing in Biblical Interpretation', article in JAAR, 41 (1973), pp. 30-48.

> I am my beloved's
> and his *desire* is for me (RSV).

Where RSV has 'desire', NEB and *The Holy Bible* have 'longing'. Happy girl! The translators have no problem here: they allow that the man and the woman in the Song are, quite simply, in love.

The same cannot be said of Eve in Gen. 3.16. Only RSV has the word 'desire' (see above). Here are the other two versions:

> You *shall be eager for* your husband (NEB)

> and thou *shalt be subject* to thy husband (HB)

The RSV reading calls for no further comment. The NEB rendering is rather ugly and the meaning is not quite clear. *The Holy Bible* translation is unacceptable. Furthermore, although the RSV uses the same word, 'desire', in Song 7.11 and in Gen. 3.16, nevertheless, the footnote to 3.16 reveals a malaise. The footnote defines woman's *sexual desire* as *her motherly impulse*! Well, poor Eve! One asks why this difference from the 'desire/ longing' of the Song? Is it to be explained by a cultural difference[18] in our society, which cannot condone woman's desire for man but considers man's desire for woman legitimate (Song 7.11)? Is it because translators are unfavourably prejudiced against Eve, who is notoriously accused of having done the wrong thing?

Turning now to the word משל, 'rule', this verb occurs many times in the Hebrew Bible. In Genesis the great and lesser lights (the sun and the moon) are said to 'rule' the day and the night (1.16); Cain 'rules' sin (4.7); Abraham's servant 'rules' his household (24.2); Joseph 'rules' his brothers (37.8). Among the many occurrences outside the book of Genesis, one occurrence is of particular interest for the present discussion: in Isa. 3.12 there is a reference to women 'ruling' the people. This usage shows that Hebrew משל is not gender specific. And the translations for Gen. 3.16? Here are the readings:

> and he shall *rule over* you (RSV).

> and he shall *be your master* (NEB).

> he shall *be thy lord* (HB).

---

18. An example of cultural difference: in a ritual performance of the African people, the Peul, the men don shells and feathers. They roll their eyes and chatter their teeth to attract the attention of the women whose attire is comparatively drab. It is up to each woman then to single out the man who stirs her desire.

The gender-specific translations, 'he shall be your master' (NEB) and 'he shall be thy lord' (HB), can be traced back to the Greek Septuagint[19] (see also the Latin Vulgate).[20] They emphasise male domination over woman in a hierarchy in which man's position is seen to be superior. Furthermore, the footnote to 3.16 in the RSV shows that this dominant position is understood to extend beyond the sexual relationship. The complete footnote reads: 'This divine judgement contains an old explanation of woman's pain in childbirth, her sexual desire for her husband (i.e. her motherly impulse), and *her subordinate position to man in ancient society*' (my emphasis). The footnote indicates that *male domination* is understood to apply beyond the sexual, marital relationship: the woman of antiquity was socially inferior. The case of *Joyner v. Joyner* has shown how, as recently as the nineteenth century, Gen. 3.16 was used to justify male abuse. Note that in contemporary society, equal rights is still a moot question.

Conclusion

The second part of this paper has intimated that Gen. 3.16 addresses woman's sexual desire for man and man's control of woman's sex life and birth-giving capacity. It has shown that, in the Garden of Eden story, phrases such as 'eager for' or 'subject to' one's husband colour female desire to woman's disadvantage, while the RSV footnote to Gen. 3.16 is tantamount to a denial of female sexual desire. The paper has also shown that Hebrew מָשַׁל, 'rule', has become gender specific in translation, thus emphasizing 'male' rule; and that where male rule has been recognized as absolute, the authority of Gen. 3.16 has been used to justify male abuse of women.

One is tempted to ask why these unfavourable prejudices with regard to the woman in the Garden. Is it because the story is generally considered to treat of sin and punishment with Eve as the source of the world's woes? (Robert Alter). Is it because woman's desire is a source of puritanical embarrassment? Is it because, Bible translation being a male preserve, male translators, unconsciously or otherwise, express here a down-with-women, up-with-men stance? Whatever the reason for these misogynous tendencies, they tend to gather strength as different cultural views and

---

19. Greek κυριεύσει. 'Mastery is synonymous with masculinity in most of the Greek and Latin texts that survive from antiquity.' S. Moore and J.C. Anderson, 'Taking it like a Man: Masculinity in 4 Maccabees', *JBL* 117.2 (1998), pp. 249-73 (272).

20. Latin *dominabitur*.

translations succeed one another. I conclude by quoting in full Gen. 3.16 from *The Holy Bible*. Of the versions mentioned, it is the most condemnatory as far as Eve is concerned. The emphasis (mine) indicates those words in the translation that end up belying the Hebrew text. *The Holy Bible* translation is set out below in parallel to the same verses from *At the Start... Genesis Made New* to bring out the differences (with apologies to Ronald Knox).

To the woman he said	To the woman he said
Many are the pangs, many are the *throes*	Increase, I will increase
I will give thee *to endure*;	your pains and your conceivings
with pangs thou shalt give birth to children	With pains you shall breed sons
and thou shalt *be subject to* thy husband;	For your man your longing
he shall be *thy lord* (HB).	and he, he shall rule you (*ATS*).

MURDER SHE WROTE OR WHY TRANSLATION MATTERS:
A RESPONSE TO MARY PHIL KORSAK'S
'TRANSLATING THE BIBLE'

Caroline Vander Stichele

What motivates a woman to translate the Bible? And does it make a difference? In 1876 a translation of the Bible was published, written by Julia Evelina Smith.[1] Living in the nineteenth century on a farm in Connecticut, she started translating the Greek New Testament, and ended up translating the whole Bible: the Vulgate, the Septuagint as well as the Hebrew Bible, five times in total. She did so on her own, with nothing but a small reading circle to support her in her work, armed with only the lexicon and the King James translation, and no other ambition than to understand the Word of God in its original language: 'I wanted every reader to see the exact original and nothing else through my rendering as through glass.'[2] External circumstances made her finally decide to publish her work.

Hardly ten years later the Revised Version appeared, the product of an all-male committee. While the work of Julia Smith was hardly noticed, the RV became, as Mary Phil Korsak puts it, 'a cultural as well as a religious monument'.[3] More than a century later, Korsak publishes her own

---

1. Julia Evelina Smith, *The Holy Bible: Containing the Old and New Testaments: Translated Literally from the Original Tongues* (Hartford: American Publishing Company, 1876).

2. Susan J. Shaw, *A Religious History of Julia Evelina Smith's 1876 Translation of the Holy Bible: Doing More Than Any Man Has Ever Done* (San Francisco: Mellen Research University Press, 1993), p. 209. A short presentation of Julia Evelina Smith's life and work can be found in Marla J. Selvidge, *Notorious Voices: Feminist Biblical Interpretation 1500–1920* (London: SCM Press, 1996). pp. 213-26.

3. M.P. Korsak, 'Translating the Bible', p. 134. There is, however, no consensus on this point. According to Strauss, neither the RSV nor the ASV challenged the KJV. 'Both were overly literal and failed to match the majesty of language and the style of

translation of the first book of the Bible, sharing with Julia Smith a passion for translation and a fascination with the Bible. But there is more. Both Julia Smith and Mary Phil Korsak want to 'see' for themselves.

Source Text and Target Text

In the first part of her article, Korsak explains how she perceives her task as translator of Genesis. She states that she wants to stick as closely as possible to the source text and tries to translate the characteristics of that text into the target language, in order 'to narrow the gap between the original Hebrew and the English version'.[4] Word patterns from the source text should recur in the target text. In order to achieve such lexical correspondence, she chooses 'an English word that can systematically carry the weight of a particular Hebrew word'.[5] In this she follows the example of André Chouraqui and others who have been working along the same lines.[6]

The same translation strategy was also used by Smith, but in so far as Smith's focus was on a translation of the source text, which had to be as literal as possible, this sometimes resulted in an obscure and not so attractive English version. Korsak, to the contrary, aims at producing an English translation that reflects the poetry of the underlying Hebrew source text. Restoring the text is the task she has set herself but, in so doing, she also found herself 'inventing *a new language*, a poetic language, which, when developed in many details, can convey a fresh perception of the book of Genesis'.[7] This fresh perception is reflected in the title she gave to the translated book: not Genesis or 'In the beginning', but *At the start*.[8] It is

---

the KJV.' Mark L. Strauss, *Distorting Scripture? The Challenge of Bible Translation and Gender Accuracy* (Downers Grove, IL: InterVarsity Press, 1998), p. 13.

4.   M.P. Korsak, 'A Fresh Look at the Garden of Eden', *Semeia* 81 (1998), pp. 131-44 (132).

5.   Korsak, 'Translating the Bible', p. 136.

6.   Korsak also refers to Martin Buber and Franz Rosenzweig in German, Edmond Fleg and André Chouraqui in French, Everett Fox in English, Mirja Ronning in Finish and 'The Amsterdam School' in Dutch. Cf. M.P. Korsak, 'Genesis: A New Look', in A. Brenner (ed.), *A Feminist Companion to Genesis* (FCB, 2; Sheffield: Sheffield Academic Press, 1993), pp. 39-52 (42).

7.   Korsak, 'Translating the Bible', p. 138.

8.   M.P. Korsak, *At the Start... Genesis Made New: A Translation of the Hebrew Text* (European Series. Louvain Cahiers, 124; Leuven: Leuvense schrijversaktie, 1992).

also reflected in the layout of the text and in the rendering of the name(s) of God and the first human beings.

Yet, Korsak has more than just a linguistic interest in translating from Hebrew into English. She also wants to bring to the fore 'issues of embedded patriarchal ideology and authority in biblical writings and translations'.[9] She has set herself the task of a detective investigating a murder. She wants to go back, so to speak, to the scene of the crime in order to find out what has happened there. Smith and Korsak part ways at this point as well. Smith seems to have been less concerned with crafting an inclusive translation of sorts and more preoccupied with a literal rendering of the text. As Shaw points out, Smith's

> motives for translation came from Adventist theology, which claimed Scripture as the prophetic voice calling out to the believer, and her interest had been to see the thematic connections from Alpha to Omega, and not to create a vehicle by which to challenge the patriarchal status-quo [sic].[10]

I will come back to this issue but, first, will discuss Korsak's view on translation as a work of restoration. As she articulates it, her translation is an attempt 'to restore the Hebrew vocabulary through the medium of English';[11] or, as Moody puts it in the Introduction to her book, 'an English modified and refined by the characteristic qualities of the Hebrew original'.[12] What is not clear to me, however, is why it is important to *restore* the Hebrew vocabulary (or Greek or any other original language) to begin with? I wonder if this is a merely romantic fascination with the original language and/or text to be translated.

I don't have a problem with romantic fascination as such, but with the idea that we can have direct access to the original, an idea that underlies the notion of restoration. In my view, the translator always brings her—or, more often, his—own world to the text. This world includes her perception of the text to be translated, her views on translation, her knowledge of other translations of the relevant text, her own social and cultural background, her perception of the culture to which the text itself belongs—to

---

9.   Korsak, 'Translating the Bible', p. 132.

10.   Shaw, *A Religious History*, p. 261. As Selvidge, however, remarks: 'Yet, it would appear that Julia's very life choices challenged the patriarchal status quo... She may not have used the word "patriarchal" but she surely recognized the absence of women among the hierarchy within Christianity.' Selvidge, *Notorious Voices*, p. 218.

11.   Korsak, 'Translating the Bible'.

12.   D. Moody, 'Foreword' to Korsak, *At the Start*, p. xii.

name just a few factors. Expressions such as 'its *primitive* strength', or 'its *popular* character',[13] refer to qualities attributed to the source text. They are not inherent to the text itself, but rather reflect a certain appreciation of the text. The use of the word 'primitive' raises the question: Who defines this, and what is the point of comparison? And to call a text 'popular' similarly makes one wonder: For whom is that the case, and what are the criteria applied?

The notion of restoration also determines Korsak's methodological choice for a contextual approach. In order to concentrate on 'what the text "says"', as compared to what the text 'means',[14] she focuses on form rather than meaning. Although she admits that 'it is impossible to pin down the original',[15] Korsak wants to stay as close as possible to the source text, using techniques that ensure 'the transfer of Hebrew word patterns to the target language'.[16]

Yet, this focus on what the text 'says' tends to obscure the act of inter-pretation, as well as the interests of the translator, which are always part and parcel of the translation process. These interests can be explicit or implicit. Korsak states that her translation 'does not intend to convey any explicit ideology'.[17] The formulation is careful. It expresses an awareness that ideology can still be present implicitly and independently of the translator's intentions. I think this is not just a *possibility*, however, but a *fact*, since texts always reflect the cultural values and prejudices of their writers. Translations are no exception to this rule.

Moreover, I wonder if Korsak's effort to render the content, form and music of the Hebrew text is not inspired somehow by a desire to be *faith-ful* to the source text. Concessions are made in the target language to achieve such fidelity. But why is fidelity so important? Here I agree with Pippin, who observes: 'If the Bible is held as a "sacred text", then this issue of fidelity is especially important, since there is often an obsession with the Word of God, a desire to hear God's voice.'[18]

---

13. Korsak, 'Translating the Bible', p. 135.
14. Korsak, 'Genesis: A New Look', p. 43.
15. Korsak, 'Translating the Bible', p. 141.
16. Korsak, 'A Fresh Look', p. 133.
17. Korsak, 'Translating the Bible', p. 141.
18. T. Pippin, 'Translation Happens: A Feminist Perspective on Translation Theories', in H.C. Washington *et al.* (eds.), *Escaping Eden: New Feminist Perspectives on the Bible* (New York: New York University Press, 1999), pp. 163-76 (171).

I do not want to deny that the source text is important; rather, the question for me is why this should be the case. The source text may well be the scene of the crime one has to go back to, as it is the final test for every reading and translation of the text. It is the place of confrontation with the facts, knowing very well that one can never be sure about these facts. They can be manipulated, explained away in different ways, perhaps there never was a crime to begin with. Moreover, the text is no safe ground to stand on. It is unstable and fluid, as it has to be recreated from existing manuscripts. Still, every reading/translation needs to be verified, over and over and over again, turning every text into a never-ending story.

Korsak's article illustrates my point, as she seeks to uncover how translations 'accentuate or mitigate an androcentric bias which is characteristic of the source texts'.[19] As Anneke de Vries has demonstrated in her book *Het kleine verschil* ('the small difference'), a direct relation can be found between the translation strategy chosen and the stereotypical representation of men and women in the translation. The freer a translation is in relation to the source text, the more easily gender stereotypes pop up in the translation.[20]

Is this a matter of ideology? Of course it is. Is it 'possible to discern ideological influences in translated Bibles, which serve the cause of patriarchy at the expense of womankind'?[21] Of course it is possible, but that will be a matter of interpretation, and does not guarantee that any alternative reading will be free of ideology. Another reading will, rather, be informed by a different ideology, feminist or otherwise.

Inclusive Language

I would like to illustrate this point by taking a closer look at two examples Korsak discusses in her article: the translation of הֹאדם, and the names occurring in Gen. 2.21-23 and 3.20. In her translation Korsak has chosen for a consistent translation of הֹאדם with 'groundling'. She justifies this choice by referring, on the one hand, to the etymological link between הֹאדם and הֹאדמה 'ground', and on the other hand, to the difference between אדם and איש.

---

19. Korsak, 'Translating the Bible', p. 132.

20. A. de Vries, *Het kleine verschil: Man/vrouw-stereotypen in enkele moderne Nederlandse vertalingen van het Oude Testament* (Kampen: Kok, 1998).

21. Korsak, 'Translating the Bible', p. 141.

As far as the first argument is concerned, Korsak prefers the translation 'groundling' over 'earthling' because she has chosen to translate אדמה systematically with 'ground' and ארץ with 'earth'.[22] As far as the second argument is concerned, Korsak notes that the translation of both האדם and איש with 'man' obscures the difference between the two words as well as the relation, established through assonance, between איש and אשה, which she renders as 'man' and 'wo-man'. This is no doubt a nice translation of these three terms in Gen. 2.21-23, because the shift that occurs in the source text is thus reproduced in the English translation. And yet, in translating האדם as 'groundling', Korsak clearly gives precedence to the generic meaning of the word.[23] There are good reasons to do so, but it is nevertheless a choice and one that is necessarily based on a judgment about the meaning of this word. The distinction between what the text 'says' and what it 'means' can therefore not be made as easily as Korsak suggests. Every act of translation is also and necessarily one of interpretation, a judgment that can be made only by taking into account the meaning of what is said.

But there is more. As Korsak states: 'the translator's lexical choices reveal significant consequences for gender issues'.[24] This statement makes clear why Korsak prefers a translation different to the more traditional ones. Julia Smith has definitely been less ingenious and more traditional at this point, in that she translated האדם systematically with 'the man', as does the RV as well. *The Woman's Bible*,[25] however, took another approach, rendering האדם in different ways: with the name 'Adam' in v. 21 ('And the Lord God caused a deep sleep to fall upon Adam') and v. 23 ('And Adam said'); and with 'man' and 'the man' in v. 22 ('And the rib which the Lord God had taken from *man*, made he a woman, and brought her unto *the man*'). What this translation reveals is that, besides having a generic meaning, האדם has other meanings as well, meanings that cannot be so neatly separated from one another, in so far as האדם also appears as an individual and as a male character. The translation with Adam in vv. 21 and 23 thus reflects how האדם features as an individual in the text.[26] But האדם is also

22. Korsak, 'Genesis: A New Look', p. 48.
23. Korsak, 'Translating the Bible', p. 139.
24. Korsak, 'Translating the Bible', p. 139.
25. E. Cady Stanton, *et al.*, *The Woman's Bible* (repr.; Salem: Ayer, 1986 [1895–98]).
26. Korsak uses the name Adam in Gen. 4.25, where אדם appears for the first time as the proper name of an individual, 'Adam'. The proper name is not accompanied by the definite article ה (cf. 'A Fresh Look', p. 136). However, there are three occasions

used on occasion to refer to the male character over against the female, as is for instance the case in 2.25: 'the groundling and his woman'; and in 3.20: 'The groundling called his woman's name Life (Eve).'

This brings me to the second example I would like to discuss, namely the translation of names in Gen. 2.21-23 and 3.20. As far as divine names are concerned, Korsak's policy is to keep their Hebrew character by transliterating, rather than translating them. Thus, the Hebrew אלהים is rendered with Elohim and יהוה with YHWH. Korsak justifies this choice as follows: 'These names have rich religious and cultural connotations.'[27] In a note accompanying the first occurrence of YHWH in *At the start*, she explains that 'the personal name of the God of the Hebrews is not pronounced'. Korsak further suggests reading instead 'Adonai', 'Yahweh' or 'the Lord' in its place.[28] She also points out that the *Tetragrammaton* YHWH respects the transcendent character of this name in Hebrew tradition.[29] It is interesting to note here that Smith made an equally unusual choice in rendering יהוה consistently with 'Jehovah', while both the RV and *The Woman's Bible* keep the traditional rendering 'the Lord'.[30] As far as Korsak is concerned, the motivation underlying her decision is clearly theological, although a feminist concern for a less exclusively male image of God plays a role as well.[31]

Korsak's approach differs from this with respect to names of human characters. In that case, the familiar rendition in English is kept, but they are translated when they prove to be somehow meaningful in Hebrew. The English version of the name follows the translation in brackets. Korsak does this for instance with the name Eve (Gen. 3.20), which she translates as 'Life'. The advantage of this procedure is that the name's explanation, 'for she is the mother of all that *lives*' (italics mine), retains the relation to the actual name.[32] This forms another interesting correspondence with Smith, who translates this verse as follows: 'And Adam will call his wife's

---

where אדם appears without the article and is nevertheless translated with 'groundling';—in 1.26, 2.25 and 5.2. In 1.26 and 5.2 'Adam' appears added between brackets.

27. Korsak, 'Translating the Bible', p. 140.

28. Korsak, *At the Start*, p. 5.

29. Korsak, 'Genesis: A New Look', p. 42.

30. Shaw, *A Religious History*, p. 202. Shaw points out that this reading was also preferred in the American edition of the RV.

31. Korsak, 'A Fresh Look', pp. 140-43.

32. Korsak, 'Genesis: A New Look', p. 41.

name Life, for she was the mother of all living.'[33] Both *The Woman's Bible* and the REV, however, have the traditional rendering of the name with 'Eve'. As Korsak notes, 'because it has been so long omitted from the texts and probably also because of all the negative commentary aimed at Eve, the meaning of this name has generally been forgotten'.[34] In this case, a return to the name's original meaning can serve as a corrective to ingrained interpretations, in which Eve has become associated with sin, guilt and death. Or, as Shaw remarks with respect to Smith's translation (a remark that holds true for Korsak as well):

> If the suffragists and the feminists, both of that day and this, wanted to claim any feminist renderings at all in Julia's Translation, it would have to be regarding her choice of the word/name 'Life' for the Hebrew word universally rendered 'Eve' in Genesis 3.20 and following... One cannot help but notice the difference it can make to hear and image the name/word of Life as the proto-mother for all living.[35]

The choice made by both Korsak and Smith at this point is to highlight the meaning of the name. For Korsak the reinsertion of Eve's name, translated as 'Life', is important from a feminist viewpoint. Such a return to the literal meaning of the source text, however, is not always an advantage. There are, indeed, occasions where the translation is less inclusive than the source text. This is the case, for instance, when האדם or ἄνθρωπος are simply translated with 'man'; and the distinction between איש or ἀνήρ consequently gets lost in the process. There are also cases where explicitly masculine terminology is used in the source text, such as 'sons' or 'brothers', and the question remains whether these terms are meant in an exclusively male or in a more general, inclusive sense. This issue is related to that of cultural differences. What is taken for granted in one culture or time may not be self-evident or even contested in another culture or time. Here a literal translation runs the risk of glossing over such hermeneutic problems. 'Sons' remain 'sons' and 'brothers' remain 'brothers', because that is what the text says. But with this terminology, a patriarchal ideology is reinscribed or reinforced in the translation, because language is used that was originally perceived as inclusive but now as exclusive.[36]

33. Shaw, *A Religious History*, p. 287.

34. Korsak, 'Translating the Bible', p. 140.

35. Shaw, *A Religious History*, p. 205.

36. For a more elaborate discussion of issues concerning inclusive language in English Bible translations see: E.A. Castelli *et al.*, 'Special Section on Feminist Translation of the New Testament', *JFSR* 6.2 (1990), pp. 25-85; V.R. Gold *et al.*, *The*

A literal rendering of the text may be considered unproblematic when it concerns Homer, but not when it concerns the Bible. The reason is that the Bible is not considered just another ancient book, and its translations are not meant for private use only. Biblical texts are part and parcel of public discourse. As such, they reflect and shape people's identity. The more the Bible matters, the higher rise the emotions when its translation is at stake. Translation, then, becomes a battleground where different ideologies compete for recognition and approval. The historical winners of this power play for the One and True Word are the so-called authorized versions, which reduce all others to the status of non-authorized sub-versions. These sub-versions, however, are subversive in demonstrating that the Word is not as One or as Unified as it may seem. Subversions cultivate the awareness of relativity and choice. They are iconoclastic, because they challenge the identification of one translation with the Word of God; but they are also stimulating, because they invite the reader to take a fresh look at the text.

The independent translator no doubt enjoys a freedom of choice of which other translators can only dream, limited and controlled as their creativity is by rules and time-tables. The more people are involved in a translation, the greater the risk that the outcome is a compromise between all parties involved.

What then can a feminist translator do? What is it that she wants to do? In my view, she can make a difference—*not so much in telling a different story, as in telling the story differently*. That is what Julia Smith did. This is what Mary Phil Korsak does.

New Testament and Psalms: An Inclusive Version (Oxford: Oxford University Press, 1995), pp. vii-xxii; and M.L. Strauss, *Distorting Scripture?*

The Translation of Elijah: Issues and Challenges

Everett Fox

Allow me to begin by expressing my gratitude to the organizers of this workshop. I have not visited Amsterdam since 1976, when I had the privilege of meeting Dr Frits Hoogewoud and spending a few hours at the university. Over the years, however, I have felt a kinship with the Bible translators and exegetes of this country, and am happy on this occasion to have the opportunity to demonstrate that kinship.

In a meeting such as this, we may all share certain presuppositions on the art and science of translation; alternatively, we may disagree on fundamental principles. I view my task here today as laying out, in the context of a work in progress, what I perceive to be one fruitful approach. I have espoused it over the years in order to try and provide a corrective to certain widespread tendencies to be overly idiomatic. But it is, needless to say, only one approach. As a translator I naturally bring certain convictions to working on any section of the Hebrew Bible; these I view as adding a voice to the larger conversation. To use a musical analogy: over 60 years ago, in this country, one could hear both Toscanini *and* Mengelberg conduct Beethoven; since then, debates have raged, but hopefully, Beethoven has been served.

I have chosen to examine the Elijah stories from a translator's standpoint for three reasons. First, they are, stylistically speaking, from the 'classical' period of biblical Hebrew prose, whose texts hold a particular attraction for me. Second, I am at present working on the book of Kings, as part of a larger translation project on the 'Early Prophets'.[1] Third, I could not resist a delicious pun. The scene of Elijah's ascension into heaven in 2 Kgs 2 has long been referred to in English as the 'translation' of Elijah, stemming from the still-current dictionary definition—indeed, the primary one—of the verb 'translate' as 'to move from one place or condition to another, specifically

---

1. To appear as *The Early Prophets* (Schocken Bible, 2; New York: Schocken Books) in 2003.

'a) *Theol[ogical]*, to convey directly to heaven without death...'[2] So Elijah has been translated, as it were, from the beginning. Despite the attempt at pedantic humor, however, there is something serious and relevant to be made of the pun. The Elijah story as a whole is a narrative about appearing and disappearing, about trying to understand (2 Kgs 2), about survival under difficult circumstances (including persecution), about crossing from one river bank to another, about the problem of serving two masters (1 Kgs 18), and about the appointing of a successor. All these images suggest major issues and challenges for translators, particularly those who work with the Bible.

Let us begin by characterizing the Elijah material. Placement is always of great import in the Hebrew Bible. These particular narratives stand at roughly the mid-point in the book of Kings, between the glory days of the United Monarchy and the demise of both Israel and Judah. In George Savran's scheme,[3] as part of the narratives about the Omride dynasty they fall in the center of the chiastic arrangement of the book of Kings. They interrupt the stylistic uniformity of the usual chronological formulae found in Kings, suggesting a crucial historical or ideological moment, in much the same way that the accounts of Hezekiah and Josiah will do later on. We approach the text, therefore, with a heightened sense of what is at stake.

The style of these stories is of course crucial to their translation. It is easily identifiable as what Frank Polak has recently called the 'rhythmic-verbal style of the Classical stratum' of biblical literature.[4] Polak lists four criteria for evaluating biblical texts: '(a) the use of subordinate clauses (hypotaxis), (b) the length of the noun string, (c) the number of explicit syntactic constituents in the clause, and (d) the frequency of reference by means of pronouns and deictic particles'.[5] He goes on to characterize the Elijah stories, among others, as consisting 'of short clauses, containing only a small number of explicit syntactic constituents...hypotaxis and long noun strings are rare, whereas reference by pronoun and deictic particles is frequent'.[6] I shall not for the moment deal with Polak's conclusion that this classical style shows the strong influence of oral or oral-based

2. *Webster's New World College Dictionary* (New York: Macmillan, 1997), p. 1421.

3. George Savran, '1 and 2 Kings', in Robert Alter and Frank Kermode (eds.), *The Literary Guide to the Bible* (Cambridge, MA: Harvard University Press, 1987), p. 148.

4. Frank H. Polak, 'The Oral and the Written: Syntax, Stylistics and the Development of Biblical Prose Narrative', *JANES* 26 (1999), pp. 59-105 (78).

5. Polak, 'Oral and Written', p. 59.

6. Polak, 'Oral and Written', p. 59.

literature, yet it will be obvious that given what I, building on the approach of Buber and Rosenzweig, do with biblical texts presupposes the importance of those texts as they are read aloud.

A facet that seems to me to typically accompany Polak's 'classical style' is the frequent usage of repetition, both in occasional phrases and in what Buber famously called the *Leitwortstil*.[7] The Elijah stories make full use of *Leitwörter*, both within separate chapters and scenes and overarching all of the included narratives (1 Kgs 17–19; 21; 2 Kgs 1–2). In this they resemble, among others, two other biblical passages, the Samson cycle (Judg 13–16) and the opening of the Joban folk tale (Job 1–2). In both of those cases, the narrative is so tight stylistically that it is constructed of relatively few words; the repetitions build up the text, which only has to add new elements from time to time to create an explosive effect that is masterful when viewed from the end.[8] While the Elijah cycle is not quite as compressed in its vocabulary, it does exhibit the overall tendency of these texts.

This is the first element to be approached in the translation of the Elijah stories. A careful reading of our texts—which has been done by many interpreters, given the number of solid studies that have appeared in journals and commentaries over the past several decades—will readily reveal a number of *Leitwörter* that thread through the narratives and indeed help them to cohere: דבר, אכל, and the two pairs היה/נפש *and* מות/הרג. The notion of 'the word of YHWH' is central to the texts, setting the divine word, and its representative, the prophet, against the person and even the institution of the monarchy. The דבר announces the coming drought (1 Kgs 17.2) and sends Elijah on the road (17.5); in the mouth of the widow of Tzarefat (17.24), and then before the Israelites assembled at Carmel (18.36), it confirms Elijah's standing as a prophet; it comes to Elijah at Horeb (19.9); it illustrates Ahab's repentance (21.27, 28); and it is at issue in Ahaziah's idolatry and death (2 Kgs 1.16, 17). The fact that it does not appear in 2 Kgs 2 at all is perhaps merely a sign that Elijah's task is over.

'Eating' appears repeatedly in these stories, not surprisingly: Israel's decision about whom to worship is connected to the issue of nurturing

---

7. Martin Buber, 'Leitwortstil im Erzählung des Pentateuchs', in Martin Buber and Franz Rosenzweig, *Die Schrift und ihre Verdeutschung* (Berlin: Schocken, 1936), pp. 11-38.

8. Cf. Everett Fox, 'The Bible Needs to be Read Aloud', *Response* 33 (11.1) (Spring 1977), pp. 5-17 (9-11); E. Fox 'The Samson Cycle in an Oral Setting', *Alcheringa: Ethnopoetics* 4.1 (1978), pp. 51-68.

(and note the thrice-repeated use of קלל in chs. 17 and 18) and survival. Moreover, it ties in with the two word-pairs related to life and death, which are consistent motifs in the narrative. Together they convey the idea that prophetic words, and the prophetic vocation, are a matter of life and death, both for the people of Israel and for the prophet himself. Hauser sees a further issue at stake: the potency of YHWH versus Baal as an arbiter of life and death.[9]

But while we may argue about the thematic importance and interpretation of a word or phrase, what is the translation issue here? It is simply that, while idiomatic, contextual rendering of specific words is undoubtedly the most fluent, clearest, and most nuanced way to translate, *Leitwörter* need to be represented by single English words, so that the thematic connections are not lost. Much of the time this will be possible, albeit with some concomitant loss of richness, although occasionally one runs into an insoluble situation. The dramatic events of 1 Kgs 1, for instance, do not allow us to say in English that 'fire came down from the heavens / and ate up him and his fifty (men)' (v. 10); the language would be stretched too far. But the translator must nevertheless take care to make those distinctions that are possible, for example between 'cause (one's) death' (המית) and 'kill' (הרג)—even if there are not semantic differences between them, it is still important to maintain the texture of the text.

A second translation element, and challenge, concerns the rendering of proper names. Buber and Rosenzweig, to their credit, established the principle that the meaning of names—specifically, their paranomastic use through what is often folk etymology—should be incorporated into the translated text itself whenever relevant. They are not always consistent on this matter, and in my own case, readers over the years have urged me to add more. This would be helpful in the case of the Elijah stories. Jezebel's name, for instance, cries out to be explained. Scholarly opinion leans in the direction of the name being a shortened form of 'Ahi-zebel' or 'Abi-zebel', 'the Deity is Exalted', or that it means 'Where is the Exalted-One?' But that cannot be its usage in our story and in connection with Jezebel's other appearances, which demand that we interpret the name as a devastating pun: 'Un-exalted'.[10] Elijah's own name, of course, is not irrelevant, any

---

9.   Alan J. Hauser, 'Yahweh versus Death—The Real Struggle in 1 Kings 17–19', in Alan J. Hauser and Russell Gregory (eds.), *From Carmel to Horeb: Elijah in Crisis* (JSOTSup, 85; BibLit, 19; Sheffield: Almond Press, 1990), pp. 11-89.

10.   The suggestion that it relates to Heb זבל, 'dung', is unlikely, given that such a form is attested only in post-biblical Hebrew—although 'trash', used in colloquial

more than is Obadiah's; the only question for the translator is when to insert their meaning. I have customarily done it the first time the name appears. Ahab is more problematic, if only because it is harder to give a satisfactory rendering of אח-אב; 'Father's Brother' or 'Like the Father/ Deity' do not appear to add anything to an understanding of either the character or the story. More fruitful, perhaps, and seldom used (Buber–Rosenzweig does not), is a rendering of נחל כרית (17.3) as 'Wadi Kerit/Cutoff', given the use of כרת at a number of points in chs. 17–19.[11] I would not, on the other hand, look for a translation of Kishon ('belonging to the god Kish'?); there what is significant is the connection with Deborah's victory over the Canaanites in Judg. 4.

There are several specific troublesome passages in the narrative that we may consider here. The first is Elijah's taunt to the prophets of Baal in 18.27. Most English translations have Elijah describe Baal as being busy, or involved in thought, or on a journey (so, with variations, KJV, NIV, RSV, NJPS). Recent commentaries, however, have understood שיג לו. as 'urinating', and so view the entire passage as scatological. This makes good sense; the Hebrew Bible does not flinch from making stinging judgments on other gods, and sometimes does resort to what might be called 'bathroom humor', albeit of a dark kind (cf. Judg. 3.21 onwards, the story of Ehud and Eglon). But of equal importance to the sense is the sound play that occurs in the passage. A taunt, after all, typically contains a rhythmical element as well as a logical one; children, for instance, will use rhymes and/or chant a taunt repeatedly.[12] On this basis, I would suggest for our passage something like: 'Or has he got business—or is he doing his business—or is he on his way (there)?'[13] What is lacking in this translation is brevity, and the translator must be prepared to revise as newer and better solutions present themselves.

American English to describe a low-class person of dubious moral character, is an attractive possibility. For the translation of names see also Korsak's article.

11. Cf., e.g., Robert L. Cohn, 'The Literary Logic of I Kings 17–19', *JBL* 101/3 (1982), pp. 333-50 (346).

12. A notorious example from American history is the presidential campaign of 1884, where Republican candidate James G. Blaine was assailed with cries of 'Blaine! Blaine! James G. Blaine! Continental liar from the state of Maine!', which Democrats countered with a taunt based on Republican candidate Grover Cleveland's admission of fathering an illegitimate child, 'Ma, Ma, where's my Pa? Gone to the White House, Ha, Ha, Ha!'

13. Cf. Jerome T. Walsh, *1 Kings* (Berit Olam; Collegeville, MN: Liturgical Press, 1996), pp. 248-49.

Another aspect of the Carmel confrontation holds interest for the translator. Elijah's exhortation to the people in v. 21, עד מתי אתם פסחים על שני
הסעפים, when it is not taken figuratively (e.g. the NIV's 'waver between
two opinions'), is sometimes understood as 'How long will you limp on
two crutches?' The later (v. 27) usage of the verb פסח to describe the Baal
prophets' dance then becomes 'they limped around the altar which they had
made'. The NJPS, in this case closer to Buber–Rosenzweig than usual,
renders 'keep hopping between two opinions', with the footnote 'Lit. "on
the two boughs"', and the later passage as 'they performed a limping
dance'. My own inclination would be toward 'hopping on two branches/
boughs', and 'they hopped frantically', to indicate the change in *binyan*.
But it is possible that 'limping' is more accurate (cf. the usual biblical sense
of 'lame'), and that the translation should be read accordingly.

Perhaps the most famous of all Elijah passages, and indeed one of the
signal moments in biblical literature, is the theophany on Mount Sinai in
ch. 19. Here the number of problems for the translator abound. Even
before reaching the infamous קול דממה דקה, there is the issue of what to
do with a rather odd syntactical sequence:

ויאמר
צא ועמדת בהר לפי יהוה
והנה ה'עבר
ורוח גדולה וחזק מפרק הרים ומשבר סלעים לפני יהוה
לא ברוח יהוה
ואחר הרוח רעש
לא ברעש יהוה
ואחר הרעש אש
לא באש יהוה
ואחר האש קול דממה דקה.

The major Bible translations uniformly render the negative sequences as
'but the LORD was not in the wind/earthquake/fire', despite the absence
of a conjunction in the Hebrew. And indeed, as part of normal narrative
syntax, we would expect something like ויהוה לא ברוח.

The King James translators, to their credit, set *but* in italics, as is their
custom with words not appearing in the Hebrew. But the issue had already
been imaginatively joined by the medieval exegete David Kimhi, who in
his commentary on Kings notes that 'the Voice' announces each time that
God is not in the particular natural phenomenon. The Stone Edition
Tanach, a translation based on rabbinic readings of the Bible, follows
Kimhi's lead, and renders the passage as follows:

> And behold, HASHEM was passing, and a great, powerful wind, smashing mountains and breaking rocks, went before HASHEM. 'HASHEM is not in the wind!' [Elijah was told]. After the wind came an earthquake. 'HASHEM is not in the earthquake.' After the earthquake came a fire. 'HASHEM is not in the fire.' After the fire...[14]

But while this at least acknowledges a difference in form, its eisegetical character has no warrant otherwise in the text.

Some modern commentators have also noted the anomalous character of the text here and have attempted to cast their English accordingly. So, for instance, the rendering of Herbert Brichto:

> Lo, YHWH in procession! At the behest of YHWH, a mightily fierce wind, splitting off crags and shattering boulders. Not in the wind, YHWH! After the wind—an earthquake. Not in the earthquake, YHWH! After the earthquake. Not in the quake, YHWH! After the quake, fire. Not in the fire, YHWH!...[15]

This rendering, which imitates the Hebrew word order, makes little sense in English; the punctuation makes it appear as if the narrator is addressing God. Better is the attempt of Jan Tarlin:

> Yahweh passing by. And a great and strong wind breaking the mountains and shattering the cliffs before YHWH—not in the wind is YHWH. And after the wind, an earthquake—not in the earthquake is YHWH. And after the earthquake, a fire—not in the fire is YHWH.[16]

Buber–Rosenzweig tries a slightly different approach, attempting to typographically reflect the rhythm of the passage:

> *Da,*
> *vorüberfahrend ER:*
> *ein Sturmbraus, gross und heftig,*
> *Berge spellend, Felsen malmend,*
> *her vor SEINEM Antlitz:*
> *ER im Sturme nicht—*
> *und nach dem Sturm ein Beben:*
> *ER im Beben nicht—*

---

14. *The Stone Edition Tanach* (New York: Mesorah Publications, 1996), p. 861.

15. Herbert Chanan Brichto, *Toward a Grammar of Biblical Poetics: Tales of the Prophets* (New York: Oxford University Press, 1992), p. 141.

16. Jan Tarlin, 'Toward a "Female" Reading of the Elijah Cycle: Ideology and Gender in the Interpretation of 1 Kings 17–19, 21, and 2 Kings 1–2.18', in A. Brenner (ed.), *A Feminist Companion to Samuel and Kings* (FCB, 5; Sheffield: Sheffield Academic Press, 1994), pp. 208-17 (216).

und nach dem Beben ein Feuer:
ER im Feuer nicht—
aber nach dem Feuer...

At once the advantage of a 'colometric' approach is clear. The tone of the passage approaches the mystical; one can almost imagine, not a normal narrator or storyteller, but an actor declaiming on stage. It is possible that the unusual word order of the Hebrew serves to point up a feature of how the narrative is to be spoken; since there is no way of transcribing performance practice known to us from pre-Masoretic texts, the structure of the text here may be signaling for the narrator to slow down, in order to emphasize the point being made.[17] In a modern, conventionally printed book, the only way to get this across without special symbols or fonts is through line division, and so, in the footsteps of Buber–Rosenzweig, I would suggest that the scene play thus:

> Now here, YHWH crossing by:
> a wind great and strong,
> crushing hills, smashing boulders in the presence of YHWH—
> YHWH is not in the wind;
> now after the wind, an earthquake—
> YHWH is not in the earthquake;
> now after the earthquake, a fire—
> YHWH is not in the fire;
> and after the fire...

Alternatively, the refrain could read, 'in the wind, YHWH is not...in the earthquake, YHWH is not...in the fire, YHWH is not'; but if the above rendering is read dramatically and slowly, the point will be sufficiently made.

The great mystery of the Elijah story, and one of its many climaxes, follows immediately. We are unprepared for what occurs, for the Bible is full of noisy or striking theophanies, from the meeting at Sinai in Exod. 19 to the acclamation of God in Ps. 29—both of which feature the usage of קול, accompanied by other visible and aural natural phenomena (cf. also Deut. 5.19-23). To trace the English translation of קול דממה דקה is to trace a history of changes in theological perception. Tyndale, as recorded in 'Matthew's Bible' of 1537,[18] renders the phrase 'small still voice'—an

---

17. I am grateful to Professor Ed Greenstein for discussions on this point, as well as for bringing to my attention the article cited in n. 19.

18. David Daniell (ed.), *Tyndale's Old Testament* (New Haven: Yale University Press, 1992).

interesting indication of the lineage of the KJV's immortal 'still small voice', and an illustration of how close and how far a particular translation may be to 'getting it right'.

There seem to be as many as four schools of thought about the phrase, as expressed in translations over the past 30 years or so. One trend is to understand it as the expression of a natural phenomenon, to be taken as providing a contrast to the meteorological pyrotechnics often associated with Baal. Hence one finds renderings on the order of 'a sound of a gentle blowing' (NASV, 1995 Update) and 'the sound of a gentle breeze' (JB). A second approach is to see in the phrase an indication of God's speaking, albeit in muffled tones, à la 'a gentle whisper' (NIV) and 'the breath of a light whisper' (Moffatt). Another tack steers a path between the first two, as in 'a low murmuring sound' (NEB) and 'a tiny whispering sound' (NAB). Finally, there is what I would term the paradoxical approach, which understands the phrase as a *mysterium*, albeit not *traemendum*: 'a sound of sheer silence' (NRSV).

How is the translator to navigate such a complex legacy? The likelihood of finding something truly new would not seem to be great—nor should that be the sole objective. About the Hebrew there are a few observations to be made: קוֹל can certainly mean either 'sound' or 'voice', yet it is the latter which is almost always indicated in biblical theophany scenes. In the Carmel scene of ch. 18, the word has already played a prominent role, so that would seem to be the logical choice. דממה can mean 'silence', but also appears to signify alternately the 'calm after the storm' (Ps. 107.29), which makes eminent sense here, or, based on a number of biblical passages and cognates, 'wailing' or 'murmuring'.[19] This last usage, suggested by Baruch Levine, demonstrates the verbalization of mourning in ancient Israel, in such passages as Lam. 2.10, and also clarifies Job's vision in 4.16:

> Something stood up, whose appearance I did not recognize;
> A form [loomed] before my eyes;
> I heard a *droning voice* (דממה וקול)[20]

Most interesting is the case of דקק, which everywhere else in the Bible refers to something thin (lit. 'crushed') that can be felt (hair, grain, dust,

19.　This second meaning is posited by Baruch Levine in 'Silence, Sound, and the Phenomenology of Mourning in Biblical Israel', *JANESCU* 22 (1993), pp. 89-106.

20.　Levine, 'Silence, Sound', p. 101. Levine acknowledges his debt to H.L. Ginsberg around the idea that דממה is audible.

etc.). So why would a writer utilize 'thin' to describe a sound? Robert Coote perceptively points out that this may be an allusion to the Manna of the wilderness narratives (Exod. 16.14); since the Elijah stories frequently talk of God's nurturing the prophet and the people with food, it makes sense to suggest that the moment of his intimate communication with Elijah hearkens back ever so slightly to nurturing images from Israel's past.[21]

We are thus left with 'voice' and 'thin', and the dilemma of what to use for דממה. The situation is further complicated by the need, noted above, to reflect the rich play of sound found in the phrase; דממה דקה has something of the mourning style found in Lamentations, with its opening *-ah* words, and in addition is chiastic (מ-מ, ד-ק, ק-ד). Finally, is it possible for one to decide definitively between the theologically intriguing 'silence' and the alternatives?

Up to this point I have arrived at no inspired solution. Stephen Prickett[22] may well be right that the King James translators, with their use of 'a still small voice', have caught the essential mystery of the situation, and their rendering has stood up remarkably well for almost four hundred years. Its simplicity and intimacy appeal to readers, who may see something of themselves in Elijah. At the risk of abandoning the comforting and the familiar (and the inspiring), however, I would suggest that the wind/-earthquake/fire sequences encourage us to understand the phrase as something on the order of 'the voice of a thin whisper' or 'a thin, murmuring voice'. I should add that I find this solution both emotionally unsatisfying and aesthetically inadequate, and fervently express the hope that a small voice will someday provide me with the true solution.

For a final set of illustrations of translation 'issues and challenges', let us now turn to a complete story, the Naboth narrative of 1 Kgs 21. It has long been held that this episode was not originally part of the Elijah materials, since both its vocabulary and its major concern—Elijah as social critic in the manner of the later literary prophets—deviate from what precedes and follows it. Recently it has been suggested[23] that it is an

21. Robert Coote, 'Yahweh recalls Elijah', in Baruch Halpern and Jon D. Levenson (eds.), *Traditions and Transformations: Turning Points in Biblical Faith* (Winona Lake, IN: Eisenbrauns, 1981), pp. 115-20 (120).

22. Stephen Prickett, *Words and the Word* (Cambridge: Cambridge University Press, 1986), pp. 6-17.

23. Marsha C. White, *The Elijah Legends and Jehu's Coup* (BJS, 311; Atlanta: Scholars Press, 1997), pp. 32-43.

example of a synthetic story about Elijah, that is, one built entirely on the pattern of the David and Bathsheba narrative in 2 Sam. 11–12, and is an attempt to model our prophet after Nathan (just as most of the other texts in Kings portray him as a Moses *redivivus*). An examination of translation problems may help to clarify this characterization. I shall follow the sequence found previously in this paper: *Leitwörter*, proper names, and specific words or phrases.

It is clear from even a cursory reading of the tale that it contains one major leading word, the stem נתן, 'give'. Its repetition at close quarters (nine times in seven verses) leaves no doubt that the writer wishes to teach a major lesson through its use, and it is not hard to fathom what that might be. 'Giving' is the opposite of 'taking'; and 'taking' was precisely what 1 Sam. 8 warned of when Israel's first king was chosen. Kings are takers by nature, and power corrupts. Ahab, villain though he may be in the book of Kings, is remarkably restrained in his response to Naboth's refusal, but Jezebel, the villain of at least this version of the story (contra 2 Kgs 9), seizes the moment, along with life and property, declaring that, in contrast to the impotent king, she will acquire the desired plot of land. The vineyard is not Naboth's to give or 'give away', but neither is it the queen's to give, and thus the usage of the verb in v. 7 is quite ironic. Yet some of the standard English translations have decided that 'give' is too dull here, and seek a more natural English. The NJPS, NIV and NJB all use 'get', and the NAB chooses 'obtain'. NJPS in particular chooses a wide range for נתן, in an attempt to be idiomatic:

> 6 So he told her, 'I spoke to Naboth the Jezreelite and proposed to him: Sell me your vineyard for money…'
> 7 His wife Jezebel said to him… 'Rise and eat something, and be cheerful; I will get the vineyard of Naboth the Jezreelite for you…'
> 15 …she said to Ahab, 'Go and take possession of the vineyard which Naboth the Jezreelite refused to sell you for money…'

But the verb occurs in such concentrated fashion that it is clearly a *Leitwort*, and such usage needs to be respected in translation, even at a slight cost of style. Naboth's refusal to 'give' over his property is successfully overcome by Jezebel's determined plan, and by her subsequent 'gift' of the land to Ahab in v. 15. One could even include the story's final use of the verb in v. 22, where it clearly means 'make' (God will make Ahab's dynasty like Jeroboam's and Baasha's), in the overall scheme of the chapter, and argue that Jezebel's seizure of the vineyard will be countered by YHWH's pronouncement of doom upon the House of Omri/Ahab. How the translator can convey the wordplay here is a difficult problem; to say 'I will give your house to be like the house of Jeroboam' is not, to say the least, passable English. But if one wants to preserve an important nuance of the text, and maintain the time-honored biblical principle of a punishment that matches the crime, it may be necessary.[24]

Another general observation concerning the vocabulary of ch. 21 is its affinity to the Bathsheba episode. Here the translator may easily coordinate our chapter with that one, rendering such verbs as שלח, שכב, שים, שות and אכל, and such words as ספר with an appropriate single English word. In addition, the phrase in 21.21,

הנני מביא עליך רעה,

might be said to echo Nathan's unusual rhyming curse in 2 Sam. 12.11,

הנני מביא עליך רעה [מביתך].

Despite this the NIV, which is usually sensitive to such issues, renders the two passages differently:

> 2 Sam. 21.11   Out of your own household I am going to bring calamity upon you....
>
> 1 Kgs 21.21   I am going to bring disaster on you....

Yet the Naboth story is not merely a slavish copy of an earlier one. True, the two accounts are quite parallel in structure, vocabulary, and general import; but a further look at the language of 1 Kgs 21 reveals that it echoes other parts of the David stories as well. David has stones (vv. 10-11) thrown at him by Shimei (2 Sam. 16); 'worthless men' (בני בליעל, vv. 10, 13) and the insulting imagery of dogs (v. 23) appear throughout the books of Samuel (1 Sam. 25.17, 25; 2 Sam. 16.7; 20.1; and 1 Sam. 17.43; 24.15; 2 Sam. 3.8; 9.8; 16.9); and the striking metaphor of 'peeing against the wall' (משתין בקיר, v. 21) is reminiscent of the Nabal narrative (1 Sam. 25.22, 34). All these allusions suggest that not only is Ahab's crime reminiscent of the Bathsheba incident, but that monarchy in general brings with it the long-lived dangers of injustice and violence.[25] But we are permitted to reach this conclusion in a translation only when the allusions are adhered to in the target language. And that means that the translator

---

24. Another classic example of such language is Gen. 6.11-13, where the root שחת is utilized.

25. The point is further supported by the fact that David and Ahab each break four of the last five of the Ten Commandments.

must do his or her work conscientiously, letting the reader make the connections by recognizing multiple occurrences of the same word or expression.

Of the names that occur in ch. 21, only one is new, that of the victim. Given the story's propensity for meaningful names, one might be expected here. The only suggestion I have come across that shows promise is Yair Zakovitch's 'name midrash' of נבות as an abbreviation for the chapter's significant phrase נחלת אבות.[26] I admit to some reluctance concerning this approach, although Zakovitch supports it with other examples from the Psalms and Ben Sira. As a translator, however, all I am willing to do is to supply a note at the bottom of the page.

A few individual moments will serve to round out the discussion. Jezebel's not idle boast in v. 7, אני אתן לך את כרם נבות היזרעאלי, is taken by most modern English translations as simply, 'I will give/get you the vineyard of Naboth'. An exception to this is the NJB, 'I myself shall get you the vineyard…' Such an emphatic rendering is fully justified, even demanded by the Hebrew construction (cf., e.g., the discussion by Niccacci[27]); it might better be served in English by '*I* will get you the vineyard'—I, the imperious queen, in contrast to you, Ahab, the 'sullen and enraged' king.

The latter phrase, סר וזעף,[28] will also point out the linkage that has been forged between this story and the surrounding ones. It has occurred in the chapter immediately preceding ours (20.43). Likewise, the expression ועזוב ועצור in v. 21 has already been heard in 14.10. There are also linkages to the other Elijah stories, however tenuous. The ubiquitous דבר יהוה, which was noted above as central to the Elijah account, here occurs twice (vv. 17 and 28). So despite the nature of chapter 21 as a separate story with a Deuteronomistic flavor, there has been some attempt to integrate it into this point in the book of Kings.

I do not wish to give the impression that all or even most of the translation problems that arise in this story are solvable. For example, the

---

26.　Yair Zakovitch, 'The Tale of Naboth's Vineyard, I Kings 21', Addendum to Meir Weiss, *The Bible from Within* (Jerusalem: Magnes Press, 1984), pp. 379-405 (387).

27.　Alviero Niccacci, *The Syntax of the Verb in Classical Hebrew Prose* (JSOTSup, 86; Sheffield: JSOT Press, 1990), pp. 23-27.

28.　I obviously do not take זעף in the sense of 'angry'; it seems to me that the emotions being played out by Ahab are much more akin to upset and depression. Cf. Gen. 40.6 for similar usage.

wonderful correspondence between Jezebel's קוֹם רֹשׁ in v. 15 and YHWH's answering קוֹם רֵד in v. 18 is not easily transferable into English beyond 'Arise, take possession' and 'Arise, go down'. But that rendering fails rhythmically, and there is nothing to be done but to admit defeat (Buber–Rosenzweig seeks a more visual solution, with *Erhebe dich, / ererbe... Erhebe dich ,/ stieg hinab...*). A more serious problem concerns the syntactical form of v. 12, קָרְאוּ צוֹם. As Alexander Rofé has pointed out,[29] a text in good classical Hebrew would read וַיִּקְרְאוּ, following the narrative sequence of verbs that it does, beginning with v. 8 ('She wrote... And she sent... She wrote... They did...'). His conclusion, in conjunction with some other observations about the language of ch. 21, is that the chapter is a Persian period story which includes this 'fine instance of a semantic "blunder" by a late, post-biblical author who was trying to imitate good Classical Hebrew'.[30] Now even if we grant this historical judgment, the translator is faced with an additional difficulty: the unenviable task of conveying in English the stylistic shift between the earlier וַיִּקְרְאוּ and the later קָרְאוּ. To my mind it cannot be done, although some have proposed differentiating between normal prose style and archaic poetry such as Exod. 15.[31]

In the end, the translation of the Elijah stories, like that of the rest of the Hebrew Bible, rests on personal choices and the scholar's judgment at the time of translating. Unlike the theatrical or musical performer, he or she does not have the luxury of almost instantaneous rethinking and revision, and is in some ways a prisoner to the relative finality of the printed page. But a translation keyed to the feel of the Hebrew text, if properly introduced and annotated, may nevertheless have the opposite effect—to free the reader/listener to reappraise the text through a more nuanced appreciation of it, even in another language, and even despite a certain degree of awkwardness and strangeness. In so doing, it reminds us that the biblical text, while relatively fixed, nevertheless partakes of the recreation inherent in all great literature.

29. Alexander Rofé, 'The Vineyard of Naboth: The Origin and Message of the Story', *VT* 38/1 (1988), pp. 89-104 (100).

30. Rofé, 'The Vineyard'.

31. David Daiches paraphrases the Song at the Sea in 'old alliterative Anglo-Saxon heroic style' in his *Moses: The Man and His Vision* (New York: Praeger, 1975), p. 95.

'THE TRANSLATION OF ELIJAH': A RESPONSE TO EVERETT FOX

A.J.C. Verheij

Dear Professor Fox, dear colleagues, ladies and gentlemen:
Allow me to begin by saying that, despite your prolonged absence from this city, your work has not gone unnoticed here. You have mentioned your 'kinship with the Bible translators and exegetes of this country'.[1] And indeed, many of us are quite familiar with your writings—particularly those of us who are working together within the framework of the *Societas Hebraica Amstelodamensis*, founded by the late Professor Martinus Beek. One eloquent testimony to this evident kinship is in the recent publication, *The Rediscovery of the Hebrew Bible*.[2] This volume contains a 'large conversation', to quote your own expression, in which your work[3] plays a prominent part. But let me refer, additionally, to your article of 1981.[4] These publications, just like your contribution of today, reveal a deep and lasting kinship with the work of Martin Buber and Franz Rosenzweig.[5]

Two 'Schools'

The debate between the rival 'schools' of formal and functional equivalence in Bible translation has been particularly passionate in the Netherlands

---

1. Cf. E. Fox, 'The Translation of Elijah' *et al.* p. 156.
2. J.W. Dyk *et al.* (eds.), *The Rediscovery of the Hebrew Bible* (Amsterdamse Cahiers voor Exegese van de Bijbel en zijn Tradities Supplement Series, 1; Maastricht: Shaker, 1999).
3. E. Fox, *The Five Books of Moses: Genesis, Exodus, Leviticus, Numbers, Deuteronomy: A New Translation with Introductions, Commentary, and Notes* (London: Harvill, 1995).
4. E. Fox, 'A Buber–Rosenzweig Bible in English', *Amsterdamse cahiers voor exegese en Bijbelse theologie* 2 (1981), pp. 8-22.
5. M. Buber and F. Rosenzweig, *Die Schrift und ihre Verdeutschung* (Berlin: Schocken, 1936).

during the last 30 to 40 years or so. Professor Rogerson referred to this debate in his paper earlier in this conference. The passion, I think, stems from specific theological and pastoral concerns, each 'school' honestly claiming, and wanting, and finding it very important, to present modern-day readers with the best translation possible (whatever that may mean) of the Bible. The content of the debate itself is of course much more general. After all that has been said and written about it, I need not discuss this here. The debate, briefly, has to do with the position of the translator and the translation as mediators between the source text/language/culture/reality on the one hand (including, perhaps, for some, a divine, transcendent reality), and their target counterparts on the other. Professor Korsak called this position 'tragic' this morning. The debate on the new Dutch Bible translation[6] shows that it is not enviable—to say the least.

In a gross simplification we might say that a formally equivalent translation, such as advocated in the Netherlands by the so-called Amsterdam 'school' and the *Societas* just mentioned, takes its stand relatively close to the source text. The rival 'school' of functionally equivalent translation seems to feel more comfortable at the target side of the spectrum.

This has important implications for the demands that the translation makes on its readers. A translation of the 'Amsterdam' type tends to require much intellectual effort of its audience. As you yourself have stated it, the purpose of a translation of the Buber type is, 'to draw the reader into the world of the Hebrew Bible through the power of its language'.[7] You also write that 'the reader must be prepared to meet the Bible at least halfway'.[8] The reader, then, is not supposed to turn away from a text that is strange, difficult, or even—to use your own expression—'not passable' stylistically. The reader is supposed to understand that reading requires active participation. Most importantly, I think, the reader is supposed to accept that there is a world of texts, that texts are a reality in its own right, and that it makes sense to explore the 'texture of the text', its internal coherence, as well as its external relations with other texts. To many people, including potential or actual readers of the Bible, even cultured ones, this may not be obvious at all. At the same time, it is the very essence of your paper.

---

6. Cf. A.B.M. Naaijkens, 'Vertaalkritiek en de Nieuwe Bijbelvertaling', *Met Andere Woorden* 19/1 (2000), pp. 18-33; and *Nieuwe Bijbelvertaling: Tegen het licht gehouden* (Haarlem: NBG, 1999).

7. Fox, *The Five Books of Moses*, p. ix.

8. Fox, *The Five Books of Moses*, p. xix.

Apart from theoretical considerations that make a functionally equivalent approach more or less 'obsolete', as Dr Crisp put it yesterday,[9] a
translation of that type is perhaps more indulgent towards its readership,
less inclined to educate, more willing to create common ground with a
large audience, and more willing to adopt usage that makes the text look
familiar and accessible. It is more 'user friendly', as it were. And ultimately, it is the propositional content of the text that is supposed to matter
here, more than its textual properties such as its register, the length of its
clauses, repetitions of sounds, words or phrases. You gave the example of
the stylistic shift between ויקראו and קראו. Yesterday, Professor de Regt
spoke about the growing sensibility for style within the functionally
equivalent approach. Yet I think that a translator from this 'school' might
react to your observation by saying: it may be true, but is it relevant to my
readers? Such a question, in my view, is legitimate, pertinent and to the
point.

In fact, I find it increasingly difficult, personally, to take a well-argued
stand in this debate. Postmodernism strikes again, I am afraid: much
depends on who you are, where you are, and whom you are trying to serve
with your work. And besides, there is of course no dichotomy in this
matter, but rather, a continuum of approaches containing many shades and
hues.

Leading Words

In any event, your paper is clearly on the 'Amsterdam' side of this continuum, and to be sure, by education and inclination, this is my position as
well. Much of your delightfully concrete presentation is, in fact, a close
reading, a textual analysis of the stories of Elijah and Naboth's vineyard.

The most intriguing question, it would seem to me, is the question of the
Leitwörter, 'leading words'. This question is immediately relevant to the
topic of translation: the rendering of any given word, if I understand you
correctly, depends on whether this word is a leading word or not. If it is,
all its instances should be represented by a single English word, 'so that
the thematic connections not be lost'. If it is not, a 'contextual rendering'
is to be preferred as 'the most fluent, clearest, and most nuanced way to
translate'.[10] So, very much is at stake here. There is a choice between
thematic connections on the one hand, and fluency, clarity, nuance, on the

---

9.   Cf. Crisp's essay, pp. 37-49 in this volume.
10.   Cf. Fox, 'The Translation of Elijah' p. 156-69.

other. And there is a hierarchy between the two as well, thematic connections being more important than fluency. All this depends on the leading word status of a particular given word.

So what makes a word a leading word? It is my impression that the frequency of occurrence is a major factor here, but that otherwise it is to a large extent in the eye of the beholder, that is, the exegete or the translator. In the story of Naboth's vineyard, your paper singles out the verb נתן qal, 'to give', as a very obvious 'major leading word', suggesting, by the way, that there may be such things as minor leading words. It is its frequent repetition, 'at close quarters' and in a 'concentrated fashion', which prompts this judgment. According to the logic of your argument, then, it should be rendered identically in all its occurrences in this story.

However, there is a verb that is almost twice as frequent in this story, namely the verb אמר qal, 'to say'. In addition, there is a verb that is almost as frequent as נתן, namely דבר pi., 'to speak'. Indeed, the frequent use of direct discourse in rapid dialogues gives this story much of its character and coherence. Still, your paper does not mention אמר as the first major leading word, nor does it single out דבר as a minor one. Now, one might object, saying that אמר is too frequent generally for it to function as a leading word in any text. And indeed, אמר is the most frequent verb even in the Hebrew Bible as a whole. But then, נתן is in the top five of frequent verbs as well.[11] It is a very common verb indeed, a fact that would seem to undermine its potential as a leading word. נתן also has a wide range of meanings, so that, for instance, the NIV's idiomatic—functionally equivalent— renderings which your paper criticizes, can be seen as perfectly acceptable.

To quote one of your examples,[12] the NIV renders Jezebel's words thus:

> I will get the vineyard of Naboth the Jizreelite for you.

A literal version, and indeed my version, would read:

> I will give the vineyard of Naboth the Jizreelite to you.

But what exactly is it that is preserved in the literal version and lost in NIV? Is it really the link to Samuel's denunciation of the greedy king, in 1 Sam. 8? (As your paper mentions, this is actually a link that runs over the semantic opposite of giving, namely taking.) Can we conclude from the Hebrew

---

11. A.J.C. Verheij, *Bits, Bytes, and Binyanim: A Quantitative Study of Verbal Lexeme Formations in the Hebrew Bible* (Orientalia Lovaniensia Analecta, 93; Leuven: Peeters, 2000), p. 36.

12. Cf. Fox, 'The Translation of Elijah', in this volume.

that Jezebel perversely sees herself as being in possession of the vineyard already, so that she can give it to Ahab? Or would that amount to reading things into the text rather than from it? These are questions, really, not answers, let alone proofs of the rights or wrongs of one side or the other.

A Subtle, Soundless Voice

It has, of course, been impossible for me to ignore the challenge put forward in your paper, to find a suitable rendering for the famous phrase, ואחר האש קול דממה דקה, of 1 Kgs 19.12. But I am afraid a 'true solution' will indeed be very hard to find, even if, as a non-native-speaker of English, I am hardly in the position to say this. As you mentioned, Elijah is not the only one in the Hebrew Bible to hear something of this kind. Eliphaz, in the fourth chapter of the book of Job, reports on a strange night-time experience. First there is silence (דממה) and, subsequently, Eliphaz hears a 'voice' (קול) speaking to him. Or this may be a hendiadys, as some dictionaries—and Buber–Rosenzweig—suggest, so that what he hears is a דממה וקול, a silent, soundless voice. In any event, there seems to be something distinctly mysterious about this expression, which any rendering would do well to preserve. In the case of Elijah, we might think of something like 'a fragile whisper', 'the sound of subtle stillness', 'a subtle, soundless (silent) voice'.[13] It is difficult, and it will remain difficult.

In fact, I am confident—or rather, I hope—that questions such as these will be allowed to keep us busy and off the streets for whatever is going to be our share of the twenty-first century. Thank you very much for your stimulating paper.

---

13. Cf. the expression, 'une voix aussi subtile qu'un silence' J. Derrida, *Adieu à Emmanuel Levinas* (Paris: Galilée, 1997), p. 197. I am grateful to Dr H.W. Sneller for this reference.

ON BIBLE TRANSLATIONS AND COMMENTARIES

Adele Berlin

Biblical translation and commentary is the quintessential form that the study of the Bible has taken over the course of history and continues to take in our own time. While translation and commentary may occur separately, they are both parts of the same exegetical process. This type of exegesis, usually done verse by verse, while not the only form of biblical study, remains the dominant one; and so it is by considering the nature of this exegesis that we may best consider the nature of our enterprise as biblical scholars. I am going to make some observations about translations and commentaries, mainly about those in English on the Hebrew Bible, that seem simple and obvious. I do so because things are never as simple as they seem, and because by considering the ways we read and write commentaries we are really considering the ways we make and transmit meaning.

My primary concern is modern translations and commentaries, but I will make some passing observations about earlier ones because stepping out of our own context often gives us a better perspective on it. I will set up some distinctions only to blur them later, because it is always instructive to consider how things are different and how they are the same.

Before moving to a consideration of what we do when we read or write commentaries, let me point out that we seem to be doing it in ever-increasing volume. This attention being lavished on the biblical text is especially noteworthy given the fact that in educational circles no one piece of literature can claim special privilege, and the 'literary canon' is dissolving. Attention is more likely to be spread widely, to encompass lesser-known literary pieces, rather than to be lavished on one particular work.[1] Yet commentaries on the Bible are proliferating at an unbelievable rate. Just consider the following list of one-volume and multi-volume commentaries currently available and/or in production. These are only the

1. Even among biblical scholars, there is growing interest in the more obscure works of the late biblical and postbiblical periods.

better-known ones written in English, and I have not included those on the New Testament alone, or the study Bibles that contain mini-commentaries: Anchor Bible; Berit Olam; *The Expositor's Bible Commentary*; *Harper's Bible Commentary*; Hermeneia; International Critical Commentary; The International Theological Commentary; Interpretation; *The Interpreter's Bible and The New Interpreter's Bible*; *The Jerome Biblical Commentary and The New Jerome Biblical Commentary*; JPS Torah Commentary; New International Commentary on the Old Testament; Old Testament Library; Readings: A New Biblical Commentary; Tyndale Old Testament Commentary; *The Women's Bible Commentary*; Word Biblical Commentary.

A concomitant phenomenon is the proliferation of Bible translations. These are of two types. The first are translations of single books, scholarly and/or artistic translations, sometimes accompanied by notes ranging from brief comments to extensive commentaries.[2] Examples include Robert Alter's translations of Genesis and Samuel,[3] Ariel and Chana Bloch's translation of Song of Songs,[4] Marcia Falk's renderings of Song of Songs,[5] E.M. Good's work on Job,[6] Steven Mitchell's translations of Genesis and Job,[7] Raymond Scheindlin's Job,[8] and many others; and the volumes in series like Anchor Bible and the Old Testament Library in which the commentators also present their own translations. More ambitious in scope, but also the work of one individual, is Everett Fox's *The Five Books of*

2.   The more artistic or literary translations are often published by major publishing houses and aimed at a wider audience than the more scholarly ones generally reach.

3.   R. Alter, *Genesis: Translation and Commentary* (New York: W.W. Norton, 1996) and *The Davidic Story: A Translation with Commentary of 1 and 2 Samuel* (New York: W.W. Norton, 1999).

4.   A. Bloch and C. Bloch, *The Song of Songs: A New Translation with an Introduction and Commentary* (New York: Random House, 1995).

5.   M. Falk, *Love Lyrics from the Bible: A Translation and Literary Study of the Song of Songs* (Sheffield: Almond Press, 1982); and *The Song of Songs: A New Translation and Interpretation* (San Francisco: Harper, 1990).

6.   E.M. Good, *In Turns of Tempest: A Reading of Job with Translation* (Stanford: Stanford University Press, 1990).

7.   S. Mitchell, *Genesis: A New Translation of the Classic Biblical Stories* (New York: HarperCollins, 1996); and Mitchell, *The Book of Job: Translated and with an Introduction* (San Francisco: North Point Press, 1987). An earlier version of the translation was published as *Into the Whirlwind* (Garden City, NY: Doubleday, 1979).

8.   R. Scheindlin, *The Book of Job: Translation, Introduction, and Notes* (New York: W.W. Norton, 1998).

Moses.[9] In the more scholarly of these volumes, the commentary predominates, taking up far more space than the translation. The proportion is reversed in the artistic translations, where the translation is the main focus and the notes or comments play a secondary role.

The second type is the translations by teams of experts, like the *Tanakh* (=NJPS), New English Bible, Revised English Bible, New Revised Standard Version, New American Bible, New International Version. (Note how many are new or revised versions of older translations, some of those not so very old themselves.) New linguistic, historical, and even literary knowledge is only part of the story. The truth is that the 'canonical' English translations have lost their power. The magnificence of the King James no longer resonates with many readers, although some still prefer it. What they prefer, however, is not actually the original King James Version, but an updated version that is easier for the modern English reader. Whether we are updating older translations or translating anew, we need to retranslate the Bible to reflect our own concerns and tastes, rather than rely on a previous generation's translation.

All of this exegetical activity is encouraging because it tells us, first of all, that the Bible is still a foundational document whose meaning is important to many readers; and, second, that new academic trends and socio-religious needs necessitate new ways of reading the Bible.

I will devote the rest of this essay to three areas of discussion: the relationship between text and commentary; modern interpretive approaches and how they are changing; and ecumenism and multiculturalism in biblical exegesis.

The Relationship between Text and Commentary

From a formal point of view, the commentary is separate from the text, as its visual form in printed editions suggests. Except for some interlinear translations and grammatical crutches, intended as crib sheets for students, the reader's eye must leave the text and find the commentary somewhere else on the page or on following pages. The format may present a segmented section of the text, a pericope or a chapter, followed by a commentary or commentaries, as in many modern publications; or it may present a

---

9. E. Fox, *The Five Books of Moses: Genesis Exodus, Leviticus, Numbers, Deuteronomy: A New Translation with Introduction, Commentary and Notes* (The Schocken Bible, 1; New York: Schocken Books, 1995).

running text with a running commentary or commentaries, as in the hyper-text arrangement in the Rabbinic Bible (*Miqra'ot Gedolot*). Whatever the arrangement, the commentary is visually distinguished from the biblical text. It is clearly not integral to the text but stands outside of it: a metatext.

But the notion of commentary as metatext may be violated in at least two ways. The commentary may become a text in its own right, as it does when there are supercommentaries on it. That is, the commentary becomes the object of study, rather than the biblical text on which it is based. This also happens when we study the history of biblical interpretation. The inquiry is not aimed to discover the meaning of the Bible, but rather the meaning that previous exegetes ascribed to it. I note that the history of interpretation is currently enjoying a resurgence of attention, no doubt due to the fact that postmodern scholars have abandoned the idea that a text has one meaning in favor of the view that it has multiple meanings. There is little point to a search for the one correct meaning of a text if that mean-ing does not exist. Those multiple meanings become much more interest-ing because they shed as much light on their authors and audiences as they do on the text.

In a rather different context, the exegesis in the commentary may become fused with the text. This is most obvious in religious communities that direct the interpretation towards their own beliefs or traditions. For example, in some Orthodox Jewish circles, the Torah is studied with Rashi's commentary, and for many students in these circles Rashi's inter-pretation comes to be synonymous with the meaning of the text. It is easy to see this process occurring in a context far removed from most of us, but it occurs more often than we realize and may, indeed, be inevitable. To the extent that we are persuaded by the commentary, it embodies for us *the* meaning of the text. I am touching upon the thorny issue of how commu-nities of readers make and validate meaning, an issue I will not pursue here. The point that I want to make in terms of commentaries is that, while commentaries are usually visually distinguishable from the text, their interpretations may not always be mentally distinguishable from the text. But the visual presentation reminds us that, theoretically at least, text and commentary are distinct.

Compare commentaries with translations. If commentaries are inter-pretations that stand alongside the text, translations are interpretations that seek to replace the text. They obviously do so for those who cannot read the text in its original language. And they do so not only as a matter of convenience, as in comparative literature courses, but in ways that have major repercussions for large communities. I think here of the adoption of the Vulgate by the Roman Catholic Church, or the veneration of the King James Version among English-speaking Christians. (As the joke goes, 'If the King James was good enough for St Paul, it's good enough for us'.) In fact, awareness of the equivocal relationship between the text and its translation goes back to the first translation of the Bible, the Septuagint, and its validation in the *Letter of Aristeas*.

Since in normative Jewish public recitation the Hebrew text of the Bible has never been displaced by a translation, ancient and modern Jewish translations have remained subordinate to it. The Targum, however, was held in great respect by the Jews; it was considered part of the Oral Law and contained authoritative interpretations. It is fascinating to see the delicate balance that the rabbis attempted to maintain between the biblical text and its Aramaic translation.

In rabbinic times, the Targum was used in three settings: the synagogue, private study, and the school. In the synagogue, the Targum accompanied the public reading of the Torah. Philip S. Alexander summarizes the process stipulated in rabbinic sources:

> As the biblical lessons were read out (both Tora and Haftara) they were simultaneously rendered into Aramaic... Every effort had to be made to avoid confusing the targum with the written text of Scripture. The Scripture reader and the translator must be two different people. The Scripture reader had to be clearly seen to be *reading* from the scroll; the translator had to recite the targum from memory: he was not allowed to use a written text in synagogue, nor was he permitted to glance at the Tora scroll—'lest the people should say that the translation is written in the Tora'. Nor was the reader allowed to prompt him if he faltered. Translation was simultaneous but targum was not allowed to overlay Scripture: Scripture and targum were delivered alternately...[10]

While this clearly shows that a distinction was maintained between text and translation, Alexander also notes the opposite tendency in the public reading.

> The reader and translator stood side by side. Only small portions of the original were read against the translation, and while the translation and original were not allowed to overlap, ideally there should be no pause between

---

10. P.S. Alexander, 'Jewish Aramaic Translations of Hebrew Scripture', in M.J. Mulder (ed.), *Mikra: Text, Translation, Reading and Interpretation of the Hebrew Bible in Ancient Judaism and Early Christianity* (Assen: Van Gorcum; Philadelphia: Fortress Press, 1988), pp. 217-53 (238).

> Scripture and targum; Scripture and targum were intended to form one con-
> tinuous, seamless text; they interlocked to make a single unit.[11]

The same interdependence and separateness of Targum and Scripture is seen in private study. In preparing the weekly portion privately, in anticipation of hearing it in the synagogue, one was bidden to read it 'twice in the Bible (*Miqra'*) and once in the Targum' (*b. Ber.* 8a). Once again, the Targum accompanies the biblical passage but remains separate from it, and slightly inferior to it in status.

When a translation replaces the text, that is, becomes the text, it provides the possibility of another type of metatext: a commentary on a translation. Examples based on modern translations are the New Century Bible Commentary, based on the Revised Standard Version, the Cambridge Bible Commentary on the New English Bible, and the JPS Torah Commentary, based on the NJPS translation. When the author of such a commentary is not the author of the translation, tensions may arise between the translator's interpretation and the commentator's interpretation. The commentator may critique the translation, or argue against it. The commentator engages with the translation just as an exegete engages with another exegete's interpretation.

Translations sometimes are called upon to replace parts of the text even for those who know the original language, especially if the translations are old enough, literal enough, and/or if they solve textual problems. In fact, much of the work of textual criticism consists of replacing the Masoretic Text (MT) with readings from the Ancient Versions. The quest purports to be a restoration of the original text underlying the MT—that is, the replacement of the extant text by a hypothetical *Ur-text*; but the result is a composite of the MT and Hebrew translations of words in the Ancient Versions—the later being translations of translations.[12] It may be no accident that most text critics who use the Ancient Versions in this way grew up in Christian traditions where the MT had been replaced, at least liturgically if not theologically, by the LXX, the Vulgate, the KJV, or other English translations.

We often forget that a translation is a form of commentary, especially when it is literal; but when a translation becomes freer, or departs too radically from the literal rendering of the text, it becomes unmasked for what it

---

11. Alexander, 'Jewish Aramaic Translations', pp. 238-39.

12. I have discussed this matter at greater length in Adele Berlin, *Zephaniah* (AB, 25A; New York: Doubleday, 1994), pp. 23-31.

is—someone's interpretation. Again, a look at the Targum is instructive, for the Targum is often a paraphrase, at times quite expansive, rather than a literal rendering. A particularly egregious example is the Targum Rishon on Est. 6.12. The MT reads המן נדחף אל ביתו אבל וחפוי ראש 'Haman hurried home, mourning and head covered'.

This is rendered in the Targum Rishon as 'Haman hurriedly went to his house, mourning for his daughter, and with his head covered, as one mourning for shame and his disgrace' (Grossfeld's translation[13]).

The idea that Haman was mourning for his daughter rather than for his own fallen state, was anticipated in the Targum's rendering of the previous verse:

> As they were walking [i.e. Haman leading Mordecai on the horse] opposite the house of the wicked Haman, Shlakhtevath, his daughter, looked down from the roof, and it appeared that the man walking on the road was Mordecai, while the man riding on the horse was her father. So she took a pot of excrement and flung it on his head. He raised his head and said to her: 'You, too, my daughter, you embarrass me.' Whereupon, immediately she fell from the roof and died from the balcony chamber.[14]

This story is not idiosyncratic to the Targum. It is cited in the Talmud (*b. Meg.* 16a) and in other midrashic collections, and is part of the exegetical milieu reflected in the Targum Rishon. It provides a particularly dramatic example of the principle that all translations operate within an exegetical milieu and partake of it. We should not dismiss this translation as a flawed effort to render the MT into Aramaic; rather we should understand it for what it is: a midrashic explanation of the sense of a biblical passage, as it was accepted by the Aramaic-speaking Jewish community. Translation is an abbreviated form of exegesis: exegesis that does not have the space to explain or justify itself. In fact, individual modern translators have a hard time writing a translation without accompanying explanation, as we see from the recent translations like those of Alter, Bloch, Scheindlin and others.

The reverse is also true. For those writing a commentary in a language other than Hebrew, there is almost a compulsion to translate the Hebrew text before commenting upon it. I can think of few commentaries that do not contain a translation by the commentator (except those, as mentioned above, that are based on standard translations). This is another proof that

---

13. B. Grossfeld, *The Two Targums of Esther* (Collegeville, MN: Liturgical Press, 1991).

14. Grossfeld, *The Two Targums*, pp. 72-73.

translation is an aspect of exegesis. In fact, much of modern commentary is an explanation or justification of the translation, or an expansion of it.

E.M. Good confronts this issue directly in his *In Turns of Tempest: A Reading of Job with a Translation.*

> The second part of this book presents a reading of the Book of Job; the first part presents the Book of Job that the second part reads. Because most English-speaking readers do not know Hebrew, the book must be presented in an English translation. Even good English translations, however, have serious flaws. To refer readers to them would necessitate constantly interjecting disagreements with this rendering or that one. So I present my own.
>
> Does the world need another translation of Job? The question can be answered in the affirmative only on grounds that (1) this translation is better than, or as good as, others; or (2) this translation is necessary to what follows it. I cannot make the first claim with a straight face, though I think mine is better in some respects than others. I can make the second claim. Only one translation always agrees with me: my own. That is the only excuse for attempting it, and it may be my translation's sole virtue and major fault.[15]

Good is forthright, in a tongue-in-cheek way. The excuse that his readers do not know Hebrew is, however, just an excuse. What he is really saying is that translation is part and parcel of exegesis, when it is done in a language different from the original language of the text. Hebrew-writing exegetes do not translate the Hebrew Bible, of course, but they often paraphrase it, and may occasionally translate an obscure or difficult construction into a different language known to their readers.[16] It now begins to appear that the distinction I made earlier between commentary, which stand alongside the text, and translations, which replace the text, has become blurred. Both translation and commentary 'interpret and recreate the text'.[17]

Interpretive Approaches and How They Are Changing

Many of the commentary series that I listed earlier were begun two or three decades ago, and their editorial statements of purpose, still unchanged, reflect the interpretive approach of that time. The Hermeneia

---

15. Good, *In Turns of Tempest*, p. 12.

16. Rashi renders some terms in Old French and A.B. Ehrlich inserts German renderings into his *Mikra Ki-feshuto* (New York: Ktav, 1969 [1899–1901]).

17. Gerald Hammond, 'English Translations of the Bible', in R. Alter and F. Kermode (eds.), *The Literary Guide to the Bible* (Cambridge, MA: Belnap, 1987), pp. 666-49 (647), says of translation that 'it both interprets and recreates the text it addresses'.

series, for example, is 'designed to be a critical and historical commentary' utilizing 'the full range of philological and historical tools, including textual criticism...the methods of the history of tradition...and the history of religion'. The Anchor Bible tells us that it is 'an effort to make available all the significant historical and linguistic knowledge which bears on the interpretation of the biblical record'. These two well-regarded series are emblematic of mid-twentieth-century biblical scholarship, which was philological and historical. For most of the twentieth century, and even now in certain circles, this was the model of scholarship drawn from the Humanities and was considered the only way to interpret the Bible.

The historical approach implies more than just general knowledge of the historical background and the realia of everyday life. It means discovering the precise moment in history from which a piece dates; the exact event or situation that gave birth to it; who wrote it and why. The kind of background information that students of modern literature come by easily and take as a starting point, became the main focus of biblicists and absorbed most of their energy, because this information is extraordinarily difficult to uncover for ancient texts.

The historical approach and the discovery of the author, even if he is an anonymous construct, leads quickly to the question of authorial intention. I want to pursue this issue a bit further: first as it applies to the writer of the biblical text and then as it applies to the writer of the commentary.

I begin with a statement by John Bright, a scholar better known in academic circles for his commentaries and historical studies than for his book entitled *The Authority of the Old Testament*, from which I am about to quote.[18] In this book, published in 1967, Bright aligns his scholarly practices with his religious faith. As a Protestant, Bright denied the church the right to control biblical interpretation; yet he was reluctant to grant to each individual reader, no matter what his/her level of learning, equal authority to interpret Scripture. He reserved full rights of interpretation for members of the academic guild and those who accepted the academic way of doing things. His explanation of how the Bible is to be interpreted is remarkable for its clarity and for its self-assuredness:

> As scholars today would unanimously agree, there is but one admissible method for arriving at the meaning of the biblical text: the grammatico-historical method. That is to say, the text is to be taken as meaning what its words most plainly mean in the light of the situation (historical situation or

18. John Bright, *The Authority of the Old Testament* (Grand Rapids: Baker Book House, 1967).

life situation) to which they were originally addressed... It becomes, therefore, the task of the student to determine as accurately as he can, with the
aid of all the tools that lie at his disposal, what Isaiah or Jeremiah... *actually
intended to say*. In this way alone can the true meaning of the biblical word
be arrived at.[19]

One can detect more than a bit of Protestantism in this back-to-the-
original-meaning movement, for it has echoes of *sola scriptura* as it neatly
bypasses the interpretation of the church. But, the search for the literal
meaning in its original context predates the Reformation and is not limited
to Protestants.[20] In modern times, even the Roman Catholic Church
espoused this approach. The 1943 encyclical, *Divino afflante Spiritu*, made
a place for the study of the literal sense, the determination of the character
and context of the sacred author and the forms of expression that he
employed. Following this lead, the 1968 edition of *The Jerome Biblical
Commentary*, a work by Roman Catholic scholars, was written 'according
to the principles of modern biblical criticism' (p. xvii) and takes upon
itself 'to interpret the Scriptures as accurately as possible according to the
mind of the men who wrote them' (p. xviii).

On the secular literary scene, too, the notion that the text's meaning was
synonymous with the author's intention was an assumption shared by
interpreters of all literary texts until quite recently, notwithstanding the
advent of 'the intentional fallacy', first proposed in 1946 by W.K. Wimsatt
and Monroe C. Beardsley.

Again, the study of the Bible reflects the general intellectual milieu in
which it is situated. As academic currents change, so will the study of the
Bible. Nowadays, the Humanities and the Social Sciences are providing
new insights about literature and literary theory, cultural and political perspectives, cognitive processes, and about the construction of knowledge
itself. Scholars in all disciplines are more concerned with the way they
make meaning. Biblicists, to the extent that they see themselves as partici-
pants in modern intellectual life, will and should incorporate this new
knowledge, and the new approaches that accompany it, into their study of
the Bible. There is already ample evidence that this is occurring, even
within established commentary series, although it is not loudly pro-
claimed. A few new series, though, have made a point of their innovative

---

19. Bright, *Authority*, p. 42. (Emphasis in the original.)

20. J.D. Levenson, *The Hebrew Bible, the Old Testament and Historical Criticism*
(Louisville, KY: Westminster/John Knox Press, 1993), p. 90.

approach to commentary. Readings: A New Biblical Commentary adver-tises that it 'represents a refreshing departure from the traditional concerns and modes of discourse of the commentary genre'. The departure is reflected in the form, which is not a verse-by-verse commentary but rather a discussion, or 'reading' of large sections of text.[21]

Berit Olam does not call itself a commentary, but bears the subtitle 'Studies in Hebrew Narrative & Poetry'.[22] It is, nonetheless, a commentary and the Library of Congress cataloging data rightly considers it one. Like many recent commentaries, these emphasize literary issues more than historical and philological ones.

It is not only a question of adding, say, literary or psychological data to the historical and linguistic information already provided. Nor is it just a question of new approaches or methodologies, although these, to be sure, are having their impact. I would cast the change in a broader theoretical perspective that I call a movement away from the contraction of meaning and toward the expansion of meaning. This expansion—a broadening of the scope of investigation—is noticeable with increasing frequency even within individual volumes, and is surely evident when we look at the total range of interpretations being put forth.

The expansion of meaning occurs in several related ways. First is the consideration of meaning across time: the history of the interpretation. In addition to considering the meaning of a passage for the original audience, one may consider its meaning for a later editor, for an audience shortly after the work was canonized, and, in theory, for any audience that has sought meaning in the passage. In practice, however, those who study the history of interpretation rarely include its most recent history in their purview. This type of expansion of meaning is driven mainly by develop-ments from within biblical studies, like the rise of redaction criticism and canonical criticism, and the growing interest in the Second Temple period. The flowering of Jewish Studies has also contributed to this effort, as has the availability of critical editions of ancient and medieval texts. The fortunate result is that the study of interpretation is gaining importance in its own right. That is, Bible scholars are not only interpreting the Bible;

---

21. This is not altogether new, since many older commentaries also have 'readings' of large sections, in addition to line-by-line exegesis.

22. I am critical of the use of 'Hebrew' when it is 'Hebrew Bible' that is meant. 'Hebrew Narrative and Poetry' takes in much literature beyond the Bible, from rabbinic times until today, but one would not know it from this subtitle.

they are more engaged in learning how earlier interpreters have done so. As this happens, earlier commentaries become texts, not only metatexts, for they themselves will become the subject of examination. Ironically, for most of this century biblical scholars have had a great interest in the history of the biblical text but little interest in the history of its interpretation. That is slowly changing.

Postmodern trends in literary theory and cultural studies are propelling changes that also result in the expansion of meaning. The emphasis here is generally on the present or recent past, and on diverse ethnic, religious, and sociopolitical communities of readers. Expanded definitions of 'text' and 'interpretation' lead me to include under this rubric interpretations in various media, in the visual and performing arts, as well as interpretations through the written or spoken word. The field of biblical interpretation has suddenly become very rich.

A slightly different aspect of the expansion of meaning is the presentation of multiple interpretations by an exegete, especially when there is a crux, but even whenever there is an interesting alternative. It is becoming more acceptable for a commentator to present the possibilities without necessarily choosing among them. Actually, the practice of providing alternative interpretations is not new, but had been more limited in scholarly commentaries during the height of the historical-critical school. Historical-critical scholars sought the 'true' meaning, of which there could be only one, so they were not generally sympathetic to entertaining too many possibilities. Under the influence of postmodernism, many today prize not so much the 'right answer' but rather any answer that can be cogently argued and supported with acceptable proof. The corollary is that there are many right answers. Increasingly I sense, although I cannot document it statistically, that even commentators who use the historical-critical approach are more likely to offer a greater variety of plausible explanations and can tolerate greater ambiguity or lack of certainty in their interpretations.

It is not altogether clear yet where this will lead, but already commentaries, individually and certainly as a group, are beginning to make reference to a greater variety of possibilities for the original meaning, and to cite portions of the early and recent history of interpretation. The trend may be to present a menu of interpretations and let the reader choose among them. The future may hold multivocal and multimedia commentaries.

Ecumenism and Multiculturalism in Biblical Exegesis

While modern literary critics have loudly discredited the search for the author's intention, they continue to search for it, although, of course, in an entirely new guise. It has become fashionable for modern authors to declare their ethnic and gender credentials and to confess their biases. And if they fail to do so, their reviewers will do it for them. Modern critics also look for these attributes in earlier authors and use them to uncover the authors' agendas. The motives of the author, nowadays generally perceived as political, point the way to the meaning of the work.

In biblical studies this process operates in the reverse direction. Because we know nothing about the biblical authors outside of what we can deduce from their works, we must first interpret the meaning of the works in order to understand the motives of the authors, so we find ourselves in a hermeneutic circle. Nevertheless, biblical scholars, in tangent with their peers in the Humanities, are beginning to uncover the political and religious ideologies of the biblical writings, and their analyses are providing a new dimension to our understanding of these books.[23]

Actually, 'the intentional fallacy' is something of a red herring. Its home is in New Criticism, a movement that saw a literary composition as an autonomous object, independent of its author's biography or its place in the historical world. Poststructuralism, and especially New Historicism, have changed that view, and once again see the value of knowing the historical or political milieu from which a composition emerged. Historical-critical studies of the Bible are under attack by postmodernists not for their attempts to understand the times and authors that produced the Bible, but because they seek an objective truth about the meaning of the Bible. The postmodernist is skeptical about any claim to have found *the* meaning and is suspicious of interpreters and their motives. Postmodernism views interpretation as a political act, and often finds the analysis of the interpreter's intention more interesting than whatever meaning the text may have once had. This is a search for authorial intention one step removed from the original author. In this spirit I will make some general observations on the motives of the authors of biblical commentaries in the recent past and in the present.

The first observation, alluded to before, is that biblical scholars have

---

23. These studies range from the healthy to the extreme, but this is not the place to critique them.

adopted the goals and methods of the secular academy, and, in large measure derive their legitimacy from the secular academy. Although these goals and methods may have, at their inception, stood in sharp contrast to religious dogmas, it was not long before biblical scholars devised ways of harmonizing their secular practices with their religious beliefs. The passage by John Bright that I cited earlier is a classic example. To his mind, the demands of the scientific study of the Bible are in absolute harmony with his Protestant beliefs. Most Protestants would undoubtedly agree, for in some ways the historical-critical approach serves the needs of a Protestant agenda.[24] On the other hand, the focus on the original meaning of the Hebrew Bible, clearly a non-Christian work with a non-Christian message, countermands the Christian need to see the Old Testament as a forerunner and adumbration of the New Testament. A Christian interpretation, and for that matter any religious interpretation, must view the meaning of the Bible as transcending its original sense or the intention of its author. Or, to put it even more bluntly, it must equate its own interpretation with the original meaning. It is difficult, if not impossible, to harmonize a truly historical-critical approach with a religious approach. Nonetheless, attempts at harmonization are not easily abandoned. David Noel Freedman takes the effort a step beyond Bright, hoping that religious dogma may change under the influence of the scientific study of the Bible.[25] This is not scholarship being brought into line with religion, but religion being brought into line with scholarship.

The point that I am making is that among biblical scholars there is a complex and largely unacknowledged interaction between one's academic and religious tenets. This interaction comes into sharper focus as the academic tenets change, as they are now doing.

We may characterize an overarching tenet of the middle of the twentieth century as the suppression of difference, to be compared with the tenet at

24. See M. Greenberg, 'Reflections on Interpretation', in M. Greenberg, *Studies in the Bible and Jewish Thought* (Philadelphia: Jewish Publication Society of America, 1995), pp. 227-34; and also Levenson, *The Hebrew Bible*.

25. '...biblical exposition may win a respectful hearing among the dogmatics and ecclesiastics. Its message may find a way into the areas of faith and practice. Just as the liturgy has been studied and revised in the light of ancient tradition, so doctrine itself can be scrutinized in the light of biblical truth. Adaption and adjustment to the changing conditions of life have always marked the Church.' D.N. Freedman, 'Modern Scripture Research and Ecumenism', in J. Huddlestun (ed.), *Divine Commitment and Human Obligation* (Grand Rapids: Eerdmans, 1996), pp. 165-71 (171). First published in *Pittsburgh Perspective* 4/3 (1963), pp. 15-22.

the end of the twentieth century—the celebration of difference. In biblical studies the suppression of difference manifests itself as academic ecumenism and the celebration of difference as academic multiculturalism. As one might expect, they both have their benefits and their disadvantages.

One of the benefits of historical-philological criticism is that anyone who knows the rules can play the game. Personal beliefs or religious affiliation, which formerly served as barriers to a shared discourse about the Bible, could be put aside in the quest for objective truth. This ecumenism is celebrated opposite the title page in the Anchor Bible:

> The Anchor Bible is a project of international and interfaith scope: Protestant, Catholic, and Jewish scholars from many countries contribute individual volumes. The project is not sponsored by any ecclesiastical organization and is not intended to reflect any particular theological doctrine.

The Hermenia series echoes this thought. It is 'international and interconfessional in the selection of authors' and the editors 'impose no systematic-theological perspective upon the series'. *The Jerome Biblical Commentary*, while modern in its approach, balked at the ecumenical selection of authors and apologetically explained that the editors felt that 'they could best serve the ecumenical needs of the times by producing a truly modern commentary by Roman Catholics' (p. xviii). In the 1968 edition, the hope was that the rest of the world would see that Roman Catholics could be just as good as other modern biblical scholars and that non-Catholics would 'find in this commentary the same scientific method and love for objectivity that characterize the best commentaries written by scholars of their own denominations'. By 1990, these goals had been realized but were still deemed important enough to preserve. *The New Jerome Biblical Commentary* did not include non-Catholics, although it did add lay contributors and women. And it reiterated the view of the 1968 edition that Catholics and non-Catholics could work together and share the same goals in their study of the Bible.

This ecumenism among biblical scholars suppressed any religious difference that existed among them, although, from time to time one could detect signs of a denominational perspective in some commentaries. This trend was very much in line with the general view in the secular academy—that religion was not to influence one's scholarly pursuits and that if one espoused sectarian interpretations it was best to keep them to oneself.

With the coming of postmodernism came the principle that one's beliefs, experiences, and especially one's particular location in terms of race, class and gender, could not help influencing one's scholarly pursuits and conclusions; and that, in fact, of objective truth was a will-o'-the-wisp. This spawned the diversity or multicultural movement, in which certain parts of one's identity that were earlier ignored or suppressed suddenly rose to the surface as the most dominant features in the creation of meaning. Concommitant with this came the shift from objectivity to advocacy. In biblical studies, as elsewhere, this is most evident in the growth of feminist interpretation, and is now being joined by increasing focus on the interpretations of various ethnic communities, especially African American, Latin American and Asian. This focus must, by definition, shift the emphasis from the original meaning, or the intention of the original author, to the meaning or meanings elicited by different communities at different times and places.

But because the academy's form of multiculturalism is stridently secular, one aspect of personal identity is largely missing, and that is the aspect of religion. That the secular academy should ignore religion is understandable, although not laudable, given its suspicion or abhorrence of anything religious. Be that as it may, religion is multiculturalism's last frontier, and I predict that it will soon be discovered and colonized. However, that biblical studies should ignore religion is, in light of its history and of the nature of the book that forms its centerpiece, truly amazing. Now, to be sure, there has been much more interest in traditional Christian and Jewish exegesis, as part of the history of interpretation; and midrash and the medieval Jewish commentaries have become rather popular because of their contributions to the postmodern notion of multivalence and polysemy in texts. But what about the religious bias of the modern exegete? Few people are asking overtly if and how modern exegesis is influenced by the religious persuasion of the exegete. This question was always in the minds of the reader, but in the ecumenical days, it was taboo to raise it in the academy. Nowadays, I would expect that it would be more openly discussed, but I see only a glimmer of interest among some feminist and some Jewish biblical scholars. Feminists have had to acknowledge the ethnic and social differences among themselves, and in the sphere of religious studies they have had to acknowledge their religious differences. Jewish scholars have harbored the misgiving that the historical-critical approach was at best Christian and at worst anti-Semitic.

This is uncharted territory for biblical scholars, dangerous because it threatens to unravel the unspoken agreement among them that academic scholarship is objective, but potentially beneficial in that it can more honestly recognize differences among exegetes. The new academy will not make everyone the same; it will accept everyone in his or her difference. Another danger is the Balkanization of biblical scholarship into various ethnic and religious constituencies. One of the paradoxes of multiculturalism is that at the same time that it opens the door to formerly excluded groups, it risks tolerating a new type of exclusivity. Religious exclusivity has long been present in biblical studies; it predates ecumenism and was not entirely banished by it. I have noted the problem that *The Jerome Biblical Commentary* had with religious ecumenism; I would add the same for the Jewish Publication Society's translation and commentary, and the lack of gender ecumenism in *The Women's Bible Commentary*. This type of exclusivity is both old and new. In its new form it mirrors events in the larger contemporary society, even beyond the academy, where minorities reserve the right to be exclusive even as they demand inclusiveness from the majority.

We have yet to see how all of this will play out in the field of biblical studies. A new generation of scholars is poised to take the lead, with energy and enthusiasm, with ideas and ideologies, and with scholarly tools and technologies beyond the wildest dreams of earlier generations. The struggle over ways of finding or constructing meaning in the Bible is a sign of the vitality of the Bible and of the disciplines that are engaged in its study.[26]

26. Some of the material in this paper is also contained in 'Observations on Biblical Interpretation in the United States on the Eve of the 21st Century' in *Studies in Bible and Exegesis. Vol. 5. Presented to Uriel Simon* (Ramat Gan: Bar Ilan University Press, 2000), pp. 385-93.

BIBLIOGRAPHY

Aaron, D.H., 'Early Rabbinic Exegesis on Noah's Son Ham and the So-Called "Hamitic Myth"', *JAAR* 63/4 (1995), pp. 721-59.

Adam, A.K.M., *What is Postmodern Biblical Criticism?* (Minneapolis: Fortress Press, 1995).

Ade Ajayi, J.F., *Christian Missions in Nigeria, 1841–1891: The Making of a New Elite* (Evanston, IL: Northwestern University Press, 1969).

Aichele, G. *et al.*, *The Postmodern Bible* (New Haven: Yale University Press, 1995).

Alexander, P.S., 'Jewish Aramaic Translations of Hebrew Scripture', in M.J. Mulder (ed.), *Mikra: Text, Translation, Reading and Interpretation of the Hebrew Bible in Ancient Judaism and Early Christianity* (Assen: Van Gorcum; Philadelphia Fortress Press, 1988), pp. 217-53.

Allen, Charlotte, *The Human Christ: The Search for the Historical Jesus* (New York: Free Press, 1998).

Allert, C.D., 'Is a Translation Inspired? The Problems of Verbal Inspiration for Translation and a Proposed Solution', in Porter and Hess (eds.), *Translating the Bible*, pp. 85-113.

Alter, Robert, *The Art of Biblical Narrative* (New York: Basic Books, 1981).

—*The Davidic Story: A Translation with Commentary of 1 and 2 Samuel* (New York: W.W. Norton, 1999).

—*Genesis: Translation and Commentary* (New York: W.W. Norton & Co., 1996).

Alter, R., and F. Kermode (eds.), *The Literary Guide to the Bible* (Cambridge, MA: Harvard University Press, 1987).

Aricheia, D.C., 'Theology and Translation: *The Implications of Certain Theological Issues to the Translation Task*', in Stine (ed.), *Bible Translation*, pp. 40-67.

Bailey, Randall C., and Tina Pippin (eds.), *Race, Class, and the Politics of Bible Translation* (Semeia, 76; Atlanta: Scholars Press, 1996).

Barrett, D., *Schism and Renewal in Africa* (Nairobi: Oxford University Press, 1968).

Bauer, W., *Griechisch-Deutsches Wörterbuch zu den Schriften des Neuen Testaments und der frühchristlichen Literatur*, 6. völlig neu bearbeitete Auflage herausgegeben von Kurt Aland und Barbara Aland (Berlin: W. de Gruyter, 1988).

Bediako, K., 'Epilogue', in Schaaf (ed.), *On Their Way Rejoicing*, pp. 243-54.

—'Understanding African Theology in the 20th Century', *Bulletin for Contextual Theology in Southern Africa & Africa* 3/2 (1996), pp. 1-11. (Previously published in *Themelios* 20/1, pp. 14-20).

Berlin, A., *Zephaniah* (Anchor Bible; New York: Doubleday, 1994).

Bevans, S.B., *Models of Contextual Theology* (Faith and Cultures Series; Maryknoll, NY: Orbis Books, 1992).

Bloch, A., and C. Bloch, *The Song of Songs: A New Translation with an Introduction and Commentary* (New York: Random House, 1995).

Blyden, Edward Wilmot, *The Three Needs of Liberia: A Lecture Delivered at Lower Buchanan, Grand Bassa Country, Liberia, January 26, 1908* (London: C.M. Phillips, 1908).

Bockmuehl, M., 'A Commentator's Approach to the "Effective History" of Philippians', *JSNT* 60 (1995), pp. 57-88.

Bonner, G., 'Augustine as Biblical Scholar', in Lampe (ed.), *The Cambridge History*, I.

Brenner, A., and J.W. van Henten (eds.), *Recycling Biblical Figures* (STAR, 1; Leiden: DEO Publishing, 1999).

Breukelman, F.H., and B.P.M. Hemelsoet, 'Van "Nieuwe Vertaling" naar "Groot Nieuws". Over het grondbeginsel van bijbelvertalen', *Amsterdamse cahiers voor exegese en Bijbelse theologie* 6 (1985), pp. 9-22.

Brichto, Herbert Chanan, *Toward a Grammar of Biblical Poetics: Tales of the Prophets* (New York: Oxford University Press, 1992).

Brichto, Sidney, *The Peoples Bible* (London: Sinclair–Stevenson, 2000).

Bright, J., *The Authority of the Old Testament* (Grand Rapids: Baker Book House, 1967).

Brown, R.E., J.A. Fitzmyer, and R.E. Murphy, *The Jerome Biblical Commentary* (Englewood Cliffs, NJ: Prentice-Hall, 1968).

—*The New Jerome Biblical Commentary* (Englewood Cliffs, NJ: Prentice Hall, 1990).

Bruce, F.F., *The English Bible* (London: Methuen, 1961).

Buber, Martin, and Franz Rosenzweig, *Scripture and Translation* (trans. Lawrence Rosenwald with Everett Fox; Bloomington: Indiana University Press, 1994 [ET of *Die Schrift und ihre Verdeutschung*, 1936]).

Buber, Martin, 'Leitwortstil im Erzählung des Pentateuchs', in Martin Buber and Franz Rosenzweig, *Die Schrift und ihre Verdeutschung* (Berlin: Schocken, 1936), pp. 11-38.

—*Moses* (The East and West Library; Oxford: Phaidon Press, 1946).

Bush, Peter, 'The Art of Translation' (The British Council Literary Translation Exhibition, www.literarytranslation.com, 1999).

Cady Stanton, Elizabeth *et al.* (eds.), *The Woman's Bible* (repr.; Salem: Ayer, 1986 [1895–98]).

Carroll, Robert, and Stephen Prickett (eds.), *The Bible: Authorized King James Version* (The World's Classics; Oxford: Oxford University Press, 1997).

Carroll, Robert, 'As Seeing the Invisible: Ideology in Bible Translation', *JNSL* 19 (1993), pp. 79-93.

—'Cultural Encroachment and Bible Translation: Observations on Elements of Violence, Race and Class in the Production of Bibles in Translation', in Bailey and Pippin (eds.), *Race, Class, and the Politics of Bible Translation* (Semeia 76; Atlanta, GA: Scholars Press, 1996), pp. 39-53.

—'Desire Under the Terebinths: On Pornographic Representation in the Prophets—A Response', in A. Brenner (ed.), *A Feminist Companion to the Latter Prophets* (FCB, 8; Sheffield: Sheffield Academic Press, 1995), pp. 275-307.

—'He-Bibles and She-Bibles: Reflections on the Violence Done to Texts by Productions of English Translations of the Bible', *BibInt* 4 (1996), pp. 257-69.

—'Lower Case Bibles: Commodity Culture and the Bible', in J.C. Exum and S.D. Moore (eds.), *Biblical Studies/Cultural Studies*, pp. 46-69.

—' "Strange Fire": Abstract of Presence Absent in the Text. Meditations on Exodus 3 (for George Steiner on his 65th Birthday)', *JSOT* 61 (Sheffield: Sheffield Academic Press, 1994), pp. 39-58.

Carson, D.A., 'New Bible Translations: An Assessment and Prospect', in Kee (ed.), *The Bible in the Twenty-First Century*, pp. 37-67.

Castelli, Elizabeth, *et al.*, 'Special Section on Feminist Translation of the New Testament', *JFSR* 6.2 (1990), pp. 25-85.

Chagall, Marc, *Le Message Biblique* (Nice: Musée du Message Biblique. Musée Cimiez).

Clarke, Adam, *The Holy Bible, with a Commentary and Critical Notes* (London: Ward, Lock & Co., 1825), vol. 1.

Clarke, K.D., 'Original Text or Canonical Text? Questioning the Shape of the New Testament Text We Translate', in Porter and Hess (eds.), *Translating the Bible*, pp. 281-322.

Cohn, Robert L., 'The Literary Logic of I Kings 17–19', *JBL* 101/3 (1982), pp. 333-50.

Combrink, H.J.B., 'Translating or Transforming—Receiving Matthew in Africa', *Scriptura* 58 (1996), pp. 273-84.

Conzelmann, H., and A. Lindemann, *Interpreting the New Testament: An Introduction to the Principles and Methods of New Testament Exegesis* (trans. S.S. Schatzmann; Peabody, MA: Hendrickson, 1988).

Coote, Robert, 'Yahweh Recalls Elijah', in Baruch Halpern and Jon D. Levenson (eds.), *Traditions and Transformations: Turning Points in Biblical Faith* (Winona Lake, IN: Eisenbrauns, 1981), pp. 115-20.

Cormie, L., 'Revolutions in Reading the Bible', in D. Jobling, P.L. Day and G.T. Sheppard (eds.), *The Bible and the Politics of Exegesis* (Cleveland: Pilgrim Press, 1991), pp. 173-93.

Dahunsi, E.A., 'The Problem of Translating the Bible into African Languages', in Mveng and Werblowsky (eds.), *Proceedings, 1972*, pp. 117-20.

Daiches, David, *Moses: The Man and His Vision* (New York: Praeger, 1975).

Daniell, David (ed.), *Tyndale's Old Testament* (New Haven: Yale University Press, 1992).

Danquah, J.B., *The Akan Doctrine of God* (London: Lutterworth Press, 1944).

Davidson, R.T., *Life of Archibald Campbell Tait, Archbishop of Canterbury*, II (London: Macmillan, 1891).

de Waard, J., 'Vertalen: Een culturele transpositie', *Wereld en Zending* 19/3 (1990), pp. 254-58.

Derrida, J., *Adieu à Emmanuel Levinas* (Paris: Galilée, 1997).

Die Bybel. Nuwe Vertaling (Bybelgenootskap van Suid-Afrika, 8th edn, 1998 [1983]).

Doughty, D.J., 'Pauline Paradigms and Pauline Authenticity', *JHC* 1 (1994), pp. 94-128. See also www.depts.drew.edu/ihc/doughty.html

Draper, J.A., 'Great and Little Traditions: Challenges to the Dominant Western Paradigm of Biblical Interpretation', *Bulletin for Contextual Theology* 3/1 (1996), pp. 1-2.

Duthie, Alan S., *How To Choose Your Bible Wisely* (Paternoster Press/Bible Society, 2nd edn, 1995).

Dyk, J.W., *et al.* (eds.), *The Rediscovery of the Hebrew Bible* (Amsterdamse Cahiers voor Exegese van de Bijbel en zijn Tradities Supplement Series, 1; Maastricht: Shaker, 1999).

Ehrlich, A.B., *MikraKi-feshuto* (New York: Ktav, 1969 [1899–1901]).

Ehrman, B.D., *The Orthodox Corruption of Scripture: The Effect of Early Christian Christological Controversies on the Text of the New Testament* (Oxford: Oxford University Press, 1993).

Eisen, A.M., *Taking Hold of Torah: Jewish Commitment and Community in America* (Bloomington: Indiana University Press, 1997).

Éla, J., 'Christianity and Liberation in Africa', in Gibellini (ed.) *Paths of African Theology*, pp. 136-53.

Ellingworth, P., 'Exegetical Presuppositions in Translation', *BT* 33/3 (1982), pp. 317-23.

—'The Scope of Inclusive Language', *BT* 43/1 (1992), pp. 130-40.

Exum, J.C., and S.D. Moore (eds.), *Biblical Studies/Cultural Studies: The Third Sheffield Colloquium* (JSOT, 266; GCT, 7; Sheffield: Sheffield Academic Press, 1998).

Falk, M., *Love Lyrics from the Bible: A Translation and Literary Study of the Song of Songs* (Sheffield: Almond Press, 1982).

—*The Song of Songs: Love Poems from the Bible* (New York: Harcourt Brace Jovanovich, 1977).

—*The Song of Songs: A New Translation and Interpretation* (San Francisco: Harper, 1990).

Fasholé–Luke, E.W., 'The Quest for African Christian Theology', *JRT* 32/2 (1975), pp. 69-89.

Fogarty, G.P., *American Catholic Biblical Scholarship*. II. *A History from the Early Republic to Vatican* (San Francisco: Harper & Row, 1989).

Fowl, S.E., 'The New Testament, Theology, and Ethics', in J.B. Green (ed.), *Hearing the New Testament: Strategies for Interpretation* (Grand Rapids: Eerdmans, 1995), pp. 394-410.

Fox, Everett, 'The Bible Needs to be Read Aloud', *Response* 33 (11.1) (Spring 1977), pp. 5-17.

—'A Buber–Rosenzweig Bible in English', *Amsterdamse cahiers voor exegese en Bijbelse theologie* xx (1981), pp. 8-22.

—*The Five Books of Moses: Genesis, Exodus, Leviticus, Numbers, Deuteronomy: A New Translation with Introductions, Commentary and Notes* (The Schocken Bible, 1; New York: Schocken Books, 1995).

—*In the Beginning* (New York: Schocken Books, 1983).

—'The Samson Cycle in an Oral Setting', *Alcheringa: Ethnopoetics* 4/1 (1978), pp. 51-68.

Fraade, S.D., 'Rabbinic Views on the Practice of Targum, and Multilingualism in the Jewish Galilee of the Third–Sixth Centuries', in L. Levine (ed.), *The Galilee in Late Antiquity* (New York: The Jewish Theological Seminary of America, 1992), pp. 253-86.

Frazer, J.G., *The Worship of Nature*, I (London: Macmillan, 1926).

Freedman, D.N., 'Modern Scripture Research and Ecumenism', in J. Huddlestun (ed.), *Divine Commitment and Human Obligation* (Grand Rapids: Eerdmans, 1996), pp. 165-71. (First published in *Pittsburgh Perspective* 4/3 [1963], pp. 15-22).

Gérard, Albert S., *Four African Literatures: Xhosa, Sotho, Zulu, Amharic* (Berkeley: University of California Press, 1971).

Getui, M.N., 'The Bible as Tool for Ecumenism', in Kinoti and Waliggo (eds.), *The Bible in African Christianity*, pp. 86-97.

Gibellini, R., 'African Theologians Wonder…and Make Some Proposals', in Gibellini (ed.), *Paths of African Theology*, pp. 1-8.

Gibellini, R. (ed.), *Paths of African Theology* (London: SCM Press, 1984).

Glancy, J.A., 'House Readings and Field Readings: The Discourse of Slavery and Biblical/Cultural Studies', in Exum and Moore (eds.), *Biblical Studies/Cultural Studies*, pp. 460-77.

Gold, Victor Roland, *et al.*, *The New Testament and Psalms: An Inclusive Version* (Oxford: Oxford University Press, 1995).

Good, E.M., *In Turns of Tempest: A Reading of Job with Translation* (Stanford: Stanford University Press, 1990).

Green, James, *An Inquiry into the Principles which should Regulate the Selection of a Word to Denote 'God' in the Language of a Heathen Race; With Special Application to the Case of the Zulus*.

Greenberg, M., *Studies in the Bible and Jewish Thought* (Philadelphia: Jewish Publication Society of America, 1995).

Greenspoon, L., 'Response', in Kee (ed.), *The Bible in the Twenty-First Century*, pp. 68-75.

Grimm, Wilhelm, 'Bericht über das deutsche Wörterbuch (1846)', in Jacob Grimm and Wilhelm Grimm, *Über das Deutsche, Schriften zur Zeit-, Rechts-, Sprach- und Literaturgeschichte* (Leipzig: Verlag Philipp Reclam jun., 1986), pp. 209-20.

Grossfeld, B., *The Two Targums of Esther* (Collegeville, MN: Liturgical Press, 1991).

Haacker, Klaus, 'Dynamische Aequivalenz in Geschichte und Gegenwart', in Carsten Peter Thiede (eds.), *Bibeluebersetzung zwischen Inkulturation und Manipulation* (Paderborn: Institut für Wissenschaftstheoretische Grundlagen Forschung, 1993).

Hammond, G., 'English Translations of the Bible', in Alter and Kermode (eds.), *Literary Guide*, pp. 647-66.

Hatim, Basil, and Ian Mason, *The Translator as Communicator* (London: Routledge, 1997).

Hauser, Alan J., 'Yahweh Versus Death—The Real Struggle in I Kings 17-19', in Alan J. Hauser and Russell Gregory (eds.), *From Carmel to Horeb: Elijah in Crisis* (JSOTSup, 85; BibLit, 19; Sheffield: Almond Press, 1990), pp. 11-89.

Hebblethewaite, Margaret, *Fresh Beginnings* (Review in *The Tablet*, 5 March 1994).

Henten, J.W. van, and A. Brenner (eds.), *Family Relations as Represented in Early Judaisms and Early Christianities: Texts and Fictions* (STAR, 2; Leiden: DEO Publishing, 2000).

Hillesum, Etty, *Journal 1941–1943* (French trans. P. Noble; Paris: Edition du Seuil, 1988).

Hoffmann, Eva, *Lost in Translation: A Life in a New Language* (London: Minerva, 1991).

Hofstadter, Douglas R., *Le Ton beau de Marot: In Praise of the Music of Language* (New York: Basic Books, 1997).

Horsley, R.A., 'Historians and Jesus: Scripts in the Official and Popular Traditions', *Bulletin for Contextual Theology* 3/1 (1996), pp. 4-7.

Isichei, E., *A History of Christianity in Africa: From Antiquity to the Present* (Grand Rapids: Eerdmans; Lawrenceville: Africa World Press, 1995).

Jagt, K.A.van der, 'Equivalence of Religious Terms across Cultures: Some Problems in Translating the Bible in the Turkana Language', in Strine (ed.), *Bible Translation*, pp. 131-53.

Jakobson, Roman, 'Closing Statement: Linguistics and Poetics', in Th.A. Sebeok, *Style in Language* (Cambridge, MA: MIT Press, 1964), pp. 350-77.

Jonge, H.J. de, '*Novum Testamentum a nobis versum*: The Essence of Erasmus' Edition of the New Testament', *JTS* NW 35 (1984), pp. 394-413.

Kamesar, A., *Jerome, Greek Scholarship, and the Hebrew Bible: A Study of the Quaestiones Hebraicae in Genesim* (Oxford: Clarendon Press, 1993).

Kanyoro, M., 'Indigenizing Translation', *BT* 42/2A (1991), pp. 47-56.

Kee, H.C. (ed.), *The Bible in the Twenty-First Century* (American Bible Society Symposium Papers; PA: Trinity Press International, 1993).

Kinoti, H.W. and J.M. Waliggo (eds.), *The Bible in African Christianity: Essays in Biblical Theology* (African Christianity Series; Nairobi: Acton, 1997).

Knox, Ronald, *The Holy Bible* (London: Burns & Oates, 1949).

Kocijančič, Gorazd, 'He Who Is and Being: On the Postmodern Relevance of Eastern Christian Apophaticism', in Robert F. Taft (ed.), *The Christian East: Its Institutions and Thought* (Orientialia Christiana Analecta, 251; Rome: Pontificio Instituto Orientale, 1996), pp. 631-49.

Korsak, Mary Phil, 'A Fresh Look at the Garden of Eden', *Semeia* 81 (1998), pp. 131-44.

—'Genesis: A New Look', in A. Brenner (ed.), *A Feminist Companion to Genesis* (FCB, 2; Sheffield: Sheffield Academic Press, 1993), pp. 39-52.

—*At the Start... Genesis Made New: A Translation of the Hebrew Text* (Louvain Cahiers, European Series, 124; Leuven: Leuvense schrijversaktie, 1992).

Kraemer, Hendrik, *The Christian Message in a Non-Christian World* (London: Edinburgh House Press, 1938).

Kwang-sun Suh, David, 'A Biographical Sketch of an Asian Theological Consultation', in Kim Yong-Bock (ed.), *Minjung Theology; People as the Subjects of History* (Singapur: Commission on Theological Concerns, Christian Conference of Asia, 1981), pp. 17-40.

Kwok, Pui-Lan, 'On Color-Coding Jesus: An Interview with Kwok Pui-Lan', in R.S. Sugirtharajah (ed.), *The Postcolonial Bible* (BibPostcol, 1; Sheffield: Sheffield Academic Press, 1998), pp. 176-88.

Lampe, G.W.H. (ed.), *The Cambridge History of the Bible*, II (Cambridge: Cambridge University Press, 1970).

Lee, D.A., 'Touching the Sacred Text: The Bible as Icon in Feminist Reading', *Pacifica* 11/3 (1998), pp. 249-64.

Levenson, J.D., *The Hebrew Bible, the Old Testament and Historical Criticism* (Louisville, KY: Westminster/John Knox Press, 1993).

Levine, Baruch, 'Silence, Sound, and the Phenomenology of Mourning in Biblical Israel', *JANESCU* 22 (1993), pp. 89-106.

Loewe, R., 'The Medieval History of the Latin Vulgate', in Lampe (ed.), *The Cambridge History*, II, pp. 102-54.

Long, Asphodel, *In a Chariot Drawn by Lions* (London: The Women's Press, 1992).

Long, B.O., *Planting and Reaping Albright: Politics, Ideology, and Interpreting the Bible* (University Park, PA: Pennsylvania State University Press, 1997).

Louw, J.P., 'Die Nuwe Afrikaanse Bybelvertaling: Kritiese Evaluering—Nuwe Testament', in J.P. Louw, W. Vosloo and V.N. Webb, *Die Taal van die Bybel en die Predikant* (Universiteit van Pretoria Teologiese Studies, 1; Pretoria: NGKB, 1986), pp. 1-11.

Lowe, Raphael, 'Jewish Exegesis', in R.J. Coggins and J.L. Houlden (eds.), *A Dictionary of Biblical Interpretation* (London: SCM Press, 1998), pp. 346-54.

Luz, U., *Matthew in History: Interpretation, Influence, and Effects* (Minneapolis: Fortress Press, 1994).

Luzbetak, L.J., 'Contextual Translation: The Role of Cultural Anthropology', in Stine (ed.), *Bible Translation*, pp. 108-19.

MacCulloch, D., *Thomas Cranmer: A Life* (New Haven: Yale University Press, 1996).

Macky, Peter W., *The Centrality of Metaphors to Biblical Thought* (Lewiston, NY: Edwin Mellen Press, 1990).

Magessa, L., 'From Privatized to Popular Biblical Hermeneutics in Africa', in Kinoti and J.M. Waliggo (eds.), *The Bible in African Christianity*, pp. 25-39.

Maluleke, T.S., 'Black and African Theologies in the New World Order: A Time to Drink from Our Own Wells', *JTSA* 96 (1996), pp. 3-19.

Marshall, I. Howard, *The Gospel of Luke: A Commentary on the Greek Text* (Exeter: Paternoster Press, 1978).

—'Introduction', in Marshall (ed.), *New Testament Interpretation*, pp. 1-18.

—*New Testament Interpretation: Essays on Principles and Methods* (Exeter: Paternoster Press, 1979).

Martey, E., *African Theology: Inculturation and Liberation* (Maryknoll, NY: Orbis Books, 1993).

Mbiti, J.S., 'The Bible in African Culture', in Gibellini (ed.), *Paths of African Theology*, pp. 27-39.

—*Bible and Theology in African Christianity* (Nairobi: Oxford University Press, 1986).

—*Concepts of God in Africa* (London: SPCK, 1970).

McKnight, E.V., *Post-Modern Use of the Bible* (Nashville: Abingdon Press, 1988).

Meeks, W.A., 'A Hermeneutics of Social Embodiment', *HTR* 79/1-3 (1986), pp. 176-86.

Meisner, N., 'Aristeasbrief', in *Jüdische Schriften aus hellenistisch-römischer Zeit*, II (Gütersloh: Gerd Mohn, 1973), 1, pp. 38-43.

Mesters, Carlos, 'The Use of the Bible in Christian Communities of the Common People', in Sergio Torres and John Eagleson (eds.), *The Challenge of Basic Christian Communities* (Maryknoll, NY: Orbis Books, 1981), pp. 197-210.

Metzger, B.M., *The Text of the New Testament: Its Transmission, Corruption, and Restoration* (Oxford: Clarendon Press, 2nd edn, 1968).

Meyers, Carol, *Discovering Eve: Ancient Israelite Women in Context* (New York: Oxford University Press, 1988).

—*Miqra'ot Gedolot* (3 vols; Jerusalem: Schocken Publishing House, 1959)

Mitchell, S., *The Book of Job: Translated and with an Introduction* (San Francisco: North Point Press, 1987). An earlier version of the translation was published as *Into the Whirlwind* [Garden City, NY: Doubleday, 1979]).

—*Genesis: A New Translation of the Classic Biblical Stories* (New York: HarperCollins, 1996).

Moffatt, James, *The Bible: A New Translation* (New York: Harper and Brothers, 1935).

Moody, David, 'Foreword', in Korsak, *At the Start*, pp. xi-xiii.

Moore, S., and J.C. Anderson, 'Taking it like a Man: Masculinity in 4 Maccabees', *JBL* 117/2 (1998), pp. 249-73.

Mugambi, J.N.K., 'The Bible and Ecumenism in African Christianity', in Kinoti and Waliggo (eds.), *The Bible in African Christianity*, pp. 68-85.

Müller, M., '*Hebraica Sive Graeca Veritas*: The Jewish Bible at the Time of the New Testament and the Christian Bible', *SJOT* 3/2 (1989), pp. 55-71.

Mveng, Engelbert, 'Impoverishment and Liberation: A Theological Approach for Africa and the Third World', in Gibellini (ed.), *Paths of African Theology*, pp. 154-165.

Mveng, E., and R.J.Z. Werblowsky (eds.), *Proceedings of the Jerusalem Conference on Black Africa and the Bible, April 24–30, 1972*.

Naaijkens, A.B.M., 'Vertaalkritiek en de Nieuwe Bijbelvertaling', *Met Andere Woorden* 19/1 (2000), pp. 18-33.

Ndungu, N., 'The Bible in an African Independent Church', in Kinoti and Waliggo (eds.), *The Bible in African Christianity*, pp. 58-67.

Niccacci, Alviero, *The Syntax of the Verb in Classical Hebrew Prose* (JSOTSup, 86; Sheffield: JSOT Press, 1990).

Nichols, A.J., 'Bible Translation: A Critical Analysis of E.A. Nida's Theory of Dynamic Equivalence and its Impact on Recent Bible Translations' (PhD dissertation, University of Sheffield, 1997).

Nida, E.A., 'Breakthroughs in Bible Translating', in Kee (ed.), *The Bible in the Twenty-First Century*, pp. 195-208.

—*Exploring Semantic Structures* (Munich: Wilhelm Fink Verlag, 1975).

—'Principles of Translation as Exemplified by Bible Translating', *BT* 10/4 (October 1959).

—'The Sociolinguistics of Translating Canonical Religious Texts', *Traduction, Terminologie, Redaction: Etudes sur le texte et ses transformations* 7/1 (1994).

—*Toward a Science of Translating* (Leiden: E.J. Brill, 1964).

—'Trends in Bible Translating within the United Bible Societies: An Historical Perspective', *BT* 42/2A (1991), pp. 2-4.

Nieuwe Bijbelvertaling: Tegen het licht gehouden (Haarlem, NBG: 1999).

Nida, E.A., and Jan de Waard, *From One Language to Another: Functional Equivalence in Bible Translating* (Nashville: Thomas Nelson, 1986).

Nida, E.A., and C.R. Taber, *The Theory and Practice of Translation* (Helps for Translators, 8; Leiden: E.J. Brill, 1974).

Norton, David, *A History of the English Bible as Literature* (Cambridge: Cambridge University Press, 2000).

Nthamburi, Z., and D. Waruta, 'Biblical Hermeneutics in African Instituted Churches', in Kinoti and Waliggo (eds.), *The Bible in African Christianity*, pp. 40-57.

Obeng, E.A., 'The Use of Biblical Critical Methods in Rooting the Scriptures in Africa', in Kinoti and Waliggo (eds.), *The Bible in African Christianity*, pp. 8-24.

Oberholzer, J.P., 'Die Afrikaanse Bybelvertaling 1983—Enkele Aantekeninge', *Hervormde Teologiese Studies* 40/1 (1984), pp. 82-91.

Odendaal, D.H., Letter of the Presbytery of Monti (Uniting Reformed Church in Southern Africa), 1999, pp. 1-2.

Oduyoye, Mercy Amba, *Daughters of Anowa: African Women and Patriarchy* (Maryknoll, NY: Orbis Books, 1995).

Panagopoulos, Johannes, 'Sache und Energie: Zur theologischen Grundlegung der biblischen Hermeneutik bei den griechischen Kirchenvätern', in Hermann Lichtenberger (ed.), *Geschichte—Tradition—Reflexion: Festschrift für Martin Hengel zum 70. Geburtstag*. III, *Frühes Christentum* (Tübingen: Mohr Siebeck, 1996), pp. 567-584.

Parratt, J., 'African Theology and Biblical Hermeneutics', *ATJ* 12/2 (1983), pp. 88-94.

Payle, K.D., 'The Afrikaans Bible Translation: A Translation for *All* Afrikaans Speakers?', *NGTT* 39/1-2 (1998), pp. 122-30.

Pearson, B.W.R., 'Remainderless Translations? Implications of the Tradition Concerning the Translation of the LXX for Modern Translation Theory', in Porter and Hess (eds.), *Translating the Bible*, pp. 63-84.

Perkins, P., 'Response', in Kee (ed.), *The Bible in the Twenty-First Century*, pp. 84-88.

Pippin, Tina, 'Translation Happens: A Feminist Perspective on Translation Theories', in H.C. Washington *et al.* (eds.), *Escaping Eden: New Feminist Perspectives on the Bible* (New York: New York University Press, 1999), pp. 163-76.

Polak, Frank H., 'The Oral and the Written: Syntax, Stylistics and the Development of Biblical Prose Narrative', *JANESCU* 26 (1999), pp. 59-105.

Porter, S.E., 'The Contemporary English Version and the Ideology of Translation', in S.E. Porter and Hess (eds.), *Translating the Bible*, pp. 18-45.

Porter, S.E., and R.S. Hess (eds.), *Translating the Bible: Problems and Prospects* (JSNTSup, 173; Sheffield: Sheffield Academic Press, 1999).

Porter, Stanley E., and Jeffrey T. Reed (eds.), *Discourse Analysis and the New Testament: Approaches and Results* (JSNTSup, 170; Sheffield Academic Press, 1999).

Prickett, Stephen, *Words and The Word: Language, Poetics and Biblical Interpretation* (Cambridge: Cambridge University Press, 1986).

Punt, J., 'The Bible, its Status and African Christian Theologies: Foundational Document or Stumbling Block?', *Religion & Theology* 5/3 (1998), pp. 265-310.

Rabin, C., 'The Uniqueness of Bible Translation', in Mveng and Werblowsky (eds.), *Proceedings, 1972*, pp. 108-116.

Reichert, Klaus, '"It Is Time": The Buber–Rosenzweig Bible Translation in Context', in S. Budick and W. Iser (eds.), *The Translatability of Cultures* (Stanford: Stanford University Press, 1996), pp. 169-85.

Robert, Dana L., 'Shifting Southward: Global Christianity Since 1945', *International Bulletin of Missionary Research* 24 (April 2000), pp. 50-58.

Rofé, Alexander, 'The Vineyard of Naboth: The Origin and Message of the Story', *VT* 38/1 (1988), pp. 89-104.

Rogerson, J.W., 'The Old Testament Translator's Translation—A Personal Reflection', in Porter and Hess (eds.), *Translating the Bible*.

Rosenbaum, M., and A.M. Silberman (trans. and eds.), *Pentateuch with Rashi's Commentary* (2 vols.; London: Shapiro, Vallentine & Co., 1946).

Said, Edward, *Orientalism* (New York: Pantheon Books, 1978).

Samuelson, R.C.A., *The King Cetywayo Zulu-Dictionary* (Durban: The Commercial Printing Co., 1923).

Sanford, Mary, 'An Orthodox View of Biblical Criticism', *Sourozh* 26 (1986).

—'How Do You Read?': Theology and Hermeneutics in the Interpretation of New Testament Parables (PhD dissertation; University, 1984).

Sanneh, L., 'Gospel and Culture: Ramifying Effects of Scriptural Translation', in Stine (ed.), *Bible Translation and the Spread of the Church: The Last 200 Years*, pp. 1-23.

—*Translating the Message: The Missionary Impact on Culture* (American Society of Missiology, 13; Maryknoll, NY: Orbis Books, 1989).

—*Abolitionists Abroad: American Blacks and the Making of Modern West Africa* (Cambridge, MA: Harvard University Press, 1999).

Savran, George, '1 and 2 Kings', in Alter and Kermode (eds.), *The Literary Guide*, pp. 146-64.

Sayers, E.F., 'Notes on the Native Language Affinities in Sierra Leone', *Sierra Leone Studies* old series, 10 (1927).

Schaaf, Y. (ed.), *On Their Way Rejoicing: The History and the Role of the Bible in Africa* (trans. P. Ellingworth; African Challenge Series; Carlisle: Paternoster Press, 1994).

Scheindlin, R., *The Book of Job: Translation, Introduction, and Notes* (New York: W.W. Norton, 1998).

Schneiders, S.M., *The Revelatory Text: Interpreting the New Testament as Sacred Scripture* (San Francisco: Harper, 1991).

Schreiter, R.J., *Constructing Local Theologies* (Maryknoll, NY: Orbis Books, 1985).

Schüssler Fiorenza, E., 'Introduction: Transforming the Legacy of *The Women's Bible*', in E. Schüssler Fiorenza (ed.), *Searching the Scriptures. I. A Feminist Introduction* (London: SCM Press, 1993), pp. 1-24.

Schwartz, Werner, *Principles and Problems of Biblical Translation: Some Reformation Controversies and Their Background* (Cambridge: Cambridge University Press, 1955).

Scott, J.C., *Domination and the Arts of Resistance: Hidden Transcripts* (New Haven: Yale University Press, 1990).

Selvidge, Marla J., *Notorious Voices: Feminist Biblical Interpretation 1500–1920* (London: SCM Press, 1996).

Shaw, Susan J., *A Religious History of Julia Evelina Smith's 1876 Translation of the Holy Bible: Doing More Than Any Man Has Ever Done* (San Francisco: Mellen Research University Press, 1993).

Simms, Karl (ed.), *Translating Sensitive Texts: Linguistic Aspects* (Amsterdam: Rodopi, 1997).

Simonetti, M., *Biblical Interpretation in the Early Church: An Historical Introduction to Patristic Exegesis* (trans. J.A. Hughes; Edinburgh: T. & T. Clark, 1994).

Smith, Edwin W., *The Golden Stool: Some Aspects of the Conflict of Cultures in Modern Africa* (London: Holborn Publishing House, 1926).

Smith, Edwin W. (ed.), *African Ideas of God: A Symposium* (London: Edinburgh House Press, 1950).

Smith, Julia E., *The Holy Bible: Containing the Old and New Testaments: Translated Literally from the Original Tongues* (Hartford: American Publishing Company, 1876).

Soskice, Janet Martin, *Metaphor and Religious Language* (Oxford: Oxford University Press, 1985).

Sparks, H.F.D., 'Jerome as Biblical Scholar', in P.R. Ackroyd and C.F. Evans (eds.) *The Cambridge History of the Bible. I. From the Beginnings to Jerome* (Cambridge: Cambridge University Press, 1970, p. 513.

Steiner, George, *After Babel: Aspects of Language and Translation* (Oxford: Oxford University Press (3rd edn, 1993 [1975]).

Stine, P.C. (ed.), *Bible Translation and the Spread of the Church: The Last 200 Years* (Studies in Christian Mission, 2; Leiden: E.J. Brill, 1992).

Stine, P.C., and E.R. Wendland (eds.), *Bridging the Gap: African Traditional Religion and Bible Translation* (UBS Monograph Series, 4; New York: UBS, 1990).

Stivers, Dan R., *The Philosophy of Religious Language* (Oxford: Basil Blackwell, 1996).

Strauss, Mark L., *Distorting Scripture? The Challenge of Bible Translation and Gender Accuracy* (Downers Grove, IL: InterVarsity Press, 1998).

Stroumsa, G., 'The Christian Hermeneutical Revolution and Its Double Helix', in L.V. Rutgers *et al.* (eds.), *The Use of Sacred Books in the Ancient World* (Contributions to Biblical Exegesis and Theology, 22; Leuven: Peeters, 1998), pp. 9-28.

Sutcliffe, E.F., 'Jerome', in Lampe (ed.), *Cambridge History of the Bible*, II, p. 85.

Talmage, Frank E., *David Kimhi: The Man and the Commentaries* (Cambridge, MA: Harvard University Press, 1975).

Tarlin, Jan, 'Toward a "Female" Reading of the Elijah Cycle: Ideology and Gender in the Interpretation of 1 Kings 17–19, 21, and 2 Kings 1–2.18', in Athalya Brenner (ed.), *A Feminist Companion to Samuel and Kings* (FCB, 5; Sheffield: Sheffield Academic Press, 1994).

Tate, W.R., *Biblical Interpretation: An Integrated Approach* (Peabody, MA: Hendrickson, 1991).

Taylor, John V., *The Primal Vision* (London: SCM Press, 1963).

—*The New Testament and Psalms: An Inclusive Version* (New York: Oxford University Press, 1995).

—*The Stone Edition Tanach* (New York: Mesorah Publications, 1996).

Thiselton, A.C., 'Semantics and New Testament Interpretation', in Marshall (ed.), *New Testament Interpretation*, pp. 75-104.

Thistlethwaite, S.B., 'Every Two Minutes: Battered Women and Feminist Interpretation', in L.M. Russell (ed.), *Feminist Interpretation of the Bible* (Philadelphia: Westminster, 1985), pp. 96-107.

Trebolle Barrera, J.C., *The Jewish Bible and the Christian Bible: An Introduction to the History of the Bible* (trans. W.G.E. Watson; Leiden: E.J. Brill, 1998).

Trible, Phyllis, 'Depatriarchalizing in Biblical Interpretation', *JAAR* 41 (1973), pp. 30-48.

Turkson, P.K., 'De Taal van de Bijbel en Afrika', *Wereld en Zending* 23/3 (1994), pp. 74-80.

Ukpong, J.S., 'Rereading the Bible with African Eyes', *JTSA* 91 (1995), pp. 3-14.

Usry, G., and C.S. Keener, *Black Man's Religion: Can Christianity Be Afrocentric?* (Downers Grove, IL: IVP, 1996).

Van der Merwe, C.H.J., ' ''n Konkordante Vertaling van die Bybel in Afrikaans. Is dit Hoegenaamd Verantwoordbaar, en Hoe sal Dit Lyk?', *NGTT* 40/3-4 (1999), pp. 293-303.

Venuti, Lawrence, *The Scandals of Translation: Towards an Ethics of Difference* (London: Routledge, 1998).

Verheij, A.J.C., *Bits, Bytes, and Binyanim: A Quantitative Study of Verbal Lexeme Formations in the Hebrew Bible* (Orientalia Lovaniensia Analecta, 93; Leuven: Peeters, 2000).

Verhoef, P.A., 'Bekendstelling van die Verwysingbybel', *NGTT* 40/1-2 (1999), pp. 162-67.

Volz, H. (ed.), *D. Martin Luther: Die gantze heilige Schrifft* (Munich: Deutscher Taschenbuch Verlag, 1974).

Vries, Anneke de, *Het kleine verschil: Man/vrouw-stereotypen in enkele moderne Nederlandse vertalingen van het Oude Testament* (Kampen: Kok, 1998).

Waard, Jan de, and Eugene Nida, *From One Language to Another* (Nashville: Thomas Nelson, 1986).

Waliggo, J.M., 'Bible and Catechism in Uganda', in Kinoti and Waliggo (eds.), *The Bible in African Christianity*, pp. 179-95.

Walls, A.F., 'The Translation Principle in Christian History', in Stine (ed.), *Bible Translation*, pp. 24-39.

Walsh, Jerome T., *1 Kings (Berit Olam*; Collegeville, MN: Liturgical Press, 1996).

Wambudta, D.N., 'Hermeneutics and the Search for Theologia Africana', *ATJ* 9/2 (1980), pp. 29-39.

Webster's New World College Dictionary (New York: Macmillan, 1997).

Wendland, E.R., *The Cultural Factor in Bible Translation: A Study of Communicating the Word of God in a Central African Cultural Context* (UBS Monograph Series, 2; London: UBS, 1987).

—*Language, Society, and Translation: With Special Reference to the Style and Structure of Segments of Direct Speech in the Scriptures* (Cape Town: Bible Society of South Africa, 1985).

Weren, W., *Windows on Jesus: Methods in Gospel Exegesis* (London: SCM Press, 1999).

Westermann, Diedrich, 'The Place and Function of the Vernacular in African Education', *International Review of Mission* (January 1925).

—*The African To-day and To-morrow* (London: Oxford University Press for the International African Institute, 3rd edn, 1949).

Whang, Y.C., 'To whom is a Translator Responsible—Reader or Author?', in Porter and Hess (eds.), *Translating the Bible*, pp. 46-62.

White, C., *The Correspondence between Jerome and Augustine of Hippo* (Lewiston, NY: Mellen Edwin Press, 1990).

White, Marsha C., *The Elijah Legends and Jehu's Coup* (BJS, 311; Atlanta: Scholars Press, 1997).

Whiteman, D.L., 'Bible Translation and Social and Cultural Development', in Stine (ed.), *Bible Translation*, pp. 120-44.

Wimbush, V.L., 'The Bible and African Americans: An Outline of an Interpretive History', in C.H. Felder (ed.), *Stony the Road we Trod: African American Biblical Interpretation* (Minneapolis: Fortress Press, 1991), pp. 91-97.

Witvliet, T., *A Place in the Sun: An Introduction to Liberation Theology in the Third World* (London: SCM Press; Maryknoll, NY: Orbis Books, 1985).

Worth, Roland H., *Bible Translations: A History Through Source Documents* (McFarland, 1992).

Yorke, G.L.O.R., 'The Bible and the Black Diaspora', in Kinoti and Waliggo (eds.), *The Bible in African Christianity*, pp. 145-64.

Zakovitch, Yair, 'The Tale of Naboth's Vineyard, I Kings 21', Addendum to Meir Weiss, *The Bible from Within* (Jerusalem: Magnes Press, 1984), pp. 379-405.

INDEXES

INDEX OF REFERENCES

BIBLE

INDEX OF AUTHORS

JOURNAL FOR THE STUDY OF THE OLD TESTAMENT
SUPPLEMENT SERIES